WORLD PROTESTANTISM

WILLEM HENDRICK VAN DE POL

HERDER AND HERDER

1964
HERDER AND HERDER NEW YORK
232 Madison Avenue, New York 16, N.Y.

Original edition *Het Wereldprotestantisme*
J. J. Romen & Zonen, Roermond
This revised edition translated by T. Zuydwijk S.J.

Imprimi potest: Angus J. Macdougall S.J.
Praep. Prov. Canadae Superioris

Nihil obstat: Censor Librorum
Patrick A. Barry

Imprimatur: ✝Robert F. Joyce
Bishop of Burlington
February 15, 1964

The nihil obstat and imprimatur are official declarations that a book or pamphlet is free of doctrinal or moral error. No implication is contained therein that those who have granted the nihil obstat and imprimatur agree with the contents, opinions or statements expressed.

Library of Congress Catalog Card Number: 64–19733
©1964 by Herder and Herder, Incorporated
Printed in the United States of America

Contents

Foreword

I write this Foreword to the book of Dr. van de Pol not merely because he is my friend, but also because I believe his book will prove, if possibly a bit sobering, nevertheless definitely enlightening to many. It is good to be reminded that attitudes and convictions rooted in long and bitter history cannot easily be changed, and good to recall that the insights of the leaders of the ecumenical movement may not as yet have been shared by the vast mass of Christian people.

I confess that for long I have been bothered to understand the positive content of the word "Protestant." A dear Methodist friend, who out of sheer goodness read a manuscript for me, remarked: "Of course, there is much in it with which, *as a Protestant,* I cannot agree." It surprised me that he did not say, "as a Methodist," but "as a Protestant." Dr. van de Pol's book gave me an increased understanding of the meaning of the "Protestant" convictions, as common to men divided within that general designation. It helped me to grasp a little more clearly why, for instance, in some public hospitals in the United States, one finds the notice "Catholic Chaplain" and "Protestant Chaplain."

I suspect that some Protestants regard the divisions within "Protestantism" somewhat as Catholics regard the different religious orders within Catholicism; the varieties within "Protestantism" can, by some judgments, be regarded as minor chords, or different instruments, all sounding the same melody. To the average man sick in hospital, it would matter little whether the chaplain were Episcopalian, Presbyterian, Methodist, Congregationalist or Baptist—unless he were a Catholic; in which case he would confess, be anointed and receive Holy Communion. The average "Protestant" minister would, I imagine, gently and wisely comfort the sick man through reviving his faith in Christ's redemption of him and love of him. But the Catholic would "give him the last Sacraments." This illustration serves to bring to a focus the difference between "Catholic" and "Protestant."

And yet I wonder if this is not too great a simplification. In England, in the armed services the designations run: "C. of E.," "R.C." and "O.D.," signifying "Church of England," "Roman Catholic" and "Other Denominations." Whether this is indicative of a feeling that Protestantism is not quite so pervading an appellation as Dr. van de Pol suggests, and, especially, whether the C. of E., and Anglicans generally, are to be considered "Protestants," is a question I do not dare to try to solve. I have relatives and friends who gladly accept the term "Anglican" but vehemently repudiate the term "Protestant." Should we insist that they are really Protestants all the same, in as much as they give their allegiance to a church which itself is essentially "protestant"? Because they reject the supremacy and infallibility of the Pope, they are not thereby rightly called "Protestant," since the Eastern Orthodox also reject these doctrines. I know Anglicans who would want "the last Sacraments" if they are seriously ill, and I know some who tell me the first prayer they learned was the "Hail Mary." In our time there are "high-church" Baptists, Congregationalists, Lutherans, Methodists, Presbyterians. The exact connotation of the term is hard to assign. Probably it indicates more frequent and more "liturgical" celebration of the Eucharist, and possibly it also means greater appreciation of the "tradition" of the whole Church back to the Apostles.

I confess I am not confident—in spite of having read several books by competent scholars on "Protestantism"—that the term "protestant" can be given a positive content which would embrace all who are Christians but neither Eastern Orthodox or Roman Catholic. It is far easier to define a "Protestant" by what he rejects than by what he accepts. Let a reader note that I say "far easier" and do not say "impossible."

But, in any case, are names important? They are certainly coming to have less importance than they used to have. The Church of South India dropped the names "Congregationalist," "Anglican," Methodist" and "Presbyterian," which were the names of the uniting bodies. Should one maintain that the Church of South India is "Protestant"? The United Church of Christ which came into formal existence in 1957, was formed from what were originally the Evangelical Synod (Lutheran), the Reformed Church of the United States (Calvinist), the Congregational Churches and the "Christian" Church (this latter being a fusion of certain Methodist, Baptist and Presbyterian congregations). The last two bodies named arrived from England, their connection with the Church of England being various and complex, as Douglas Horton indicates in his fascinating book entitled *The United Church of Christ*. When the union was formed, all the old titles were dropped; a suggestion had been made that the title should be the Uniting Church of Christ, since the union envisaged continuance of the process of reunion (Horton, *op. cit.,* pp. 108–111), a suggestion rejected as "expressing a sense of unrelieved inconclusiveness" (*ibid.,* p. 111). Yet it is significant that the old names do not appear; and Dr. Douglas Horton has no hesitation in saying that the United Church of Christ deems itself to be "a Protestant Catholic Church" (p. 95). On this basis, the old associations clinging to the names "Catholic" and "Protestant" are beginning to lose their hold, though I must honestly confess that there is much in the United Church of Christ that seems to my Catholic ears to ring a Protestant bell. Attempts are being made at a new and a deeper synthesis which will be both "evangelical" and "catholic." The reunited Church proposed by Dr. Eugene Carson Blake in December 1960 was to be "both reformed and catholic." On the vexed question of the rule of faith he said this:

"The reunited Church must accept the principle of continuing reformation under the Word of God by the guidance of the Holy Spirit. A few years ago I would have felt that here was an issue on which no possible agreement could be reached. The reformation Churches have traditionally found their authority for faith and life in the Scriptures alone. So long as the wording *sola scriptura* is required, no bridge can be made between catholic and evangelical. But it is now clear in ecumenical conversations that Protestants generally have come to recognize the right place of tradition, just as catholics have generally become aware of the rightness of judging all tradition by the Scriptures as interpreted to the Church by the Holy Spirit" (Cf. *The Challenge to Reunion. The Blake Proposal under Scrutiny,* compiled and edited by Robert McAfee Brown and David H. Scott, New York 1963).

Dr. Blake wrote so before the famous discussion in Vatican II about Scripture and Tradition. It may well appear, when we see the revised text on the sources of revelation, that Dr. Blake spoke more penetratingly than he may have then realized.

Moreover, problems connected with authority in the Church are arising in new forms. The United Church of Christ, for instance, "recognizes responsibilities at home and abroad for missions, fraternal aid and service, ecumenical relations, interchurch relations and Christian unity, education, publication, the ministry, ministerial pensions and relief, evangelism, stewardship, social action, health and welfare and any other appropriate area of need or concern" (Article VIII of Constitution). These areas are cared for by "boards, commissions, councils, offices, or other instrumentalities" which perform their functions in accordance with the Constitution, By-Laws and "instructions given them by the General Synod." Thus the United Church Board for World Ministries has superseded the American Board of Commissioners for Foreign Missions, the Board of International Missions, the Commission on World Service and the Congregational Christian Service Committee. The members of the new Board for World Ministries are nominated and elected by the General Synod.

There is, indeed, in the Constitution of the United Church careful provision to safeguard the autonomy of the local church (Cf. Douglas Horton, *op. cit.*, pp. 135–36). But it is obvious that the responsibilities listed can be fulfilled only by a comparatively small group of officials who must devote themselves with a certain permanence to their tasks. Thus a certain bureaucratic centralism inevitably arises, and the strict theory of congregational autonomy applies only with considerable modification and is not easily reconciled with efficiency in administration.

Efficient administration, involving large sums of money and planning for years to come, raises problems about the relation of central bodies to local churches. This has been shown by Paul M. Harrison in his book *Authority and Power in the Free Church Tradition. A Social Case Study of the American Baptist Convention* (Princeton 1959). Theological issues about the nature of the church are involved, since decision-making tends in fact to be concentrated in a comparatively small group, which, contrary to the current ideology of the Baptists, comes to believe that the national agencies, in order to fulfill their responsibilities, must be endowed with ecclesiastical jurisdiction and authority from God (Cf. Harrison, *op. cit.*, p. 102). Thus theory and practice are not harmonious.

Something of the same situation is alleged to exist in the World Council of Churches, and the question is being asked whether in fact a small group exercises a power which formal documentation about "authority" does not justify; two former officials of the World Council have recently raised this issue in essays in the volume *Unity in Mid-Career,* edited by Keith R. Bridston and Walter D. Wagoner (New York 1963). Dr. Liston Pope and Dr. Keith R. Bridston both stress the complexity of the organizational problems involved in a world council of this size, and both regret the reduced status of the Faith and Order Commission (Cf. *vg.,* pp. 23 and 31–32). The "Staff Executive Group," it is alleged, constitutes a hierarchical control center not envisaged by legal enactments (Cf. *ibid.,* p. 37).

Roman Catholics surely have no reason to feel superior because of these as yet unsolved problems among separated brethren. The complicated questions surrounding "the collegiality of bishops" are by no means yet solved. I venture, however, the opinion that while Protestants are seeking a theological justification for an increased and increasing concentration of ecclesiastical power and authority, Catholics are seeking means of greater practical diffusion on the exercise of an authority all most loyally and gladly accept as given by God. Pope Paul VI, speaking of the second session of Vatican Council II, made special reference to "the development of the doctrine of the Episcopate, its function and its relationship with Peter.

"For us personally, it will provide doctrinal and practical standards by which our apostolic office, endowed though it is by Christ with the fullness and sufficiency of power, may receive more help and support, in ways to be determined, from a more effective and responsible collaboration with our beloved and venerable brethren in the episcopate."

To a considerable extent, possibly more than is realized, all Christian bodies are facing problems of organization in the modern jet age. The language used often differs, but not seldom the problems faced and the solutions proposed do not in practice greatly differ.

Mutual knowledge between "Catholics" and "Protestants" has increased; they have written with new understanding and new sympathy about the others. Speaking merely from memory, among Catholics who have written about Protestants the following names stand out: Lorsch, Congar, Sartory, Bouyer, Küng, Weigel, Tavard, Baum; among Protestants who have written about Catholics: R. M. Brown, Pelikon, Skydsgaard, Pawley, Cullmann, Lindbeck, von Lowenich, John Bennett, but both lists are sadly incomplete. Dialogue, especially in the United States, is being carried on at various levels and in various ways. There is a new feeling. Antagonism is giving way to mutual respect, regard and even affection. Agreements are being stressed more than differences. There is desire for understanding and growing mutual sympathy.

"We look with reverence," said Pope Paul VI, "upon the true religious patrimony which we share in common, which has been preserved and in part even well developed among our separated brethren. We note with special approval the study made by those who seek to make known and to honor the treasures of truth and of genuine spirituality possessed by separated brethren, in order to improve our relations with them."

Two things appear to have surprised the "observers" (should I say "the Protestant observers"?) at the Council: the freedom of speech used by the bishops and cardinals, and the universal friendliness with which they were greeted and treated. Through the Secretariat for Promoting Christian Unity the voices of the "observers" were heard in the Council—and in some cases their advice was accepted.

The change of feeling and attitude was declared by Cardinal Bea to be a real miracle; and Professors Oscar Cullmann and George Williams agreed that the word "miracle" was not too strong.

Probably there will be few readers of Dr. van de Pol's book who will agree with absolutely everything he says; and this applies particularly to what he says about that mystery which is called Anglicanism. A book like Eric Waldron Kempe's *Counsel and Consent* (London 1931) shows the pervading sense of history characteristic of Anglicanism, by contrast to the other churches which broke with Rome in the 16th century; a book like Leslie Paul's *The Deployment and Payment of the Clergy* (Westminster 1964) shows a lively effort to grapple with the problems of a mobile population and a welfare state. Anglo-Catholics are by no means the only Anglicans; perhaps they are not even characteristic Anglicans. Yet the Church of England cannot afford to lose them and this involves, as the Conversations with the Methodist Church plainly said, an invariability in the practice of episcopal ordination which forbids action upon the assumption that episcopacy is only a optional "extra," something of the *bene esse* or the *plenum esse,* in the Church. Anglicans, of course, can be infuriatingly vague about theological principles; but, all told, Anglicanism has retained a sense of continuity with the past, manifest in its canon law, which continental reformers lost.

And yet I must sorrowfully record my acquiescence, though not my full agreement, in Dr. van de Pol's warnings against too optimistic expectations. Periodicals like *Christianity Today* and *The Church of England Newspaper* will chasten any starry-eyed Catholic reader. Professor Alexander Schmemann's essay "The Moment of Truth for Orthodoxy," in the volume, already mentioned, *Unity in Mid-Career,* will dispel any illusions regarding Orthodox-Protestant relations in the World Council of Churches. Opposition to various proposals for reunions among Protestant churches—the Anglican, Presbyterian, the Anglican-Methodist, the "Blake" proposal, and others besides—must surely bring realization that the way to unity is beset with distressing and wearying obstacles and that nothing less than heroic efforts and a hope more than human can surmount them. Indeed, nothing less than God's omnipotence can overcome them. But unity is God's will. It is Christ's prayer. And therefore all of us may go forward in serene and energetic confidence that God's omnipotence will do what our poor human efforts cannot do, perhaps in ways that may surprise us and make us more deeply aware that our faith must not rest "on the wisdom of men but on the power of God" (1 Cor 2:5).

BERNARD J. LEEMING S.J.

Preface

THE fact that this book on world Protestantism, written nearly ten years ago, is now presented in an English-language edition seems to require some introductory remarks. We are all of us aware of the many deep and far-reaching changes which are being brought about in the life of the churches owing to certain developments of the past decades. Indeed there would be every reason to write a book on the fastly changing atmosphere in the spiritual life of very many Christians of these days. There is a tendency in our days to look forward rather than backward, to forget things that are past and to look to things to come.

This changing atmosphere seems to call for some explanation of the original intention and method of this book. What I have set myself to do is to give an impartial characterization of the four main groups of Christian churches, which—although stressing their continuity with the Church of all ages—derive their present character largely from the character and specific witness of the Reformation of the sixteenth century: the Lutheran, the Reformed, the Anglican and the later free churches. It is the conviction of the author, one based on careful comparison of the sources, that the so-called differences between the English and the Protestant Reformation are far smaller than is often suggested by those who for one reason or another want to exaggerate the distance which is supposed to exist between Anglicanism and Reformation Christianity.

What I want to make clear in this preface however is that the intention and method of this book are not primarily historical but rather phenomenological or typological. Although the characterization of the four groups of churches which are rooted in the Reformation has been given against an historical background, the book should not be read and judged as if it were a book on ecclesiastical history.

For this reason the picture of the various types of Reformation churches which has been given, and especially insofar as it is a true picture, is not in need of any revision owing to what happened during the past ten years. Although some facts had to be added from an historical point of view, these facts do not at all mean that the character of the various churches as it has been described has been changing to any great extent.

Notwithstanding this stability of character however a general remark on the present religious situation would not seem to be beside the mark. Since World War II it is increasingly becoming clearer and clearer that we are on the verge of a completely new era in the history of the human race. Imperialism, colonialism, racial discrimination, authoritarianism, religious antagonism and many other things we have been used to for ages are rapidly drawing to a definite end. The all-round crisis which has dawned upon the present generation is of necessity also deeply affecting the whole religious situation and in consequence of this also the relations between Christians of different denominations, and, not least of all, the relations between Roman Catholics and Protestants.

The work Pope John XXIII has begun in summoning a general council of all bishops in communion with the Apostolic See does not stand apart. It is rather one of the many aspects of a general situation which involves the whole of Christianity and ultimately the whole of mankind. We are being faced with the surging question whether we are living in a post-Christian, or rather a pre-Christian age. Pentecostal movements warn us that we are approaching the end of conventional Christianity, that worn-out forms of Christianity will have to give way to a completely new and vital witness to the gospel of God's revelation in Jesus Christ. The Reformation revival by which the period between the two world wars had been characterized and which had given rise to the theology of Karl Barth and his followers has not succeeded in solving the religious problems of our time. Bultmann, Tillich, Eliade, just to mention the most outstanding of those who are occupying the thoughts of modern theologians, are the exponents of a completely new approach to the Bible, to Christianity and to religion.

As Cardinal Bea has remarked, the Counter-reformation belongs to the past. But no less does the Reformation definitely belong to the past. The age-long controversy between Rome and the Reformation is gradually becoming obsolete in consequence of the up until now fully unknown character which the present religious situation with its own particular problems is assuming.

The Church in communion with Rome is embarking on a long-time period of thorough renewal. And so are many of the other Christian churches nowadays. It is through renewal on both sides that the churches are being brought closer to one another.

Therefore I would like to conclude this preface by earnestly warning against a misunderstanding, or rather an illusion, which is still widely spread among Roman Catholic Christians. It is the illusion that "non-Catholic Christians" will sooner or later be prepared to come back and submit themselves to the holy Catholic Church from which they have separated when they see how earnestly the Church is devoting herself toward a complete renewal in accordance with the will of Christ and the spirit of the gospel.

No Christian church however will admit that it ever separated itself from the one, holy, catholic and apostolic Church of the Creed. To this Church all baptized Christians belong. All Christian churches rooted in the Reformation (and not only the Anglican churches) protest against the view that they have broken away from the Church of Christ. All of them lay great stress on their continuity with the Undivided Church. Although the Christian churches are still divided on episcopacy, ministry and sacraments, it is becoming more and more evident that ecclesiastical problems are not being solved by old answers, but that a new approach based on achievements of modern biblical and historical scholarship will have to clear the way toward the full realization of the unity of all Christians in the One Church of Christ. Not by way of return or submission but by way of reconciliation and reunion based on a thorough renewal on all sides will such a unity be restored at large which is in every respect wholly according to the will and intention of Christ, as well as according to the true character and essence of his Church.

W. H. VAN DE POL

Nijmegen
Pentecost 1964

Introduction

THE schisms of the eleventh and the sixteenth centuries were both heralded by ecclesiastical and religious tensions in the preceding centuries. Each schism resulted in a separate form of Christianity existing apart from and in opposition to the Catholic Church (the Church in full communion with the Apostolic See of Peter in Rome), viz. eastern Christianity and Protestant Christianity. Each of these types of Christianity is marked by its own characteristics and identity, resulting from its own independent history of origin and development.

Protestantism even more than eastern Christianity is an intricate complex of various churches and sects, and within these churches and sects there are again new currents, movements and (as they are wont to be called today) modalities. All these various forms, types and expressions of Protestantism have common ground in that they arose and developed from the religious world of faith and thought and within the atmosphere of Protestantism itself. This means, among other things, that they all reject and oppose the Catholic Church as contrary (according to Reformation standards) to the content, spirit and intention of the gospel of Jesus Christ as attested by the Bible.

World Protestantism in its diversity is the result of a number of religious, theological and philosophical influences as well as of a variety of cultural, social and political factors which have made themselves felt, both from within and from without, ever since the beginning of the sixteenth century Reformation. In turn it has also left its mark on the western European and Anglosaxon culture in all its dimensions.

Protestantism has gradually expanded over the entire world, partly by colonization and emigration, partly by a powerful missionary activity. In the course of the past hundred years this activity has increased intensively as well as extensively; in more recent years it has also been increasingly directed toward traditionally Catholic countries.

World Protestantism by no means gives the impression of being timeworn. It seems to have overcome the religious stagnation and decline of previous centuries and appears to be enjoying a period of renewal and revival. An indication of this is a new theological reflection on the deepest essence of the gospel and of Christian faith, on the fundamental principles of the Reformation and on the religious questions which the modern world asks of Christianity. Other indications are a revivified and increasing consciousness of vocation with regard to its own people, to society and to all mankind; a new awareness of solidarity with all men without distinction, based on the love, reconciliation and forgiveness revealed by God; and finally the inauguration of various movements of an ecclesiastic and religious nature, the most important of which is the ecumenical movement.

This revival of world Protestantism does not mean merely a return to the Reformation of the past. In many respects it also means a real renovation. It aims at the future with a strong sense of purpose. The newly awakened world Protestantism prepares to overcome its own inner antitheses and disagreements and to win future mankind for the gospel.

World Protestantism has set out on the road to a distant goal, a goal which does not seem to be in the direction of the Catholic Church. In the near future it will however make itself felt in the world in such a manner that both the Catholic Church and the individual Catholic will again be confronted with it.

This will not be a confrontation with a doctrinal system, the untenability of which can be demonstrated by means of formal logic and its principles. World Protestantism is not a system but a living reality. It is, of course, possible to try to avoid an encounter or confrontation, but this path of least resistance would be a sign of weakness. What has been said of the Reformation itself applies equally well to all of world Protestantism: it is a religious effort in the present (*ein religiöses Anliegen heute*—Lortz). It does concern us and we must face it from the point of view of our own religious convictions and practices and life. It is a question that we must find an answer to.

If all Catholics were timorously to take shelter how would it ever be possible for world Protestantism to encounter the Catholic Church? How would it ever be possible to arrive at a real confrontation between Protestant man and Catholic Church? The truth of which we as Catholics are convinced can only come to light in a living, personal, existential encounter with the other.

For this reason a profound reflection on the Catholic faith and on what it means to be a Catholic will now, as well as in the future, necessarily have to go hand in hand with a proper knowledge of world Protestantism. And this holds true for every priest and for every Catholic layman who holds a responsible position in everyday life in which he will invariably encounter Protestants.

It is not the intention of this volume to refute world Protestantism, thus handing priest and layman a means of defending the Catholic view of faith. The intention is rather to give a well rounded, correctly proportioned and true to life picture of world Protestantism as it actually presents itself to us in the past and present in its rich variety of types and nuances.

If the extensive scope of this subject has prevented the writer from achieving this ideal, he has nonetheless honestly attempted, with all that lay in his power, to give a fair, impartial and objective picture.

In the chapter covering Reformed Protestantism we shall treat of the distinction which in Holland is generally indicated by the words *hervormd* and *gereformeerd*.[1] But since this distinction is difficult to express in language other than Dutch, when we speak of Reformed Protestantism in general the reader should not think of the Dutch Reformed Church in particular.

Another difficulty is the fact that the Protestant reader will feel closely allied to a definite form of Protestantism and thus get the impression that his personal vision of Protestantism has not been given its due, or that it has not been presented satisfactorily. Consequently, too, other forms may seem to have received too much attention or to have been given a too favorable interpretation.

Catholic readers may see that some of their misunderstandings and prejudices concerning Luther, the Reformation and Protestantism are found wanting. Some may find it surprising that there are so many good things to be said about all this. In this respect many a Catholic is in a position similar to that of a Protestant. After centuries of polemics and one-sided information, both Catholic and Protestant will often find it extremely difficult to obtain a correct view of the real nature of "the other religion."

An impartial investigation into the rise and development of the Reformation uncovers facts and imposes conclusions which, as Meissinger has observed in the introduction to his *The Catholic Luther,* will be difficult for both Protestants and Catholics to listen to and accept.

On both sides of the wall of division we have all too long been accustomed to listen to only one party, our own. It is however more in accordance with Christian charity to listen also to the other party, and in such a manner that one does not merely hear its testimony but actually listens to it. In any case we must refrain from clouding the truth and reality in a false sense of

---

[1] When the author speaks of *hervormd* we will refer to it as the Dutch Reformed Church. When he speaks of *gereformeerd* we will refer to it as the Reformed churches in The Netherlands. Both belong to the main type of Reformed Protestantism treated in chapter 2.—tr.

irenics. We must rather come to a point where we can, together and without scandal or grudges, courageously face reality as it is: as the historical and present reality.

It seems to be particularly difficult for Catholics as well as Protestants to arrive at a unanimous opinion about the person of Martin Luther and his role in the history of Christianity. This is not surprising since for both sides Luther is the personification par excellence of the separation and opposition which the sixteenth century Reformation effected.

It is *a priori* excluded that Catholics and Protestants should have an identical view of Luther's liability and responsibility. As long as there are Reformation Christians Luther will be looked upon as a prophet and legate of God who in a dark period of religious decline rekindled the light of the pure gospel. Catholic Christians, on the contrary, will always see Luther as the tragic if not demonic figure who—possibly misguided by good intentions—has been responsible for the desertion of a large segment of Christendom from the Church. They will see him as a man who by his passionate ragings against the pope and papists as well as by his crass misrepresentation of Catholic teachings has been responsible for the greatly distorted ideas about the Catholic faith and the anti–Roman feelings still evident among a good number of Protestants today. Fortunately recent research on Luther is considerably clarifying these matters. Meissinger even contends that there is a growing insight that Christianity in its collectivity has a common responsibility in this respect.

The purpose and method of this book about world Protestantism differ from those presented in this author's other books: *The Christian Dilemma*[2] and *Karakteristiek van het Reformatorisch Christendom* (Characteristics of Reformation Christianity).[3]

The purpose of *The Christian Dilemma* was to determine the

[2] New York: 1952.
[3] Hereafter referred to as *Characteristics.*—tr.

15

main points of difference between the Catholic Church and the Reformation. Much misunderstanding arose concerning the manner of approach to the cardinal differences between the two, even though we attempted to clarify matters in later publications.[4] It was certainly not our intention to separate word and reality or to distinguish them as contradictories. In revelation God reveals himself in his word, in Christ, in the Church, in God's salvation. Obviously both the Reformation and the Catholic Church understood this as a reality. Both agree that faith depends and is based on the proclamation of the word. The word of God is not merely an elucidation. It is efficacious; it effects something in the person who hears and believes it. It is the only means whereby the Holy Spirit moves a person to make the act of faith. When writing *The Christian Dilemma* this author thought it perfectly legitimate to presuppose all this as self-evident to any believer, Catholic or Reformed. For it is precisely in this that we find the common element in the Catholic and the Reformation foundation of faith.

The cardinal difference, however, is that according to the Roman Catholic the Catholic Church is in her one and indivisible manifestation a totally new and unique supernatural reality. In her visible manifestation, founded upon the rock of Peter, she is a supernatural reality in an ontological sense. The Catholic's act of faith in the visible Church as the Mystical Body of Christ is analogous to the act of faith in Jesus Christ as the incarnate word.

For the Catholic the visible Church is the form in which Christ continues here on earth his proclamation of the truth (infallibility of the living magisterium) and his work of salvation (sacraments imparting grace). Christ is the *minister principalis,* the actual minister and the only mediator between God and man. The pope, bishops and priests are his representatives

---

[4] Dr. van de Pol added to the English edition of *The Christian Dilemma* an appendix on the cardinal difference between word-revelation and reality-revelation.—tr.

and coworkers, his *ministri instrumentales,* his instruments in the Church upon earth. This new mystical salvific reality, at once visible and invisible, was rejected by the Reformation as nothing more than a human instrument of salvation. For the Reformation the sacraments as visible signs are means of confirming and strengthening the word received by the believer. God's reality-revelation reaches man in his existence on earth through the word and not in and through the mystical reality of the Church. The Reformation did not simply deny and reject the Church. It gave an essentially different meaning to the Church as the instrument by which the word is administered. According to the Reformation salvation comes to man through the word and not through the supernatural operation of grace that proceeds from the sacramental action of the Church as a new, real being existing on earth.

Since the terms word-revelation and reality-revelation caused some misunderstanding this author is prepared to sacrifice these terms for better ones. But he maintains his position that the cardinal difference between the Catholic Church and the Reformation lies precisely in those points in which he found this difference when he was accepted into full, visible communion with the Catholic Church.

At any rate it is not the purpose of the present book to renew the questions which were discussed in *The Christian Dilemma.* Nor does this book on world Protestantism deal with the theme of the writer's other work on the characteristics of Reformation Christianity. The latter was an effort to determine theologically the precise Reformation concept of the Christian faith. Hence whatever was not typically reformation in the original and authentic sense had to be eliminated.

The purpose and method of the present book on world Protestantism differ in all respects. This book is not written primarily for professional theologians and students, as was *Characteristics.* It is written for all persons who are interested in the ecumenical question today. For this reason quotations have been kept to a minimum.[5]

In the writing of this book we had in mind world Protestantism in its totality, Protestants in everyday life. This book is neither a history of theology nor a concise church history of Protestantism. We do not claim complete data on persons, facts and events. Dates are given only when they are required for a proper insight into the inner connections of world Protestantism and its development.

The origins of world Protestantism as it arose in Germany, Switzerland and England are described in the first three chapters. The second chapter, on Reformed Protestantism, contains some sections which refer especially to The Netherlands. Since Anglicanism is the most changeable form of Protestantism and has not yet arrived at a final stabilization, its history had to be pursued to the present. The final chapter describes the development of the Reformation up to the world Protestantism of today, so that the readers might be able to arrive at a clear picture of world Protestantism in its development, its differences, its inner connections and its eventual unity.

Because of important ecumenical developments since this book was originally prepared, the author found it necessary to revise and update thoroughly various sections of this book. Particular attention has of course been given to areas of discussion relevant to the Second Vatican Council. Examples of unionism, that is, efforts at unity within Protestant communities themselves, have also been given full consideration.

---

[5] In this translation the quotations will be given in English, and where necessary the title of books in foreign languages will also be translated.—tr.

1

Lutheran Protestantism

Causes of the Reformation

THE beginnings of the sixteenth century Reformation, the birth of Protestantism and the lasting division of Christendom which resulted are generally considered to be bound up with the person and activity of Martin Luther (1483–1546).

On Oct. 31, 1517 Luther nailed to the door of the castle-church at Wittenberg his ninety-five propositions on indulgences and true genuine contrition. Not only Lutherans but practically all Protestants celebrate this date as the official beginning of the Reformation.

Yet it is an oversimplification to attribute the Reformation to Luther alone or even to him principally. Modern research into church history has deepened man's insight into the most intricate complexity of religious, ecclesiastical, cultural, social and political causes which together prepared and promoted the outbreak of the Reformation. We shall here single out but a few elements.

The Babylonian captivity of the popes in Avignon (1304–1378), followed by the uncertainty about the lawful successor of Peter during the western schism (1378–1418); the secularized and warring Renaissance popes of the late fifteenth and early sixteenth centuries; the way in which some of these popes had cunningly acquired possession of the Apostolic See of

Peter; the manner in which they doled out important functions and handled finances; the luxury and the decline of morals at the papal court—all these facts had certainly not contributed to an appreciation of the religious sense and meaning of the papacy in the hearts of the sincere faithful.

In his *Manual of Church History* the late Cardinal de Jong of Utrecht concludes a paragraph about the Renaissance popes with the remark: "And while decadent papal Rome made merry, Luther summoned the German people to rebellion. Leo did not at once appreciate the real scope of this movement, though he finally condemned Luther in the bull *Exsurge Domine* (1520)." These tempered words put in glaring focus the actual situation of the Church which provided the background of Luther's actions.

In addition many bishops were exercising jurisdiction in secular affairs and were utterly negligent of the duties of their office. The level and nature of ordinary pastoral care of souls and the manner of life of numerous priests and religious were likewise cause for scandal. If one takes as criteria the spirit of the gospels, the sermon on the mount and the parables of Jesus and bears in mind the reasons why Jesus himself had come into conflict with the religious leaders of his time, one cannot but conclude that the situation in the Church at that time generally had little in common with Christ's intentions when he sent his disciples into the world as apostles.

Still it was not primarily the situation in the Church that incited Luther to action. Even if the abuses had been much less serious and extensive than has sometimes been supposed, even if the secular and monastic clergy had been possessed of a much higher dedication to their exercise of pastoral care and their life of piety than earlier Protestants would give them credit for, all this would hardly answer the question whether Luther's action was justified or not.

For many different elements were playing their part. Without the decline of late medieval theology and philosophy, without the late medieval shift of emphasis from a theocentric celebration of the liturgy to all sorts of man-centered devotions, and without the strong concentration of late medieval religious practice on punishment for sin, on hell and purgatory and on self-imposed penitential exercises to obtain justification in God's sight, the struggle in Luther's soul and his consequent view of the gospel are unthinkable.

It is moreover not easy to overestimate the significance of the invention of the art of printing. It took very little time to make copies of the Bible available to the general public. Wherever people began to read the Bible there was a growing conviction that the God of the gospels was different from the God proclaimed by the ecclesiastic and religious practices of the time.

The Reformation arose primarily from an inner crisis in religious life. There was a definite crisis in the manner in which man's relationship to God was envisaged and lived.

The reason this religious crisis could so easily lead to a separation from Rome and to the formation of new churches is to be found in the overall critical situation which western culture experienced in the transition from the middle ages to the new age. The spiritual climate had undergone profound changes as a result of the spread of Renaissance and humanist ideals. The Reformation itself was not related to these ideals but the change of the spiritual climate indirectly promoted the possibility of a religious revolution.

In addition there was a growing self-consciousness of nations and of individuals (nationalism, individualism, autonomy), a discovery of the person: personal nature and character, personal interests and rights, personal responsibility and calling. The individual loosened himself from the bonds of solidarity that had always made him one with the community.

Finally the interests of princes and many other political factors also played a part in the way the Reformation gained a foothold in various countries. But these incidents did no more than favor the spread of the Reformation. They should not be confused with the spiritual elements which were its more immediate causes.

Recent research into the Reformation has frequently raised another question: to what extent would reformers such as Zwingli and Calvin have made independent steps toward the Reformation movement if Luther had never lived? It is in any case important to examine how far the non-Lutheran forms of Protestantism actually depend on Luther, and to what extent they are also based on their own independent genesis and development. Some non-German researchers are inclined to say that the non-Lutheran forms of Protestantism are less dependent on Luther's teaching and action than is usually supposed.

Whatever the answer to this question it is certain that Lutheran Protestantism is the immediate fruit of Luther's actions. Lutheranism bears the personal stamp of Luther, and this applies especially to the first period of its rise. A correct understanding of original Lutheranism requires not only a knowledge of Luther's theology but also—and on an equal level of importance —an insight into the nature of his personality and religious sentiments. The latter can only be understood in the light of Luther's spirituality, i.e. in the light of Luther's personal encounter with the living God, and in the light of the fearful interior battle unto life or death which Luther, armed with the gospel, waged with God.

Luther's actions and the Lutheran Reformation are marked by the introduction not of a new theology in an intellectual sense, but of a new life, a new existence, in an existential sense. At the outset the Lutheran Reformation bore an existential character, a fact not always understood by Luther's opponents.

Lutheranism as a legitimate type of Protestantism was however influenced in its nature and being not only by Luther but also by Melanchthon (1497–1560). But since then many other influences and changes have occurred. For this reason it is incorrect to identify Lutheranism as it appears today with the teaching and spirituality of Luther himself.

22

Research on Luther

Before going further into our study of Lutheran Protestantism we must again mention the more recent research on Luther and the Luther image that has resulted from his research.

In the past four centuries Lutheranism has undergone profound changes which have at times relegated the spirit, belief, piety and intentions of Luther to the distant background. In spite of this, time and again there have been efforts to return to Luther for a reorientation. Even though these efforts did not always result in a complete grasp of the complete Luther, what was always appreciated and sought in him were those traits in which he was in harmony with the prevalent personal views of the gospel and Christianity. The very discovery of these traits, in turn, supplied the support these personal views needed at the time.

In the early eighteenth century, for example, both orthodox Lutherans and pietists had recourse to Luther. The pietists in their opposition to orthodox Lutheran scholasticism with its Aristotelianism eagerly reopened Luther's battle against philosophy. Even at that time efforts were made to project the existing antitheses into Luther himself, some holding that young Luther should be the criterion of pure Lutheranism, others that it should be the middle-aged or perhaps the elderly Luther.

So too in the course of the seventeenth and eighteenth centuries and early in the nineteenth century. Lutheran orthodoxy, pietism, the enlightenment, German idealism and German romanticism successively, in forming their own notions of the nature of religion and of evangelic Christianity, formed their own corresponding Luther image.

The third centenary of the Reformation in 1817 provided the occasion for the publication of a wide variety of writings praising Luther in many different ways as the great German hero of faith. This tercentennial literature did not rely on authentic sources but on a melange of personal religious feelings, desires, fantasies and subjective opinions. In fact it was so amateurish and jejune as to inspire the great historian Leopold von Ranke to write a critical, scientifically verified history of Luther and the Reformation based on a study of the sources proper. At first his abilities were not quite equal to this task and he was delayed in his effort. But at a more mature age he published his six-volume *A German History of the Age of the Reformation* (1839–1847).

Meanwhile interest had been aroused for a collection of all the writings, sermons, letters, notes and whatever else by Luther could be discovered in archives and libraries. The Erlangen publication of Luther's writings which had begun in 1826 was followed by the even more scientific Weimar publication, started in 1883. Volumes 56 and 57, published in 1938 and 1939, contain the reconstructed text of Luther's lectures (1515–1518) at the University of Wittenberg on Paul's epistles to the Romans, Galatians and Hebrews. This reconstructed text is based on sources which were not discovered until the first half of our century in different libraries, among them the Vatican.

The fourth centenary of Luther's birth (1883) had provided the impulse for the Weimar publication of Luther's works and for the organization of the *Association for the History of the Reformation*. In the meantime many biographies and monographs on Luther had appeared from the hands of such writers as Köstlin, Theodosius Harnack, Kolde, Albrecht Ritschl and others. While they display profound professional knowledge and scientific earnestness even these writings are not free from certain personal ideas of religion and Christianity. This should suffice to show how difficult it is even for the most knowledgeable and conscientious historians and theologians to present a picture of Luther and the Reformation that corresponds as objectively as possible to reality.

Van Rhyn, a church historian at the University of Utrecht, remarked in his comparative study on Ritschl and Luther: "The more one reads Luther, the more one gets the impression that

Ritschl emphasized the aspects that attracted him, at the expense of all else. Consequently in Ritschl we do not find Luther as he really was but as Ritschl wanted him to be." This could be applied, *mutatis mutandis,* to the entire nineteenth century interpretation of Luther.

It is no exaggeration to say that in the course of the centuries each new generation has fashioned for itself its own Luther image. That this fact has been the special focus of attention in more recent times is evident from a number of very worthwhile books treating of this subject: Zeeden, *Martin Luther und die Reformation im Urteil des deutschen Luthertums* (Martin Luther and the Reformation from the Point of View of German Lutheranism) 2 vol. 1950 and 1952; Pelikan, *From Luther to Kierkegaard* 1950; Stephan, *Luther in den Wandlungen seiner Kirche, neu bearbeitet und bis zur Gegenwart fortgeführt* (Luther in the Transitions of His Church up to the Present) 1951; Bornkamm, *Luther im Spiegel der deutschen Geistesgeschichte* (Luther as Mirrored in the History of German Spirituality) 1955.

This brings us to modern research on Luther, which in our age has entered a new phase, both from an historical and a theological point of view. The sense of reality proper to twentieth century man demands definite facts and an objective approach. Leaving aside our subjective attitudes we are now willing to ask the question: who was Luther and what did he actually teach and intend?

The first impulse in this modern research came from two Catholics who wrote on Luther, viz. Heinrich Denifle O.P., whose book appeared in 1904, and Hartmann Grisar S.J., who published in 1911. Both writers hoped to settle accounts with the Reformation by placing Luther in a rather bad light, though it must be said that Grisar's judgment was by far the milder of the two. Denifle tried to strike at the Reformation at its most vulnerable spot by showing that the man Luther deserves no respect, morally speaking. Grisar did not go so far although he did give the impression that Luther's religious crisis and certain other incidents in his later life manifest psychopathic traits.

It is now generally acknowledged that this was an incorrect evaluation of Luther's character and work. The quality of his gifts and the depth of his religiousness were not sufficiently appreciated. Partly in response to such faulty evaluation and partly stimulated by the fourth centenary of the Reformation in 1917, Catholic and Protestant historians launched into an unprejudiced investigation of the facts.

Kiefl, professor of Catholic theology at Würzburg, published a centenary study in 1917 in the periodical *Hochland* entitled *"Martin Luthers religiöse Psyche als Wurzel eines neuen philosophischen Weltbildes"* (Luther's Religious Psyche as the Basis of a New Philosophical Worldview). This was a considerable step forward in Catholic studies on Luther. It meant the rehabilitation of the man who was Luther. Not for a moment does Kiefl doubt the genuineness and depth of Luther's religiousness, nor does he bring the purity of Luther's motives and intentions into question. Profound religious impressions, partly against the background of German mysticism, convinced Luther of God's self-sufficiency. Man owes his salvation exclusively to God's mercy, forgiveness and grace. He cannot expect it from any other source. Salvation for Luther was the work of God alone. Carried to the extreme this had to lead to a departure from Catholic teaching and to a separation from the Church.

Continued Catholic research has led to the publication of Herte's three volumes entitled *Das katholische Lutherbild im Bann der Lutherkommentare des Cochläus* (The Catholic Picture of Luther as Seen from the Commentaries on Luther by Cochlaeus). Cochlaeus was a contemporary of Luther and his bitter opponent. Entirely incapable of penetrating to the real background of Luther's religious struggle, Cochlaeus more than anyone else is responsible for the vague Luther image, deformed as it is by misunderstanding and slander. For centuries this picture has been commonly accepted without question. It still circulates among Catholics of many countries.

In his three volume work Herte parades practically all books written about Luther by Catholics in Germany and other European countries in order to prove to what degree these writers were influenced by Cochlaeus' Luther image as it is known by Catholics. He accuses Denifle of setting aside the historian's neutrality, of being led by passion and bitterness and consequently of presenting a totally distorted and vague picture of Luther's personality and life. Nor is Grisar spared the criticism of having failed to live up to his intention, namely, to provide an understanding of Luther's thought and character. According to Herte the reason for this failure is the fact that Grisar's reproduction of Luther has been mixed with too many elements that must be considered incorrect, offensive, unjust and untrue.

Among those who initiated the renewed investigation of Luther the Protestant historians and theologians naturally occupy the first place. If the Catholic image of Luther had to be proved legendary because based on disparagement and antipathy it was also necessary to remove the legendary from the Protestant image, projected as it was from a standpoint of hero worship and—as far as Germany is concerned—from national pride.

This modern investigation has been greatly facilitated by the discovery of new sources.

Since 1512 Luther had been professor of exegesis of sacred Scripture at the University of Wittenberg. Under the influence of humanism this branch of the science of theology had also undergone a profound change at other universities. In Paris for example Faber Stapulensis had written commentaries on the psalms and on the epistles of Paul which were later used by Luther.

Previously sacred Scripture had been employed as a reservoir of proofs from which a writer in his treatment of a theological question could draw texts to support his thesis. Humanism on the other hand wanted to return to the sources and, by examining and determining the text as accurately as possible, see what Scripture was trying to convey.

All that was known of Luther's lectures from 1512 on was his exegesis of the psalms. Early in this century however research in the Vatican Library led to the discovery of a carefully written manuscript copy of Luther's lecture on Paul's Epistle to the Romans, a lecture delivered in 1515–1516. This copy put Ficker on the track of the original manuscript, which he published for the first time in 1908 after finding it in the National Library in Berlin.

This discovery was the first of a series. Students' notebooks containing notes of Luther's lectures on the epistles to the Romans, Galatians and Hebrews were found. These notes do not entirely agree with one another and, as far as the letter to the Romans is concerned, not even with Luther's own manuscript original. This of course is easily explained by saying that students do not always take accurate notes, but also by the fact that Luther in the ardor of his lectures frequently departed from his manuscript text and launched into improvisation.

Over a period of many years Ficker and his collaborator Meissinger labored very assiduously and with great precision over the discovered material in order to provide as well as possible a warranted reproduction of what Luther, prior to the Reformation, taught concerning the sense and meaning of the Pauline letters. Meissinger even mentions some years during which he spent two hundred library days on the examination of these texts. The results could finally be published in 1938 and 1939 as parts 56 and 57 of the Weimar publication of Luther's works.

Obviously this extensive material is the principal source for an understanding of the manner in which Luther arrived at his new insights into the Bible prior to the year 1517. Seeberg and others have even expressed the opinion that in this material it was possible to find all of Luther's ideas and teachings and that all his subsequent teaching and actions were but repetitions, elaborations and applications of the pre-1517 material. This is obviously a one-sided oversimplification. At present great emphasis is laid on Luther's publications of 1520 as well as on his later theology.

Meissinger, who knows the texts of Luther's lectures better than anyone, thinks that they display nothing that is contrary to Catholic teaching. He is of the opinion that the break with the Church came about as a result of the religious fury and bitterness of the polemics against Luther and not because of what Luther actually taught. This too is a one-sided conclusion though it certainly contains a nucleus of truth that gives food for thought.

The more recent research however has not been limited to the discovery and publication of new sources. It has also led to a more profound understanding of Luther's life and character. Among the numerous studies of him by historians of church and dogma, mention should be made of those by Scheel, Böhmer, Holl and Seeberg, and of such more recent works as those by Ritter, Stange, Meissinger, Bornkamm and Wolf.

Of equal significance is the ever growing number of monographs which treat of one single theological or ethical aspect of Luther's teaching. It is a happy phenomenon that only very few attempts are made to use Luther for the justification of private opinions. There is a very distinct general effort to arrive at a proper understanding of what Luther's teachings, intentions and activities exactly were.

Positive contributions in this direction have also been made by countries other than Germany. In Holland there was van Rhyn; in Sweden Aulèn and Wingren; in Finland Alanen and Pinomaa; in Scotland MacKinnon; and in the United States Carlson, Pelikan and Schwiebert.

Several popular Luther legends have evaporated in the face of historical truth, such as the stories about monastic conditions and about Luther's own monastic life; the story according to which Luther was supposed to have accidentally found a Bible under a thick layer of dust and that he had to smuggle this Bible into his cell; the authenticity of Luther's celebrated exclamation to the emperor: "Here I stand, I cannot do otherwise."

Some of the Luther legends are based on his own testimony. It is now evident that in his narration of past events Luther allowed himself to be led not by a sense of reality but rather by a lively fantasy that colored the objective facts. Nor does it seem that his memory was quite reliable.

The most controversial sources are Luther's *Table Talks* during which he often gave free rein to his spontaneity, his fancy and his passionate temperament. If his often crude, even barbaric manner of expression would easily offend a delicate sensibility it also often displays a frankness and unconcern that exclude any suspicion of malice, corruption or deception. Rather malice can be detected in the manner in which some opponents of Luther have exploited these "weaknesses" against the profound earnestness of his piety.

The story of Luther's experience in the tower room which he occupied is generally known. While preparing his lectures there he suddenly experienced a sense of discovery in which the real meaning of the gospel is supposed to have become clear to him, and as a result of which he is supposed to have changed into an entirely new man. The greater part of this story is based on Luther's personal testimony contained in the preface, written by him shortly before his death, to the first publication of his works. Research has established that this testimony is strongly exaggerated and that it does not correspond to the historical facts.

Meissinger even maintains to have found that the newly discovered texts exclude such a sudden conversion in Luther between 1512 and 1517. He holds that Luther's new insights developed slowly as a result of constant study. Consequently he relegates Luther's tower experience to the realm of the legendary. In any case the various researchers have not been able to arrive at a unanimous opinion concerning the year of Luther's sudden conversion—if it actually did take place.

Of far greater importance however is the fact that modern investigators have thoroughly screened other Luther legends of a much more serious nature. In this connection Bornkamm mentions the legend of the enlightenment which extolled Luther as the hero of reason and the champion of freedom of conscience. Also mentioned are the legend of idealism which pictured Luther as the creator of a new culture; the legend also of Lutheran ecclesiasticism which used Luther as the crown witness for the truth and correctness of personal convictions and views of life, but did not allow Luther to have a say for fear of an uneasy conscience. A plain, formalistic and conventional mentality will never suffice for a really profound and correct understanding of Luther. To obtain a proper view of a figure such as Luther, to understand him in his greatness as well as in the tragedy of his loneliness and failures, it was first necessary to experience the shocks of the First World War and the total spiritual bankruptcy of our own times.

The existing ecclesiastic counterpositions necessarily result in differences of opinion about Luther. Yet practically all modern investigators are agreed that their research has happily led to what Bornkamm calls "a distinct parallelism of the main lines in the theological and historical research of Protestants and Catholics alike."

Amateurism in this field has been very widespread. We have to realize that this research is still in full progress, that there are still many areas to be explored and that we have by no means arrived at a complete, well balanced picture of Luther that is scientifically warranted in all respects.

It has for example not been definitively established which of the late scholastic works Luther personally knew and studied. Obviously those works about which there is uncertainty must be thoroughly examined if we want to find out what theological and philosophical influences Luther was subjected to. Compared with those of the high middle ages the late medieval works were of little theological importance and have, since the Council of Trent, fallen into oblivion, from which they must now be rescued.

31

Although much has been written about Luther's attitude toward scholasticism, mysticism and humanism (and about his possible dependence on the Paris humanist Faber Stapulensis), modern research has hardly reached a stage that answers all scientific requirements.

One aspect of this research not yet sufficiently come into its own is the close connection between the nature and content of Luther's writings and his character and personality. In this respect Denifle and Grisar have pointed in the right direction even though they lacked the sympathy required to understand Luther and judge him fairly.

A similar connection is practically nonexistent in scholastic theologians in general and in Thomas Aquinas in particular. Scholasticism is aimed at an intellectual knowledge of truth. It tries to establish the truth by means of logical arguments. Therefore it depends strongly on philosophy. Proofs and conclusions scarcely depend on the character and personality of the scholastic theologian.

Luther's theology, on the contrary, is essentially different. He consciously and vigorously rejected and opposed intellectualism. His theology is aimed at the salvation of the sinner. It has a soteriological character, that is, it is concerned with the salvation of man. It does not reason but bears witness; it does not prove but proclaims. In this proclamation there is a question of personal encounter with the living God, i.e. of a life and death struggle with the living word of God. This word is directed not at man's understanding or intelligence but at his heart; it touches him in the very core of his being. It is at one and the same time man's condemnation and acquittal. It is not something that is intellectually understood once and for all but something that must be lived and fought through over and over again. In this view God has one individual way with each single person; the testimony of each one of the faithful—including the theologian—bears a personal stamp.

Accordingly Luther's theology is highly personal, dynamic

and existential. His theology is therefore closely connected with his personality. It does not depend on any philosophy but on the immediate and living word of God as it touches man personally in his existence as man before God. Thus it is not surprising that Luther and the scholastic theologians never had any contact in their disputations for there are few points of contact between scholasticism and the theology of Luther—the latter not to be understood as Lutheran theology.

The man Luther

Recent Protestant and Catholic findings agree fairly well on Luther's character and personality. It is obvious that Luther's character was not favorably influenced by the lack of understanding he experienced frequently and in many areas both from his supporters and his opponents. The older Luther (after about 1525) is no longer as generally sympathetic as the original young Luther. However this applies only to certain aspects of his character.

As can be seen from his successes and achievements, since his first years as a student Luther showed an indestructible zeal, a creative power and a stamina which exclude any thought of immorality of life often imagined by his enemies.

In fact Luther's life was from the very beginning characterized by seriousness, austerity and sound regularity. The integrity of his character and personality, the purity of his intentions, the unselfishness of his actions, the genuineness and depth of his piety and his extraordinary gifts of mind and heart are beyond any doubt or suspicion.

Luther was a man of feeling. His nature was warm, even childlike, simple and sincere, although it was easily inflamed, especially when his passionate temperament and sense of justice set him off in angry indignation. In those instances he often lost his self-control, raving on in an irresponsible manner. However, what was at stake in those instances was never himself but rather the cause he defended, a cause which he seriously considered as the cause of God in the interest of his neighbor's salvation.

It is a well known fact that his outbursts of anger and indignation led him more than once to a relentless denunciation of the pope, prelates and bishops and in later years of zealots (Anabaptists and other sectarians) and of rebellious peasants. Melanchthon alluded to this in his oration at Luther's funeral: "If we hear that Luther was often too coarse in his writings, we answer with Erasmus that God sent a strict physician because the disease was serious; such a champion was needed against the powerful, presumptuous opponents of the truth."

In any case Luther was profoundly aware of his sins and defects. It was hard for him to control his violent temper, subject as it was to his changing moods. Moreover he frequently fell into religious melancholy. One day he might be the champion of faith, the next he might fall prey to temptations, doubts, uncertainty. Time and again he despaired of God's grace, of his vocation and of the legitimacy of his actions.

It cannot be maintained that the serious religious crisis to which he was subject for years beginning in 1505, and for which there seemed to be no remedy, was mainly due to the papist piety and practices of those days and to ignorance of the true meaning and content of the gospel. The fact that similar fears and tensions kept recurring to the end of his life proves that his religious crisis must be considered in the light of particular predispositions connected with his entire makeup.

Both Ritter on the Protestant side and Lortz on the Catholic side find they can discern a distinct difference between young Luther and the old Luther. Even during the disastrous rebellion of the peasants, which was put down with much bloodshed, Luther's polemic, already passionate and violent, began to have malicious and embittered overtones. As Ritter says, "the deep pathos of his voice was mingled with a new, harsher, and sometimes strikingly unharmonious sound."

If his attitude toward Copernicus was reserved and that toward Zwingli stubborn, Luther's attitude toward the peasants and zealots was fanatical. Whenever it was apparent that he was no longer master of the situation he encouraged violence. He was entirely devoid of any sense of freedom of conscience in the modern meaning of the word. He demanded freedom for the true proclamation and open practice of the pure gospel. In reality this meant freedom for all who understood the gospel in Luther's sense, not for those who explained and practiced the gospel in any other manner. In the last years of his life his hatred of the Jews was particularly fierce and he advised the authorities to burn their houses and synagogues, to confiscate their properties, to subject them to forced labor or to send them into exile (cf. *About the Jews and Their Lies* 1543).

However it was in his duties toward the movement he had incited and in his attitude toward Philip of Hesse that Luther fell short more than anywhere else.

In his pamphlet *Luther, Die deutsche Tragödie* (Luther, the German Tragedy) 1521 Meissinger describes the German tragedy as the fatal result of Luther's lack of a sense of duty and responsibility toward the German people and toward the historical consequences of his actions in which he had thus far displayed courage and constancy.

Instead of taking a powerful hand in the direction of the Reformation movement when the time was ripe—after the Diet of Worms and his refusal to recant—Luther withdrew to the quiet of private life, allowing the development of events to take its own course. Meissinger contends that if Luther had fully recognized and utilized the situation and created a National Church of Germany, the country would have been saved from the Counter-reformation, from the sufferings of the Thirty Years' War and from many of the credal controversies. "The religious man that Luther undoubtedly was could not find in him the political man he should have been" (Meissinger). Ritter also finds that these were the limitations of Luther's genius: "He lacked the quiet reflective care, the reliable sense of politics required for successful action in secular affairs."

All experts are agreed that his attitude toward Philip of Hesse marks one of the most incomprehensible and dark pages of Luther's life.

From the very nature of this case Catholics have no inclination to find excuses for any of Luther's doings. For them it is especially difficult to refrain from unbalanced and unjust criticism of Luther in the face of such frightful shortcomings as he displayed in regard to Philip of Hesse. Not only had Luther allowed this landgrave to enter into a secret bigamous marriage but he had also counseled him to answer any suspicions or questions in this matter with a "good and lusty lie."

All this had taken place because of political threats by Philip, and with the approval of Melanchthon and Bucer, both of whom were even personally present at the secret wedding.

While it is true that this entire matter is quite unsavory it would be unfair to emphasize this episode in the life of Luther and in the history of the Reformation, thus casting a slur on everything Luther and the Reformation stood for. It would moreover be shortsighted and unwise. For the papacy and the Catholic Church have also known very dark periods which all too often have been thrown up at the Catholic Church in utter disregard for its true nature and purpose.

Luther as a Catholic

It is impossible in the framework of this chapter to speak extensively of Luther's entire career. This makes it all the more important to point out some of the principal moments which are important for a correct understanding of Luther's teaching and actions.

Martin Luther was born in Eisleben in 1483. In this same year his parents moved to Mansfeld, where Martin spent his youth. It is sometimes stated that the tactless and sometimes overly severe attitude of his father caused, even at a very early age, a certain aversion to anything resembling authority. However there are no reasons to suppose that Luther's youth was generally very difficult and unhappy.

In his parental home Luther learned the Catholic faith in a very primitive form. The inhabitants of German areas in those times considered fairly remote had only recently felt the influence of the Church. Moreover the cultural level could not be compared with that of France, England or The Netherlands.

Luther does not seem to have received any profound religious impressions until he was sent to school in Eisenach in 1497 (the year of Melanchthon's birth), where he lived at the home of the Schwalbe family, according to Böhmer "the most pious family of Eisenach." Here he met for the first time in his life people for whom religion was really the predominant concern, the only norm of life. In this environment Luther learned to see the distinction between Catholicism as a pure matter of routine and as a profound serious way of life. Böhmer thinks that it was here that the foundations were laid for Luther's vocation to the monastic life.

At the age of eighteen he left for Erfurt. With his exceptional talents and by industrious application he graduated after only four years of study as the first among his fellow students with the degree of master of arts.

Shortly after the celebration of this brilliant and well earned success he began to complain about a trial of sadness, a temptation of melancholy which was the prelude to the serious religious crisis from which Luther suffered repeatedly from 1505 on.

This crisis had considerable influence on Luther's further religious development. It is therefore very important to know the true causes and nature of this crisis. This matter cannot be brushed off with the statement that a person's faith cannot be judged by psychological or historical influences.

There is no doubt that Luther's psychic structure strongly predisposed him to such crisis-phenomena as mentioned above.

However this in itself is no reason to conclude to psychopathic aberrations. Still less does it give a satisfactory explanation of the origin of the crisis, for though the causes do imply a predisposition they should not be confused with that predisposition. It is also superficial to judge the religious significance of the crisis and its consequences by the predisposition. The question in such a religious crisis is one of truth and reality and must be judged by its own criteria. Even if a religious crisis does show psychopathic symptoms as a result of a certain disposition, this says nothing about the religious truth and reality in question. If it is admitted that certain facets of the gospel were discovered anew by Luther, these facets will retain their validity even if it later appears that the discovery was accompanied or stimulated by a crisis that shows certain psychopathic traits. This author does not by any means intend to suggest that such was the case with Luther. These observations are addressed to people who are easily inclined to say that Luther's teaching and actions do not deserve serious attention since they can be "explained" by a psychopathic disposition.

The cause of the disposition which was at the basis of Luther's crisis can be best typified as a spiritual short circuit between the depth and seriousness of Luther's personal religious life and the religious environment in which he became involved.

In our day and age it is very difficult to imagine the spiritual and religious climate of cities like Erfurt of those times. Philosophically as well as theologically this climate was dominated by Ockhamism, a system of thought which is not only entirely foreign to us but which could scarcely be regarded as typically Catholic at any time.

It seems to this author that all modern Luther scholars are agreed that the principal cause of Luther's crisis must be found in his Ockhamist ideas of God.

William of Ockham lived in the first half of the fourteenth century. Born in Ockham near London, he became a Franciscan monk, studied in Oxford, lectured in Paris, was imprisoned in

Avignon on charges of heresy, and escaped in 1328, together with the general of his order, to the court of Louis of Bavaria in Munich, where he died around 1350.

As the founder of nominalism he exerted great influence in the late middle ages in England and France, and especially in southern Germany. It is true that Luther did not study theology in Erfurt before 1505 but even then the entire system of education, including that of religion, was saturated with Ockhamist ideas. In Erfurt Luther was confronted with an arbitrary, unreasonably severe and impossibly demanding God. There was practically no trace of the spirit of the gospel, which is a spirit of love, of patience, of forgiveness. Luther's receptive soul, inclining to melancholy and discouragement, could offer no resistance to the Ockhamist ideas of God and to the religious practice based on these ideas.

Ockhamism held that the moral law was based not on the nature of things but on an arbitrary decree of God. There was no intrinsic value in the acts of a believer. Whether an act was meritorious or not, that is, accepted or rejected by God, depended on an arbitrary decision by God. The best that man could do was to make all possible efforts to live up to God's severe demands. Ockhamism had distinctly Pelagian tendencies for it left man to his own natural resources. It was devoid of the Augustinian and typically Catholic conception of grace as a supernatural gift and quality with which God comes to man's aid and through which God directs man to his eternal salvation. Justification and grace were conceived as a cloak with which God covered the sinner who believes. Faith, grace and justification were granted by God exclusively to those who were predestined to receive them. But even then man remained sinner and justified at one and the same time (*simul justus et peccator*). No one could know with certainty what state he was in. All that was in man's power was to do his best to avoid all sin, to make up for it or to overcome it.

Moreover the act of faith itself was of an arbitrary nature

and could in no wise be rationally justified. There was an absolute divorce between faith and reason. To believe meant to accept blindly on authority and with no rational understanding. Ockhamism was in principle anti-intellectual. It had even lost all sense of the nature and value of the divine gift and mystery of the speculative powers.

It is therefore true that the religious notions of Ockhamism led up to Luther's interior crisis. But it is no less true that the anti-intellectualism as well as the Pelagian concept of the nature of grace and the *simul justus et peccator* were transferred, though in a new evangelical context, from Ockhamism to Luther's teaching and theology.

It would obviously be a serious mistake to confuse the Ockhamist system of thought and its religious climate, which were passing phenomena, with the faith and life of the Catholic Church.

A complete and further investigation of the extensive Ockhamist literature still waits for the republication of several Ockhamist works. Meanwhile much new light has been shed on the religious situation at the end of the middle ages by the most valuable contribution of Dr. Heiko Oberman, *The Harvest of Medieval Theology*. Dr. Oberman strongly objects to nominalism being called a caricature of Catholicism. Rather he looks upon it as a "vital link" between high scholasticism and the theology of the Counter-reformation.

In any case it is certain that Luther considered the Catholic faith and religiousness from an Ockhamist point of view, so that his later fierce reactions are directed against it rather than against the true Catholic doctrine.

After his academic success of 1505 and greatly influenced by his father's wishes, Luther planned to study law. However, during his summer holidays he was more and more overwhelmed by fear—fear of sin, fear of the judgment to come and fear about the uncertainty concerning his predestination to eternal salvation. On his way back to Erfurt he was caught in a thunderstorm and nearly struck by lightning. A few days after his arrival he sold all his books and on July 17, 1505 entered the Augustinian monastery at Erfurt.

This seminary was generally known as an excellent monastery where monastic discipline was well observed without any undue excesses. There is no reason to suppose that the religious spirit and austerity there were inferior to those of our monasteries today. As research has proved sufficiently, the cause of Luther's crisis, of his reform movement and of the origin and rapid expansion of the Reformation must not be attributed to a general decadence or to serious abuses. Legends about Luther's monastic life do not prove anything against monasticism as such. If they contain any truth at all they rather attest to the unhealthy, scarcely Catholic notions which Luther had formed for himself of monastic life. It seems certain that Luther hardly lived his monastic state in an evangelic manner and that his superiors could not succeed in inducing him to a more healthy view. Throughout his life, however, Luther did retain a deep respect for two of the confessors he had become acquainted with in the monastery.

Luther received the tonsure in the year of his entrance, pronounced his vows in 1506 and was ordained a priest on April 4, 1507 in the abbey of Erfurt. He continued his studies of theology until the fall of 1508. If his training for the priesthood was marked by Ockhamist tendencies this is true to an even higher degree of his continued studies in theology. His Ockhamist formation was completed through the writings of Gabriel Biel, Peter d'Ailly and Ockham himself. And his religious disposition certainly did not profit by it. He repeatedly suffered from fears, worries and doubts. If there is any truth in the story about his hesitations during the celebration of his first Mass he must have experienced this consoling mystery in a manner which is quite contrary to the content of the prayers of the canon of the mass and to the Catholic ideas of the holy eucharist and sacramental grace.

Luther lectured in moral philosophy from October 1508 to October 1509 at the University of Wittenberg, then situated on the edge of civilization. Catholicism there had a distinctly popular character and as in many other places the veneration of relics had a very prominent place. Since the printing press had only recently been invented the number of those who were able to read and write was extremely small. As a result it was the statues, the stained glass windows and the relics that captured the imagination of the people who, through these externals, understood their common bond with Christ and with the saints.

From October 1509 to October 1510 Luther lectured at Erfurt as *sententiarius,* that is, he explained the *Sentences* of Peter Lombard (concise theological answers to questions posed by scholastic theology). Luther's copy of the *Sentences* as well as an edition of the works of Augustine which Luther studied (both richly annotated by Luther) have been preserved to this day.

During the winter of 1510 Luther accompanied the procurator of the German Augustinian order to Rome to appeal against measures taken by local authorities in connection with disagreements within the order. This trip to Rome should not be considered of great importance with regard to Luther's later development, except perhaps in the sense that the indulgences he gained there did not serve to put an end to his religious fears and worries.

Early in the summer of 1511 Luther was sent to Wittenberg to be promoted to doctor of divinity, a promotion which took place in October 1512. In spite of his protestations that he was not fit to undertake such responsibilities the vicar general of the order insisted on appointing him professor of exegesis of sacred Scripture. This function also implied the obligation to preach regularly.

In the Augustinian monastery at Wittenberg Luther had been assigned a tower-like upper story, the so-called tower room where he used to prepare the lectures he gave from 1512 to

42

1518 on the psalms and the epistles of Paul to the Romans, Galatians and Hebrews. Luther's rediscovery of the gospel took place in this period.

By the time of his arrival at Wittenberg Luther's religious crisis had become quite serious. He received much support and sympathy from the vicar general Von Staupitz whom he had chosen as confessor. Von Staupitz, a convinced Thomist, was also a follower of the *devotio moderna,* a mystical form of piety which had begun in the Low Countries and had spread to Germany. In vain did Von Staupitz try to remedy the turmoil caused in Luther's soul by the Ockhamist ideas of God. His words however left such a deep impression on Luther's subconscious that in one of his *Table Talks* in 1531 Luther exclaimed, "I have received everything from Von Staupitz! Von Staupitz started this doctrine, for he told me that I must look at the man called Christ."

Still Von Staupitz' words were not effective enough to help Luther. Whenever Luther tortured himself with the question whether he was among God's elect Von Staupitz would answer, "Anyone who wishes to argue about predestination must begin with the words of Christ. You must form in your mind the image of Christ predestined by the Father to suffer for sinners. If you have this, then predestination is in full progress"—that is, then you are personally involved and taken up in the work of divine predestination.

On another occasion Von Staupitz is supposed to have said to him, "True contrition and penance must begin with the love for God." Commenting on this in 1518 Luther wrote, "These words hit me like a stroke of lightning and pierced my soul like a sharp arrow."

Von Staupitz did nothing more than try to cure Luther by means of the consoling medicine of the gospel. It is puzzling to find that his words had no effect on Luther. We may well ask ourselves why Luther had to discover the saving and healing gospel, a gospel that was deeper and purer than the age-old gospel proclaimed by the Catholic Church from the beginning.

Luther's discovery

It would seem that there is only one way to find out what exactly was taking place in Luther's soul, what led him to his evangelical preaching, and what it was that seized his hearers and readers so profoundly as to make possible the rapid spread of the new gospel over a large part of western Europe. This approach should not begin with an investigation of the exterior situations and circumstances so as to arrive at a conclusion whether or not there were reasons for such a revolutionary movement. The only way that will lead to a real understanding of the deepest sources from which the Reformation sprang lies in an exact chronological study of all the Luther texts we have of the early period, that is, from 1512 to 1520. Hence it is easy to see the extreme importance of the discovery and publication in our age of Luther's lectures on the epistles of Paul to the Romans, Galatians and Hebrews.

It is obvious that the result of one's investigation will be strongly influenced by what one is looking for. Until recently most researchers were trying to trace how Luther's acquaintance with Augustine or with German mysticism influenced his terminology and theological considerations. Such efforts however do not touch much more than the surface, for it was not Luther's purpose to institute a new theology but a new relationship to God and a new pastoral care. The deepest causes of his preaching and activity and of the rise of the Reformation are to be found in the area of practical religion; Luther did not seek change for its own sake. The changes he effected and the new theology he supplied the impetus for are but the accidental consequences of something far more important: the awakening of a new awareness of God, a personal encounter with God. In the given ecclesiastic and religious situation Luther considered himself to have been given new and inescapable obligations that required fidelity to a new vocation and task.

In all this the words of Von Staupitz played a secondary part in that they served to awaken in Luther a distrust of the theological ideas he had acquired in Erfurt, ideas which were at the basis of his personal struggle. But Von Staupitz too was no more than human. Who then would give Luther the guarantee that his words could be trusted? Nothing less than God's own word could convince Luther that he had found favor in God's sight. And where else could this word be found than in the Bible?

For Luther personally therefore it was a most happy circumstance that from October 1512 onward he had to study and expound the sacred Scripture *ex professo*. It is doubtful whether apart from Luther there has ever been a professor of exegesis of Scripture whose professional and scientific association with the Bible had at the same time such a profoundly personal and existential character. For Luther it was a question of "to be or not to be." His interior struggle for the certainty of salvation led him therefore to a persistent and urgent recourse to sacred Scripture until it should supply him personally with the liberating word of the gospel. After all his struggles and experiences Luther was concerned only about the direct and unadulterated word of God. He wanted ultimate and strict objectivity.

In this disposition of mind, which was at the same time a new type of exegetical and theological disposition, Luther rediscovered the gospel in an entirely new way: that of personal discovery. As a message from God addressed to him personally it contained the only means of solving his personal struggle and agony of soul. Since then one of the most important characteristics of Reformation piety and belief has been this personal, direct, living, existential relation between the individual believer and the objective character of the recreating word of God as it speaks to man directly and immediately.

Reformation spirituality is based on and nourished by a daily dialogue with the Bible and as a result the theology of the reformer also received its own characteristic stamp. Truth no longer has a general, abstract, speculative and theoretical meaning but rather a highly personal, concrete, existential and practical one; the science of theology is now no longer a system of premises and conclusions. Luther was perfectly convinced that human reason by itself was incapable of achieving true and genuine knowledge of God. Any such knowledge, he held, must rest on God's self-revelation, on God's own word. This word is not directed primarily at the mind but at the heart. It effects something in man and man reacts to it and draws his practical conclusions from it, but neither the operation of the word nor man's reactions are of an intellectual nature. These events cannot be expressed in a system. They must be expressed in testimony. Luther's theology was from the very beginning marked by this testimonial character, not in the sense of a proclamation of personal opinions but in the sense of a faithful and obedient annunciation of the objective word of God, of the message of salvation which affects the lives of all men. His theology was born of a prayerful, conscientious listening to sacred Scripture. In his activity and theology Luther was not primarily concerned with his own salvation. From the moment that he discovered the gospel as a real force for the renovation of life his prime concern was the salvation of others. From its inception Luther's theology was put at the service of preaching and pastoral care.

It is an established fact that Luther's personal rediscovery of the gospel as God's saving message to men must be dated in the first years of his professorship in Wittenberg—in any case before 1517. Modern research however has rendered questionable the supposition that this rediscovery was a sudden, unexpected event. It was not the "experience in the tower" which, according to Böhmer, must be dated in the spring of 1513. Bornkamm says that rather we must think of a gradual process of maturation, although it is entirely possible that some definite date was of especial importance in this process. This could have been the day when Luther, during the preparation of his lectures, for the first time had a clear insight into the meaning of the biblical expression "the justice of God." Bornkamm denies that in this connection we should think of an emotional experience as a result of which a complete change took place. We have already pointed out that such an idea contradicts the facts and the source material at our disposal beginning with the publication of Luther's lectures. As we have remarked Meissinger, who knows this source material better than anyone, has used it as evidence to relegate the story of the "experience in the tower" to the land of legends.

The question about the ultimate cause of the low religious and moral level among the majority of the people had occupied Luther's attention since 1512. In that year Luther wrote a sermon for the prelate of a Premonstratensian monastery, a sermon read on the occasion of a synod. The theme of the sermon is the improvement of the life of the people and in it Luther rejects all sorts of exterior palliatives. Even in this sermon he names the manner of preaching as the principal cause of the prevailing ecclesiastic and religious situation. As long as the gospel is not preached as a living and powerful word of God, he contended, any efforts at improvement will be ineffective. There is only one cure: the direct, pure word of God which no one can escape.

The final paragraph of the sermon contains some distinct expressions of the exclusive character of Luther's preaching. In one sentence the word *solus* (alone, exclusively) is mentioned four times. As the context clearly shows this word is not intended quantitatively but qualitatively. Former apologists have often given the impression that this emphatic *solus* of Luther and the Reformation indicates an arbitrary choice, a one-sided stress on one definite religious factor to the exclusion of all other less important ones. This is a mistaken supposition. Luther wanted to return to the heart of the matter. There are numerous opinions and ways of doing this which man has concocted for himself, and which therefore lead to nothing. What matters only is

47

what God has said and done, the way which God has shown us through Christ.

The closing paragraph referred to above reads: "So it is that everyone who shall have invoked the name of the Lord is saved: but only he who believes invokes him; only he believes who hears the word of truth; only he who hears the gospel hears the word of truth; only he hears the gospel who hears the priest as a messenger of God."

This final statement that only he hears the gospel who hears the priest as a messenger of God proves that in 1512 Luther still considered the objective gospel and the subjective act of faith as dependent on the priestly, authoritative proclamation in and by the Church.

The most important problems modern research on Luther will have to occupy itself with for some time are the questions: how did Luther's personal rediscovery of the gospel lead to a break with the Catholic Church in which he himself was a priest, and was this break a necessary consequence of the rediscovery? Also, was the gospel as Luther had gradually come to consider it after 1512 really contrary to the teaching of the Catholic Church? There is a growing number of Catholic as well as Protestant researchers who doubt that it was.

Should the answer be that a world of misunderstanding and prejudice prevented contact between Luther and his opponents, it should not be regarded as not really being a matter of great importance. If it was a question only of a misunderstanding, the misunderstanding was so profound that it simply had to arise when two so vastly differing spiritual worlds clashed. But a definitive judgment on this matter must be left to the future.

The question that is being asked today is what precisely Luther understood by the gospel, and what Reformation Christians mean when they say that Luther rediscovered the true, original gospel, "removed it from under the bushel basket, and placed it again on the lamp stand."

The Ockhamist notion of God which Luther had made his

own while he was a student had been the cause of his being filled with fear and terror whenever he reflected on the justice of God, the *justitia Dei*. The fact that this expression occurs more than once in Paul's epistles had at the outset even deterred him from involving himself in a study of these epistles. The Book of Psalms showed Luther the way to the Epistle to the Romans when he was struck by the apparent contradiction of the psalm verse, "Set me free, Lord, in your justice." How could fallen man, burdened with the awareness of sin, be liberated by the justice of God? Is it not precisely this *justitia Dei* which holds man captive in fear because he is a sinner?

There were in particular two texts from the Epistle to the Romans which shed some light on these obscure questions:

For in (the gospel) the justice of God is revealed by an ever growing faith [literally: from faith unto faith]; as it is written, "He who is just lives by faith" (Rom 1:17).

But now the justice of God has been made manifest independently of the Law, being attested by the Law and the Prophets. It is the justice of God through faith in Jesus Christ, and upon all who believe (Rom 3:21-22).

Luther had never known or understood that the Christian faith is a matter of this *justitia Dei*. He had always understood the word in the old Greco-Roman moralistic sense of "rendering to each person what is his due." In this sense God's justice would mean that God demands of man that he always and in all things conduct himself according to the natural law and according to the revealed divine law; God then rewards good and punishes evil in strict measure according to the divine justice.

It had been Luther's idea that the gospel applies not to sinners but only to the just; only to those who, having done their best, have earned the salvation of Christ; only to those who have peace of conscience, that is, those whose consciences are not burdened by the consciousness of sin and guilt.

Luther's pangs of conscience arose from the firm conviction that even with the utmost exertion he would never really and fully be able to live up to the severe demands of God's justice.

However, it appeared to him that the *justitia Dei* in Scripture meant something entirely different from the philosophy and moral theology based on it. First of all, in the Bible there is question of the justice of God which man cannot possibly come to know by his own powers of reason, but which must be revealed by God if man is to know anything about it. This is a very peculiar type of justice which the Old Testament had already given witness to but which is fully revealed only in the New Testament. It is a justice which can only be believed; it is accepted on the authority of God's own word. And what is more it is a justice that is not based "on works prescribed by the law" but on "the placing of the act of faith." Finally the biblical justice is not a demanding and terrorizing justice but rather a giving and consoling one. It is a justice existing in God and forgivingly directed to the sinner precisely as sinner, because no sinner is ever capable of obtaining absolute justification for himself as the fruit of his own efforts. The biblical justice of God is based on the full and complete justification which here on earth has been acquired and merited only by Jesus Christ and by no other man. In his love and grace and forgiveness God grants this full and complete justification of Christ to all who believe in the gospel, that is, to all who upon hearing the gospel frankly and unconditionally admit to being sinners utterly dependent for eternal salvation on the justification merited by Christ. It is for this reason that man is justified, not by fulfilling the law but by believing in the gospel. Man is justified when he is reinstated in the right relation to God, a relation disrupted by sin.

This message of justification by faith alone was for Luther the core of the gospel, of which Paul wrote: "I am not ashamed of the gospel, for it is the power of God unto salvation to everyone who believes, to Jew first and then to Greek;" that is, first to the chosen people but later to the rest of mankind.

To any Catholic it is entirely self-evident that the written gospel is also the gospel proclaimed by the Catholic Church in the past, the present and the future. However this proclamation must not be confused with theology, a human product. The datum of revelation is the object of the reflections and considerations of theology. If thus far Reformation Christians have failed to find the written gospel in the Catholic Church this is not necessarily due to an incorrect interpretation of the gospel on their part. To a great extent it may be due to the nature, method and terminology of Catholic theology on the one hand, and on the other to a complete alienation of Reformation Christians from the life of the Catholic Church.

In any case the Catholic historian is faced with the problem that much of what was rediscovered by Luther and other reformers as entirely new was in fact purely Catholic, even if it was not acknowledged as Catholic by the reformers or by their opponents. Not only has the problem of how Luther came into conflict with the Church not been solved by the examination of Luther's newly discovered lectures on the epistles to the Romans, Galatians and Hebrews; rather it has only situated the problem correctly.

What has at any rate been ascertained is that Luther's further developments after his discovery of the biblical meaning of the *justitia Dei* took place in a continuous battle with and defense against scholastic theology. It is however highly questionable whether he sufficiently knew and understood scholasticism at its best. It is a fact though that Luther's later development is characterized by an increasing simplification and interiorization. The typically Lutheran conception of the nature of the act of faith is, according to Bornkamm, best expressed in Luther's lecture on the Epistle to the Hebrews. Bornkamm calls it "Luther's most profoundly personal document of the year when the Reformation became a fact."

Luther's conflict with the Church

Two dates are of decisive importance in the course of Luther's development and in the history of the origin of the Reformation. The year 1517 saw the definitive outbreak of the Reformation;

the year 1520 the final break with Rome. After 1517 Luther's vision of the gospel underwent no essential changes. He had acquired this vision as a result of five years of intensive biblical studies as professor of exegesis. If it can be supposed that his explanation of the Pauline epistles was contrary to the teaching of the Church, this very fact would show that in those days a professor of theology could get into personal difficulties in matters of faith simply because he could go around propounding all sorts of false teachings without being detected or disturbed.

What caused the open conflict between Luther and the Church is the fact that Luther extended his activities from lecture hall to public life. It is general knowledge that Tetzel's preaching of indugences led up to this even though the question of indulgences is not the actual theme of the Reformation. The practice of indulgences in those days did no more than supply the impetus by which the Reformation process got under way, a catalyst that promoted and hastened the Reformation movement.

Tetzel's preaching of indulgences was the most proximate reason why Luther became involved in the fields of pastoral care and ecclesiastic life. From this time on the main accent in the course of events is not on the question about the nature of the gospel (this question had been solved as far as Luther was concerned) but on the nature, function and competency of the Church.

It was Luther's vision of the Church which led to a conflict and ultimately to a definitive break with Rome. The cardinal point of difference between the Catholic Church and Reformed Christianity today is still found on this plane. Many Protestant theologians are convinced that there is an intimate connection between Luther's vision of the gospel and his vision of the Church and that the first necessarily led to the second. There are many difficult problems here which require further investigation and such investigation can be fruitful only when the sources are studied from the Protestant as well as the Catholic point of view. One has to guard against confusing the essentials with all sorts of accidentals tied down to a definite time and culture.

In any case it is a fact that the real cause of the definitive rupture lies in the consequences which Luther himself drew from his vision of the gospel with regard to the nature, authority and functioning of the Church.

In his great work on the Reformation in Germany Lortz rightly pointed out that the Church's functioning in the life of the faithful of that time was for many reasons quite defective. People had lost the sense of the true nature and of the deepest meaning of the Church as a mystery of faith, as the mystical Body of Christ. The liturgico-sacramental life had become impoverished and had given way to an individualistic and subjectivistic piety. The authority in the Church was no longer understood as a divine authority; obedience to ecclesiastic authority was no longer considered a matter of faith. The accidental form in which the Church appeared in its human manifestations was confused with the real nature of the Church in its actual and functional solidarity with Christ. This fatal circumstance made it possible that Luther's very noble pastoral concern, his solicitude for a genuine preaching of the true gospel in its saving power, finally resulted in the stubborn and deplorable break between the Catholic Church and the Reformation.

Luther's first public protest against Tetzel's manner of preaching indulgences was no doubt a testimony "for the sake of gospel and conscience." It arose from a profound pastoral concern for the spiritual and religious well being of the masses. Here Luther apparently did not act on the presupposition that being baptized and being in the Church includes in principle a participation in the grace of Christ, and that for those who are in the Church it is not a question of obtaining salvation but of maintaining it. Luther's vision of the gospel is a vision of the connection between man's sin and God's grace; between the condemnation of the sin and the acquittal of the sinner; between the proffered reconciliation, forgiveness and redemption on the one hand and, on the other the act of faith, justification and a life according to God's will and intention spontaneously born of this justification. In such a vision of the gospel the Church as a mystery of salvation does not occupy an essential place, only an accidental and subservient one. True, Christ willed that there should be a Church and he instituted the sacraments; but it is ultimately the Holy Spirit who by means of the gospel calls forth in man's heart the act of faith and accomplishes salvation.

Luther made no real distinction between the baptized and unbaptized in an ontological sense; he saw all men, believers and unbelievers, baptized and unbaptized, as lost sinners who are saved only by a conscious act of faith in the gospel's message of salvation.

Even before Oct. 31, 1517, when he posted his ninety-five theses about true contrition and conversion, Luther had frequently made mention of indulgences in his sermons. Anyone reading these sermons carefully and without prejudice must conclude that Luther's anger and dismay had primarily been aroused by the manner in which indulgences were preached and handled. Luther found it evident that the preachers of indulgences were more interested in the money than in the salvation of the faithful. But Luther seems to have been even more concerned about the false complacency the faithful had developed by the purchase of indulgences and letters of confession, as if their eternal salvation was now secure and no further application to a life of true penance and conversion was needed. The preaching of indulgences had replaced the preaching of the living and life-giving word of God. A false way of salvation was held up to man instead of the only true way of salvation God himself teaches to man through Christ. Luther was convinced that the preaching of indulgences not only failed to contribute to an understanding of the true gospel but that it positively prevented such understanding and was an obstacle to the saving act of faith. He found that the preaching of indulgences therefore truly endangered the eternal salvation of the faithful who founded their assurance of salvation on indulgences.

The question of the pastoral dangers of the preaching of indulgences was bound to result in the question about the propriety, the competency, the validity and the real or supposed effects of indulgences. This question, in turn, led to the question of the limits of the authority and powers of the pope.

Nor did it take long before the question arose about the limits of ecclesiastic censures and excommunications. To what extent did they affect the well being of the soul and eternal salvation? What are the actual effects of excommunication? Can a papal bull of excommunication separate a person from Christ and exclude him from God's love, grace and union? Is not such a transition from the plane of human judgment to that of God's judgment a transgression of human powers? Does papal jurisdiction even include by a decree of Christ's will the authority to pronounce an excommunication? After such a pronouncement is there no possibility of appeal to the decision of a general council?

These and other questions occupied Luther's mind very profoundly from 1517 to 1520. In 1518 he published a commentary on his ninety-five theses numbering more than a hundred pages. Luther considered the above questions in this commentary and also in a sermon "On the Force of the Ban" and in a long polemical tract against Sylvester Mazzolini on the power of the pope. All these writings can be found in the first volume of the Weimar edition.

Luther's theses and polemical writings did not take long to find widespread approval. The Augustinian order did not interfere with Luther. It was the archbishop of Mainz who first called Rome's attention to the rapid propagation of Luther's doctrine and to the dangerous consequences of his activities. Neither the pope nor the papal curia took the information very seriously. Still less were they able to form even the slightest idea of what Luther's primary interests were. Cardinal Cajetan, who was the one important Renaissance theologian and who had himself written a warning against erroneous interpretations and applications of indulgences, was finally appointed to call Luther to account in Augsburg—and to silence him.

From the very beginning Luther was at the mercy of two opposing forces: the desire of the Elector of Saxony to leave Luther undisturbed, and the desire of Luther's enemies to render him harmless. Cajetan's efforts to bring Luther around, now by a benevolent attitude, now by threats, and finally through the intervention of Von Staupitz, were quite understandably unsuccessful. He lacked a proper insight into Luther's spiritual structure and religious attitude, a lack also displayed a year later by John Eck in his public disputation with Luther in Leipzig.

Luther's inability to cope with the acute scholastic arguments of Cajetan and Eck is beside the point here. Luther was not concerned about irrefutable conclusions but about fidelity to conscience, about direct testimony based on God's word. Luther and his opponents in no wise shared the same presuppositions; their motives and aims were radically different. The actual point in question and which both sides ardently defended was of a totally different order and lay on a completely different plane. Understanding and rapprochement were *a priori* precluded.

The decisive year for Luther, the year when he broke with Rome, was 1520. Stimulated by the disputations with Cajetan and Eck, by the support and opposition he experienced, by the political and ecclesiastic situation in which he had become involved, and by the accumulating problems which demanded a hurried solution, Luther in 1520 displayed a hitherto unknown activity. This was the year when the major part of his principal works appeared. They were of a highly polemical nature and were charged with a passionate anger and indignation which found expression in a truly brilliant eloquence.

Although Luther wrote a number of tractates (to call them sermons would be misleading) on good works, the New Testament, the mass, the papacy, etc. three of his treatises are of greater importance. The first, written in German, was entitled *To the Christian Nobility of the German Nation on the Improvement of the State of Christianity.* The second was written in Latin and entitled *On the Babylonian Captivity of the Church —A Prelude.* In only a few weeks' time this was being read widely in many European countries. The third was *A Treatise on the Freedom of a Christian,* written in German. A Latin translation of this latter treatise was sent to the pope with an accompanying letter by Luther.

In the address to the Christian nobility of Germany Luther develops, more as a prophet than as a politician, a program of politico-social reform based on his new vision of the gospel. He envisaged a social ethics on the basis of which the Christian community in all its dimensions was to be subjected to a drastic reform and renewal. It is always worthwhile to study this document, particularly because similar questions are of interest again today.

The work on the Babylonian captivity of the Church, intended to be a prelude, is like an iconoclasm, a radical housecleaning in the Church. It proceeds from an entirely new concept of the nature of the Church, the sacraments, the sacrifice and public worship. Here too it is a matter of the consequences Luther drew from his vision of the gospel and of the nature and function of the act of faith. Luther's concept of the Church and of the place of the Church in the work of salvation is based on a new vision of the manner in which the encounter between God and man takes place. If Luther does maintain some of the traditional and "Catholic" teachings the context in which they appear and the meaning given to them are new and essentially non-Catholic.

Both the address to the Christian nobility and the treatise on the Babylonian captivity emphasize the general priesthood of the faithful. Because man hears the word of God and acknowledges it as such, in other words because he believes, he stands in direct relationship to God and thus needs no priestly intermediary at all. In fact the believer precisely as believer is himself a priest inasmuch as by being a believer he is called to testify to the gospel in word and deed. Accordingly man himself becomes an intermediary between the gospel and his fellow men who do not yet believe. This general priesthood finds expression not only in the Christian testimony or confession but also in prayer and in Christian charity and mercy. No believer is excluded or exempt from this general priesthood, which is however in no way sacramental. It has nothing to do with ordinations or orders. The entire notion of valid or invalid orders is completely foreign to the Lutheran concept of Church, office or sacrament.

It would therefore be wrong for a Catholic in judging these matters to hold fast to certain "Catholic" teachings. The treatise about the freedom of the Christian and the sermon about good works are documents concerning man's liberation from the slavery of the law, and in particular from the slavery of the precepts and duties imposed by the Church, and from the slavery of casuistic moral theology. From his vision of the gospel Luther draws conclusions about the nature, function and mutual relationship between law, sin, the gospel, redemption and liberation and good works. These new mutual connections as they are determined by Luther's vision of the gospel also presuppose an essentially new concept of conscience which, however, has little to do with the later liberal concept of freedom of conscience.

Luther's treatise on the freedom of the Christian was answered by Pope Leo X in the form of a bull of excommunication. The pope named Dec. 10, 1520 as the deadline for a possible retraction by Luther. On that date Luther publicly burned the bull, together with the book of canon law and some late scholastic writings. He did not do this on impulse or in a burst of rage. It was a planned symbolic action by which Luther wished to confirm all he had written in the preceding years about ecclesiastic authority and law. With this action Luther consciously and irrevocably discarded the past. He discarded a world of ecclesiastic and religious notions, claims and practices which he considered totally in contradiction to the spirit and true sense and meaning of the genuine gospel and the unadulterated word of God. The break with Rome and the papist Church had become accomplished fact.

At the Diet of Worms in 1521 Emperor Charles V made a final attempt to persuade Luther to revoke his writings. It was hardly to be expected that this attempt would be successful. Luther's answer was an appeal to his conscience:

Unless I can be convinced by the testimony of the Scripture or by evident reason (for I believe neither the pope nor the councils since it is a fact that they have often failed and contradicted each other), I cannot and will not revoke anything. I am convinced by the texts of Scripture which I have quoted, and my conscience is held by God's words. It is neither safe nor fitting to act against one's conscience.

Luther's life after the break with Rome

The nucleus of Luther's preaching and activity can be approached from various angles. One could take as a starting point his awareness of God, the nature and manner of his encounter and converse with God, his vision of the nature of sin, his vision of the nature and manner of the redemption, his concept of the nature of the act of faith, or his concept of the nature of Christian conscience.

Between these latter two there is a very intimate connection. In fact this connection was so close for Luther that in one of his writings he defines faith as "nothing other than a good conscience." Especially in his later years he strongly emphasizes that a good conscience depends not on good works but on faith. We shall presently refer to this after concluding the story of Luther's life.

Actually the further course of Luther's life does not present any new insights or perspectives. In 1525 appeared his treatise *On the Enslaved Will* (*De servo arbitrio*) in reply to a treatise by Erasmus on free will (*De libero arbitrio*). Luther always considered this his most important work. It deals with the assurance of a salvation found exclusively in God and not in man's weak, inconstant will.

In this work Luther denies neither the existence of man's will power nor that man can exercise his will and execute a decision of the will with respect to the created things which are subject to his will. Luther here discusses man's will only insofar as it touches his relation to God and eternal salvation. He goes to some trouble to make clear that he is not speaking of the will regenerated by the Holy Spirit but of the will of fallen man precisely as sinner and unbeliever. Consequently the treatise looks more like a rejection of the humanism and Pelagianism of Erasmus than a denial of the authentic teaching of the Catholic Church. This does not by any means however indicate that Luther's teaching on grace is Catholic.

Of great practical importance for the ecclesiastic and religious life of the nascent Lutheran church are Luther's *The German Mass* (1526); the minor and major catechism (1529); and the German translation of the Bible in 1534. The stabilization of Luther's doctrine in the form of the Augsburg Confession and later confessional writings was more the work of Melanchthon than of Luther himself.

In 1525 Luther married the fugitive religious sister Catherine Von Bora. This marriage, a happy one, was the bright spot in Luther's later life, filled as it was with worries, disappointments, friction with friends, political complications and interior struggles. In the end, like so many other great men, Luther lived and died in solitude, a misunderstood man. He died in his native Eisleben on Feb. 18, 1546 and was buried on Feb. 22 in the castle church of Wittenberg. Melanchthon delivered the funeral oration.

If in an effort to summarize we ask ourselves what really were Luther's positive teachings and intentions, we see that they are concerned principally with four aspects or facets: his vision of the gospel and of the nature of the act of faith, his vision of man's conscience, his vision of the Church and of everything pertaining to ecclesiastic life, and his vision of the Christian's place in the world.

Luther and the gospel

The gospel is God's message to fallen mankind in this world. Jesus Christ is the personification of this message. He proclaimed the gospel but by his person and work he himself is also the content of the gospel.

The gospel reveals to man the real nature of sin. It speaks of the consequences of sin, of God's wrath and judgment of sin. It speaks also of God's grace, mercy and love for the sinner precisely as sinner, of the work of reconciliation, redemption and liberation accomplished by Christ. It proclaims God's readiness to forgive and God's promise of eternal life and eternal salvation.

Christ came into this world not only that he might speak of sin, judgment, grace, forgiveness, reconciliation and justification, but also that he might by his life, passion, death and resurrection be the personal pledge of the truth of the gospel message. By his life, passion, death and resurrection he merited grace, forgiveness, reconciliation, redemption and justification for the whole human race and made all of these things living realities.

As the incarnate Son of God Christ really accomplished what no human effort, penance or ascetical or mystical practice could ever have achieved: the restoration of complete peace with God. Christ is himself the foundation of grace, forgiveness, reconciliation, redemption and justification—in short, of peace with God and eternal beatitude. Christ is himself the "rock of our salvation," unfaltering, eternal. From the moment that man hears and believes the gospel of Jesus Christ he knows once and for all that he must not seek his salvation in or through himself but only in and through Christ. From the fact that Christ is man's only means of salvation it is clear what a pitiable state of loss and sin fallen man lives in as long as he lives without Christ. Only when we see our human situation and existence in the light of the cross of Christ do we know what it really means to be a sinner. To be a sinner means that man has without reserve placed himself in the center of his own existence, that he has dethroned and banished God. All sinful thoughts, deliberations, impulses, plans, desires and deeds are symptoms of the state in which man has found himself ever since original sin.

From the point of view of moral theology there are of course many differences between people, between serious faults and minor ones. But sin, the cause of our separation from God and of eternal death, is not something quantitative; it is something qualitative, a state in which man lives. For there is no man for whom God is really, that is, unconditionally, completely, exclusively, always and in all respects the center of his human existence, determining all its expressions perfectly and totally. All men who have ever lived are equal in this: that they are sinners in the biblical sense of the word.

The only exception is Jesus Christ. For this reason Christ alone could reconcile man to God, he alone could merit and obtain true justice for man. Merit in its absolute sense of restoration and satisfaction can be attributed only to the salvific work of Christ.

The gospel addresses man precisely as sinner. Its condition: man must stop defending and exonerating himself, he must stop deluding himself about his good intentions and about his being oriented to the good. The gospel places all men under God's judgment; it demands of man an unconditional surrender to this judgment and a sincere and unqualified acknowledgment of sinfulness, that is, of his inability to repair his relationship with God. In contrast with the pride of sin the gospel demands an act of true humility—man's total surrender before the face of God.

The gospel is a solemn assurance and pledge from God based on the salvific work which Christ accomplished. If a person is too proud to clasp this saving hand and expect from Christ alone whatever he needs for his eternal salvation, he cannot possibly be reconciled with God and saved by Christ. He is much like the drowning man who rejects the lifebelt offered him because he wants to continue his hopeless efforts at saving himself.

According to Luther the real nature of the act of faith consists in this: that he who hears the gospel capitulate unconditionally to the word of God and that he acknowledge, accept and confess Christ as the sole means of salvation offered by God. Faith is not a rational acceptance of a doctrine. It is a personal, conscious act in which the sinner surrenders and entrusts himself totally to Christ and his work of salvation. This faith is the work of the Holy Spirit—not directly or independently of the proclamation of the word, but through the gospel and the word of God.

By means of the living, dynamic word of God the Holy Spirit awakens faith in the heart of each individual. The act of faith is a highly individual and conscious act. It is the function of the word to address man in the Bible in order to reveal man to himself. Through his word God takes complete possession of man as sinner. In and through the act of faith man surrenders unconditionally to God. Thus there arises a fundamentally new orientation to God from which a new life is born, a life spontaneously directed to God's will and intentions. This new life is of an ethical nature; it is not a supernatural quality infused into man but the fruit of a faith-filled acceptance of the evangelic message. In no wise does a Christian's life consist of an external and moralistic obedience to precepts and commands; it is born of an inner renewal of the heart accomplished by the Holy Spirit through the word of God. Man is justified, saved in time and eternity when, having heard and understood the gospel, he accepts it for himself personally through a real, conscious act of faith, that is, when he believes the gospel with heart and soul. Then no power of the world, the devil or hell can snatch him away from the hand of God. Neither is there any power on earth, not even that of the Church, which should ever or could ever intrude between the word of God and the person who is saved by faith in this word.

The one and only means God uses to save man is the gospel. This is absolutely sufficient, just as on the part of man it is sufficient to posit the saving act of faith. This implies that there is for man only one way of salvation, one *via salutis*. The way of salvation as conceived by Luther and the other reformers is best indicated by the three exclusives, the three *solas: sola Scriptura, sola gratia* and *sola fide*—Scripture alone, grace alone and faith alone. God speaks to man through Scripture only; objectively man is saved only by God's grace (that is, through God's gracious disposition, mercy and forgiveness); and subjectively he is saved only by faith in the gospel.

The classical expression for this Lutheran vision of faith is that man is justified by faith alone (*justificatio sola fide*) without the works of the law, that is, not by faith together with good works, and still less by good works instead of faith, but by the act of faith alone.

The question then arises whether man on his part need contribute anything toward his justification and eternal salvation. Luther's answer is negative. Not only does man not have to do anything but he cannot and even should not do anything. If man should try he would be robbing Christ of his glory. Moreover he would be building his assurance of salvation on quicksand instead of on the immovable rock of salvation: the all sufficient salvific work of Christ.

Yet this does not mean that good works are done away with. Once man has been justified by faith and has obtained peace with God there arises in him a sincere love of God and a daily awareness of gratitude. Good works spontaneously spring forth from this love and gratitude according to the circumstances of life. These good works have exclusively an ethical, not an ascetical character. They are done from love of God and neighbor and not in order to obtain something for self, whether it be greater holiness or greater reward in heaven. According to Luther and the Reformation good works are in no respect a condition or foundation of justification and eternal salvation. They are the spontaneous results of gratitude for the salvation given by God in and through Christ.

All of this also implies a certain connection between the law and the gospel. It is quite true that the law is in itself not evil; it is just and good. But its function is to convince and accuse man of his sin since no man can fulfill the law by his own power. As long as he does not know Christ and the gospel man is burdened by the slavery and the curse of the law. Christ alone, as the representative of the entire human race, really fulfilled the law. The person who believes in Christ has been redeemed by Christ from the curse of the law. Therefore Christ is redeemer, he is in no way a lawgiver. For it is impossible that Christ, who came to redeem man from the slavery of the law, would want to put him under the slavery of a new law. According to Luther it is a complete misunderstanding of the meaning and the purpose of the salvific work of Christ and of the proclamation of the gospel to speak of the new law of the gospel.

Luther and the human conscience

The above vision of the connection between the gospel, the act of faith, justification and good works led Luther to an entirely new concept of the human conscience. There is no question here of the later concept of the freedom of conscience for which liberalism unjustifiably invoked Luther.

On the one hand Luther's concept of the human conscience is closely connected with his vision of the gospel; on the other hand it played a very important part in influencing and determining his vision of the nature of the Church and his position with regard to ecclesiastic claims of authority and rights.

On the basis of sacred Scripture Luther had become convinced that every person in this world is and always remains a sinner, even as a believer. It is precisely the believer alone who knows and acknowledges that until his last breath he depends on God's grace, in the sense of God's forgiveness for the sake of Christ.

As a sinner man must succumb to God's anger. No person in this world ever sees himself as he really is unless he has a bad conscience. No one who reflects on the abyss of his actual existence before God can ever have a good conscience. Particularly at the moment of death does a person stand guilty before God, that is, with a bad or accusing conscience. This is what happens when man relies not on Christ but on himself.

Apart from faith in Christ and in the gospel there is no efficacious means of silencing one's accusing conscience and changing it into a good conscience, not even by the most severe penance or the greatest sacrifice on behalf of one's neighbor or the most noble good work. In themselves these are not entirely devoid of value but they lack the power to change a bad conscience into a good one.

The only expedient possible is for God to grant a good conscience to the person plagued by a bad conscience. God does this in his readiness to forgive without there being any merit on the part of man and independently of man's actions. This is also what the Holy Spirit does through the gospel. The gospel is the only efficacious cure for a terrified and fearful conscience. A really accusing conscience that knows why and of what it is accusing man even presupposes knowledge of the gospel, for without the gospel man has no knowledge of sin. Man has at most an awareness of moral faults and failures such as pagans can also have, but the gospel awakens the accusing conscience, creates as it were the Christian conscience which is never satisfied with what man himself has done.

When the gospel strikes the human heart it not only awakens the conscience; in and with the placing of the act of faith it also changes the accusing conscience into a good conscience. So close is the connection between the genuine act of faith and a good conscience that Luther, in his commentary on the First

Epistle of John (1527), defined faith briefly as a good conscience (*fides nihil aliud est quam bona conscientia*—faith is simply a good conscience). To the degree that man does not have faith he has a bad conscience and, as often as he counteracts his bad conscience by positing a genuine act of faith, he has a good conscience.

Accordingly the good conscience of a Christian is not founded on his good deeds but is independent of them because it is the fruit of the gospel accepted in true faith. A truly good conscience expresses itself in serenity of mind, peace of soul and assurance of salvation, in short, in "the peace of God which surpasses all understanding," the gift of God and the most precious possession of the man who believes in Christ and in the gospel. The believer does not allow himself to be stripped of this possession, no matter how much men, powers, circumstances and diabolical temptations may at times lay snares for it.

This treasure is safe only as long as it remains captive and secured in the word of God. Just as original sin was the result of man's lending an ear to a voice other than God's so too will a good conscience be in danger whenever it reckons with any human word, including that of the Church, which is not the direct and living word of God as it addresses man personally and immediately in sacred Scripture.

For the believer then each decision is a decision of conscience, and peace with God is at stake whenever the conscience forms a decision independently of the word of God. In this connection there can never be any question of compromise, opportunism or obedience to any authority whatever apart from the authority of God's word. Luther often repeats that man should never do anything which is contrary to his conscience but he does not mean to say that man must follow his private insights, his intellectual judgments of conscience which are measured by moralistic criteria. What he very emphatically means is that man must in his entire existence and in all his actions be guided and dominated by his conscience which is captured in and formed by God's word.

Man will be prevented from nourishing a bad conscience only when he allows his conscience to remain captive in God's word and when he lets himself be guided by this conscience. Insofar as the bad conscience, rightly or not, acts as accuser it can as it were be compelled to make way for the good conscience only by a genuine act of faith.

In his later years Luther was more and more inclined to see the bad or accusing conscience as an instrument of the devil. He himself suffered frequent serious temptations. It is the devil's aim to deprive the believer of his faith and in his attempts to make man afraid and desperate he awakens the bad conscience. The devil tempts man to sin and at the same time acts as man's accuser before God. At times it is only after a fearful struggle of faith that man succeeds in regaining his faith and in silencing his bad conscience by the only means available: faith in Christ and the gospel.

But a dead conscience is worse than an evil conscience. Luther thought that in his day popes, bishops and prelates had dead consciences. These ecclesiastics, he held, purposely and knowingly close their ears to the voice of the pure word of God. Their hearts are hardened like the heart of the pharaoh of Egypt. Not only do they not arrive at faith in the gospel but they invent all sorts of means to torture, enslave or dull the consciences of men. They carefully keep the people away from the living word of God by offering them stones for bread in the form of foolish legends and devotions, and thus prevent them from arriving at a personal, conscious and saving faith in the gospel.

Luther and the Church

As we have remarked earlier in this book it is possible to adduce a complicated and complex system of causes that might explain Luther's actions, his conflict with Rome and the genesis and rapid spread of the Reformation. There is no doubt that external factors played a part in all this: for instance the circumstances and the manner in which the ecclesiastic authorities reacted to Luther's first public actions. But it is obvious that the causes and motives can best be learned from what Luther himself said about them in his lectures, sermons, letters and treatises.

The conflict with the Church and the lasting breach with what Luther called "the papist church" were ultimately the result of a crisis on authority. The consequences which Luther drew from his vision of the gospel and God's word led to a personal conflict between obedience to the authority of conscience held captive in God's word and obedience to the teaching and pastoral authority of the Church.

From an entirely new and, as he thought, purely biblical and evangelical concept of authority and conscience Luther undertook to fight to the death, in vehement language, against what he held to be unjustified and godless claims to authority on the part of the pope and the papist church.

If Luther described the pope as the antichrist and with fiery indignation branded the papist church as an invention of Satan (e.g. in his *Against the Papacy at Rome Founded by the Devil*), one should think not of uncontrolled outbursts of rage but of purposely intended cries of alarm by which he wanted to warn the faithful lest they continue to be victims of a diabolical deceit.

The devil has only one aim: to drive man to perdition by leading him away from God and by having him rebel against God. The principal means he uses are lies and deceit. The devil has been a deceiver from the very beginning. Ever since his first victory over our first parents the devil has continued to twist the word of God and has tried to render it powerless and destroy it. Naturally his attacks are the fiercest against Christ and against those who believe in Christ. According to Luther the papacy and the papist church had replaced the authentic word of God by fables of their own invention which, he was ever more convinced, the devil used as his instrument to drive Christians to perdition. Luther ultimately saw nothing in the papist church but the incarnation of the deceitful attacks and plans of the devil.

In his fanatical ragings against Rome and the pope Luther was convinced that he had been called by God to destroy this bulwark the devil had constructed in the form of the papacy and the papist church, a bulwark that prevented the efficacious penetration of the gospel into the hearts of men.

The reader should not let himself be led by a false sense of irenics into believing that Luther's vision of the papist church is "naturally" no longer accepted by reasonable people of our own time. This is not intended as an accusation. Even in our own time it is a typical Protestant conviction that in the battle against Rome, waged "for the sake of the gospel and the human conscience," nothing else is at stake than the well being of the soul and the salvation of the "true believers in Christ."

This conviction is present somewhere in the subconscious of all genuine Protestants, Lutherans and others. It is awakened, strengthened and enlivened whenever at some culminating point of ecclesiastic and religious life (even in the Christian Student Movement and in the ecumenical movement), and particularly during the annual celebration of the Reformation, the militant Luther hymn is intoned:

> A mighty fortress is our God,
> A bulwark never failing;
> Our helper he amid the flood
> Of mortal ills prevailing:
>   For still our ancient foe
>   Doth seek to work us woe;
>   His craft and power are great
>   And, armed with cruel hate,
> On earth is not his equal.
>
> Did we in our own strength confide
> Our striving would be losing;
> Were not the right Man on our side,
> The Man of God's own choosing.
>   Dost ask who that may be?

Christ Jesus, it is he;
Lord Sabaoth his Name,
From age to age the same,
And he must win the battle.

And though his world with devils filled,
Should threaten to undo us;
We will not fear, for God hath willed
His truth to triumph through us:
The prince of darkness grim
We tremble not for him;
His rage we can endure
For lo! his doom is sure,
One little word shall fell him.

That word above all earthly powers,
No thanks to them abideth;
The Spirit and the gifts are ours
Through him who with us sideth:
Let goods and kindred go,
This mortal life also;
The body they may kill:
God's truth abideth still,
His kingdom is forever.

Luther's conflict with Rome led to a definitive break between the Reformation and the Catholic Church. In this connection Luther and the Reformation made a sharp distinction between the Church which is believed and the Church which is seen, between the invisible Church of creed and the visible Church of empirical reality.

Sacred Scripture, as well as the ancient Christian symbols (apostles' creed, etc.) Luther accepted, speaks of a Church. Consequently Luther had to determine what and where the Church is if the papist church is not the Church intended by Christ. What are the marks by which the Church can be known? How does the Church function? What are her motives, means and aims? What is her relation to the work of Christ and what part does she play in the life of the believer?

The most important conclusion concerning the Church drawn

from Luther's vision of the gospel and of the human conscience captive in God's word was that only God is absolute. This divine absoluteness cannot be attributed to any word, deed or authority of any man or of any human community. Only Christ's salvific work accomplished here on earth has absolute and universal authority.

The Church in its earthly manifestations is a human community. Despite its efforts to proclaim the word of God in its purity and to act according to God's will and intentions the Church will never be an absolute. In its earthly manifestations the Church, even in the person of its highest officials and representatives, can fall into error or fail in its fidelity to its vocation and task. In no respect should an absolute character be attributed to any ecclesiastic authority as if it was divine, absolutely binding authority.

Man is truly free only when he knows himself in a conscience bound and safeguarded by nothing but the living word of God. No human authority may intrude between the free and direct operation of God's word and the heart of the believer. Whenever the Church seeks to oblige the faithful in conscience to accept an ecclesiastic doctrine or to follow ecclesiastic precepts or commandments she puts herself in the place of God, hinders the free operation of the word of God, attacks man's freedom of conscience and reduces man to the slavery of the law from which Christ and the gospel had redeemed him. Nothing but God's word obliges in conscience.

Luther's vision of the Church therefore excludes definitely and radically everything resembling the Roman concepts of a hierarchy, a living teaching authority, jurisdiction and ecclesiastic law, as if these concepts were all matters to which man should consider himself obliged in conscience.

If in the earthly, empirical Church a certain organization, order, common opinion and discipline are necessary, no more than a relative and human authority can be attributed to them. While the believer remains free in all this his freedom is not a licentiousness but a strict subjection to God's word. Rather than excluding it his freedom includes a certain sense of subjection to the word, confession, institutions and measures of the church to which he belongs, just as membership in any community implies duties as well as rights. However this type of subjection, even as far as the church is concerned, lies on the human, relative plane.

Ecclesiastic subjection may in no wise intrude between God and the soul, between God's word and the individual act of faith. What the Church in her earthly and empirical manifestation says or does should never play a dominant role. Its role should exclusively be one of serving, regulating and directing. Organizational and liturgical forms are in themselves indifferent and serve the efficacy of God's word without standing in its way. When therefore in Lutheran churches some forms and usages are found (such as episcopal organization, altars, crucifixes, candles, vestments, processions) which are reminiscent of the Catholic Church, this can be explained by a certain indifference to such forms rather than by a positive acceptance of and sympathy for Catholic forms.

It cannot be emphasized too strongly that Luther's teaching about the Church had little or nothing to do with the abolition of abuses and undesirable practices in the Church. It concerned rather a totally new vision of the nature of the Church. The Church the creed speaks of, according to Luther, is not a supernatural, mysterious reality on earth which in its visible, human manifestation retains a divine character that gives it concrete and absolute claims to unconditional obedience. The Church of the creed is a spiritual and therefore invisible communion of faith. To this communion belong all true believers, that is, all those who have heard and believed the pure gospel.

It is only this spiritual communion of faith, and no visible and earthly organization whatever, that exists by divine right. Law, right and divine authority do apply, however, in this spiritual communion but the authority of God makes itself felt

73

only by means of God's word. The believer completely fulfills the law and the right of God only by making a personal and conscious act of faith in the pure gospel. In no other way does the believer have anything to do with God's law and right or with any divine authority based on it. This means a radical rejection and complete abandonment of all ecclesiastic institutions, in the sense of canon law, and an entirely new vision of man's relationship with God.

Luther did not on this account refuse to acknowledge a visible Church or churches. He distinguished between the universal Church and the particular churches. The universal Church practically coincides with Christianity of all ages and of the whole world, even though schisms and heresies have divided and disrupted it.

In this universal Church the Church of the creed (the spiritual union of all true believers) finds a poor expression. Even the papist church is part of the universal Church, no matter how depraved she may be or how she may labor under the delusion of being herself the universal Church. By the very fact that even in this papist church there are true and sincere believers this church is thereby still connected with the universal Church. But this does not mean that the papist church is a true church.

The particular churches are the separate denominations which have been formed in the course of time, partly because of existing national differences, partly because of a difference of conviction concerning the interpretation of sacred Scripture on points of the content of faith, of church ordinances and liturgy. Whether a certain denomination is considered a church in the true sense of the word can be judged by only one criterion: does the denomination proclaim the pure gospel, and are the sacraments Christ instituted (baptism, the Lord's supper, and possibly the sacrament of penance) being administered in a manner in accordance with the intention of Scripture?

The essential marks of the Church, that is, her unity, holiness, catholicity and apostolicity, may in certain respects possibly be dynamically expressed at times but of themselves they are never statically tied down to a permanent visible form. These essential marks can only be "believed." They can never be ascertained and demonstrated as visibly present. The Church of the creed always remains a hidden reality but a reality hidden in and under the externally visible, human—and therefore defective—ecclesiastic forms. Thus hidden the Church of the creed becomes all too often camouflaged by these forms.

The word of God is the only external sign by which a person is able to ascertain whether and to what extent he is at any given moment being confronted with the real Church. This is the only exclusive mark of the Church. Truly, the word of God is the only sacrament in the full and true sense of the word. Luther frequently called the word of God the real sacrament and never spoke of the other sacraments independently of the proclamation of God's word. The sacrament of baptism, the Lord's supper and penance are means to emphasize, confirm, actualize and concretize God's word. But they do not effect anything in the heart and life of the believer which has not already been accomplished by the word and the consequent act of faith.

In this connection it is also clear that in the Church as a visible, organized communion of faith there is but one office, that of preaching. The Lord's supper as a visible celebration of the community does not have the nature of a sacrifice offered by the priest for the living and the dead. The priestly office in this specifically ecclesiastic sacramental sense is abandoned by Luther. The office of preaching is one of reconciliation since the word of God which is being proclaimed is above all the word of reconciliation. Man's reconciliation with God has once and for all been accomplished by Christ. The individual's reconciliation is effected when the word of reconciliation reaches man and when it is accepted by him in faith. Only in this sense can it be said that the preacher is also priest.

From this however it should not be concluded that therefore

there is a distinction between priest and layman. To have a right order in the Church it is necessary to have the ecclesiastic office. By the mandate of the Church the preacher must proclaim the word of reconciliation. But this mandate does not cancel the obligation, vocation and privilege of any believer, whenever the opportunity arises, to witness by word and deed to God's reconciliation, thus reconciling his neighbor to God by means of the word of reconciliation. Any believer is called to be a preacher, that is, a priest of the word of God in behalf of his neighbor. This is what Luther intended by his teaching of the universal priesthood of the faithful.

It cannot be denied that in his later years Luther gave a little more emphasis to the visible and institutional aspect of the Church. He was forced to do this by the practical problems which accompanied the beginnings of a new church formation. Another factor was the tendency toward disorder and lawlessness which began to manifest itself among the people, who were not ready for a spiritual practice of the gospel. But it is not correct to say that this emphasis on the part of Luther also implied an essential change in his vision of the nature of the gospel, the Church and the sacraments. The same can be said about Luther's conflict with Zwingli concerning the real presence of Christ in the Lord's supper. Here too it was Luther's primary intention to have an unconditional faith placed in the word of Christ: "This is my body; this is the chalice of my blood." He was not in the least concerned about speculations with regard to the manner of Christ's presence.[6]

In a similar manner did Luther hold to the letter of the gospel text in his letter to Copernicus in which he abruptly rejected the latter's new astronomical insights into the revolution of the

[6] The term consubstantiation is of a later date. Moreover it presents difficulties since, because of Luther's nominalist formation, it is impossible that he should have taken *substantia* in the sense which it has in Catholic teaching on transubstantiation. Luther himself never used the term consubstantiation.

heavenly spheres (the earth and the other planets) around the sun. Quoting the words of Joshua: "Stand still, O sun, at Gabaon, O Moon, in the valley of Ajalon," Luther wrote to Copernicus: "Therefore you see that the sun moves around the earth, and not the earth around the sun." Luther would invoke only one inviolable authority—not science or the Church, but the word of God, that is, the word of the Bible.

In summary therefore we must say that Luther's vision of the Church was the necessary consequence of his vision of the gospel and of the nature of the mutual, close dependence of faith and conscience. In the concrete this means that Luther made the Church, the sacraments and the ecclesiastic office completely subject to and in all respects dependent on the living word of God so that one was at the service of the other.

In sacred Scripture this word of God addresses man directly and in an unmistakably clear manner. The word of God is the only instrument the Holy Spirit uses to arouse faith in the heart of man, thus effectively accomplishing reconciliation and peace with God, and perhaps with the aid of the sacraments but certainly not by means of the sacraments. The objective proclamation of the word together with the corresponding act of faith restore man to his original proper relationship with God (justification). The fruits of this restoration are the good works which necessarily flow from it.

Luther considered it one of the fables of the papist church that the Church should by means of the sacraments be able to infuse into the soul of man a special supernatural grace, a supernatural virtue of faith or any other virtues. The close connection between Luther's vision of the Church and his vision of the gospel makes it impossible to agree with Meissinger when he holds that the break with Rome should be attributed only to the external circumstances and events. For it is certain that the germ of the Reformation and the consequent schism lay in the insights which Luther acquired even before 1517.

Luther and the world

If Luther's vision of the Church was the necessary consequence of his vision of the gospel and of the nature and function of faith and conscience, the same is to be said about his vision of the believer's place, calling and attitude in the world.

Just as every believer is at one and the same time a sinner and a just man, so too does every believer at one and the same time stand in the world and in the kingdom of God. Just as every believer is justified precisely as a sinner, so too is every believer justified precisely as being in the world and in God's kingdom. The words sinner and justified do not indicate two different types of men, nor do they refer to two different periods in a man's life. Neither do the words world and kingdom of God refer to two distinct, essentially different and carefully separated realms. To be in God's kingdom means to be in the world not as an unbeliever but as someone who believes in and subjects himself to the word of God.

For the believer as for the unbeliever there is but one reality of which he is part and in which he has been placed by God: the reality of the natural world in which he finds himself. Luther firmly rejected any ideas about a distinction and contrast between a natural and a supernatural, between a profane and a sacred reality.

Considered against the background of Catholic teaching it is here that Luther without realizing it made the first important and decisive step on the road toward secularism, later traveled to its completion by the enlightenment, liberalism and modern humanism. Not that Luther was in any way connected with the Renaissance and humanism: far from it, for he saw in these an enemy to the pure gospel and a life of faith even more dangerous than the papist church. But by denying the reality of a new, supernatural, sacramental order of being as revealed in and through Christ and by viewing the restoration of man's relationship with God exclusively as a new relationship announced

78

by the word and realized in the act of faith, Luther utterly destroyed faith in the world of the supernatural. In doing so he also directed the believers' whole attention, precisely in those things pertaining to their life of faith, to the reality of the natural world in which they find themselves.

What was the meaning which Luther attached to faith in this connection? Faith meant for Luther that man obediently views and accepts his presence in the world and his relation to the world and to his neighbor in the light of God's word. That is to say, man wishes to see and accept the world as the naturally given reality as determined by God's decrees of creation. God has placed man in this reality: the reality of marriage, family, situation in life, occupation, people, nation, society.

By faith in God's word man knows that as a result of original sin his presence in the world implies all sorts of struggle, labor, care, sorrow and temptation. But by this same faith the believer is no less certain that it is God's will that he should be faithful to this world, that he should not desert or escape the world in which he must actualize his faith according to God's will.

For the believer presence in this world is a cross which he willingly and obediently accepts from God's hand. It means moreover a struggle of faith in which his faith is at once tried and strengthened. He would commit an act of disobedience if he should try to retreat from the world or withdraw from the vocation, struggle and affliction God imposes on him in this world. Luther was convinced therefore that he was making a positive act of faith and obedience when he violated his monastic vows, rejected his celibacy and married a fugitive religious sister.

As a consequence of his vision of the gospel Luther had come to regard celibacy, the taking of monastic vows, self-imposed heavy penances and the performance of good works not intrinsically connected with one's given situation in life or with an encounter with one's neighbor, as so many self-willed efforts

79

to arrive at a reconciliation with God by other means than those indicated by God.

On the basis of his vision of the gospel Luther also made it his principle to reject any distinction between profane and sacred in regard to persons, offices, objects and actions. According to Luther everything here on earth is profane and by faith it is rendered sacred. Therefore there is no distinction between a secular and a religious state of life, for it is precisely a life in the midst of the world which is by faith made religious and holy. There is no difference between sacred and profane occupations for the occupation of the priest is just as profane as that of "the blacksmith, the shoemaker, tailor, baker, brewer, merchant or anyone else." But by the same token each of these occupations is by faith also made a sacred occupation, because by faith it is just as much a vocation as that of a priest or preacher.

In this world state and church are not to be considered two separate entities having their own rights and powers since the same people—that is, juridically speaking, the state—are by faith the church. Sovereignty, jurisdiction and government, even in the realm of religion, belong to the state. The only task of the church is to proclaim the word of God by church services and other appropriate means, such as religious instruction and pastoral care. Finally there is no difference between worldly culture and Christian culture since all culture is worldly. According to Luther it is an illusion to think that the world, the state, politics or culture can be christianized. The believer cannot withdraw himself from the life of culture. Rather he must sanctify it by faith. For the believer therefore a worldly culture as worldly is at the same time a Christian culture by faith.

The idea that the believer should be able to build for himself a new, pious and safe world in the form of the church or monastery separate from the depraved and dangerous world is, according to Luther, an illusion. The battle between the kingdom of God and the devil is waged in the midst of the world and victory can be gained only in the midst of the world, by means of the word of God and faith. If believers think they can place themselves out of action by safely withdrawing to the sacred grounds of the church or monastery they will soon find that the devil has even more dangerous temptations and serious torments at his disposal in these sacred halls than he has in the midst of the world.

Thus the believer must persevere unto death in the world, that is, in the married state, in the family, life situation, occupation and in the life of the people, state or society, according to the gifts and abilities, the possibilities and circumstances God has destined for him. In this he is in solidarity with the entire human race. The believers in no way form a separate sacred community distinct from or above the rest of mankind. The difference between believers and unbelievers consists not in their each belonging to their own separate worlds but in their having opposite orientations, in their having diametrically opposed relations to God. However this difference in orientation, in relation, manifests and actualizes itself in the midst of the same world. For the unbeliever this means a life under the slavery and curse of the law, for the believer a life in the freedom of a Christian by faith, that is, precisely and exclusively through faith in God's word.

Luther's treatise on the freedom of a Christian begins with the paradox: "The Christian is the slave of all things and is subject to all; the Christian is the lord of all things and is subject to none." Since the Christian belongs to the world and stands under God's decrees of creation, whatever applies to any other person in the married state, in family and occupation and in the life of the people, of the nation and society applies to him as well. The Christian too is subject to God's decrees of creation. He may not withdraw from them. But as a believer, as a person who accepts any situation in life and makes his decisions of life in the light of God's word, the only truth that really sets a person free, the Christian finds himself at the same time in the full freedom of the children of God.

This applies especially to the Christian's relation to civil authority. Whatever pertains to the state, its rights and competencies Luther counts among the decrees of creation. For this reason the Christian's acknowledgment of and respect for the authority of the prince, the state or civil society is an act of faith and an act of obedience to God's word.

It cannot be denied that by his vision of the Christian's relation to civil authority Luther delivered the empirical, organized church, as far as its governmental and juridical aspects were concerned, into the hands of the state. Without intending it he contributed to the ineffectiveness of the Lutheran churches in the face of the spirit of the times, particularly under the pressure of a totalitarian regime.

Luther, Lutheranism and Protestantism

The preceding pages constitute an attempt to present objectively a brief summary of the principal elements of Luther's evangelic and reformation testimony based on Luther's own writings. They have also been intended to show the close connection that exists between these various elements. We have asked ourselves what Luther's fundamental intentions were, what moved him to his actions, what was the real core of his teaching and what was the most essential nature of his vision of faith.

With Elert we might here speak of the *evangelische Ansatz,* the actual impetus and the original, fundamental motive which led to the Reformation movement, to Lutheranism and ultimately to world Protestantism. This first beginning did not in itself have the character of a confession in the sense of a doctrinal system but it did have, above all, the character of a biblical and prophetic testimony.

It is true that a very intricate complex of causes, cultural, social and political, played a part in the rise, development and

82

spread of Lutheranism and Protestantism as well as in the foundation of new Reformation churches. It is also true that soon enough theological and ecclesiastic questions arose which have not found uniform and unanimous answers either within the boundaries of Lutheranism or among the main types of Protestantism which developed. Yet one fact is absolutely certain: all Reformation Christians (particularly in their rejection of the papist church and papist doctrine) were concerned about the same basic matter, viz. the original Reformation testimony of which, according to all Protestants, Luther was the first and principal interpreter. From this follow at least three conclusions.

In the first place it is impossible to obtain a correct insight into the history of the genesis and development of the Reformation, of Lutheranism and ultimately of world Protestantism if one does not have a profound and clear understanding of the actual meaning and range of Luther's evangelic testimony. Such understanding can be acquired only by listening patiently and without bias to what Luther himself has said and written. This means that one must know what took place in the inner life of Luther and the other reformers. Therefore it is not primarily a question of knowing external circumstances, situations and events which played only a subordinate role. Nor of course is it a matter of knowing Luther's philosophical presuppositions.

In the second place Luther's original and fundamental testimony was a dominating factor in the confessional stabilization, theological development and ecclesiastic organization of Lutheranism. No matter how diverse the later theological systems and forms of spirituality may have become, no matter how many serious tensions have occurred between various doctrinal, ethical, mystical and liberal types of Lutheranism, something common has always remained, as a result of which there has always been some continued relationship, or even unity. This common element has settled in the Lutheran and in the Protestant consciousness because of Luther's original testimony. Lutheranism—not to mention Protestantism in general—has always confronted itself with the actual nucleus of Luther's concept of the gospel whenever the original principles and intentions of the Reformation were at stake. Any revival or restoration within Lutheranism or outside it, as for example in Methodism, has taken Luther's original testimony as its point of orientation.

In the third place the core of Luther's evangelic and Reformation testimony must be considered as the actual, primary factor which gives a real unity to the various main types of Protestantism, even if they do differ in many important respects. It is in other words the basis of unity of world Protestantism. Since Luther's testimony contained at the same time a protest and rejection in regard to the Roman concepts of Church, Christianity and religion world Protestantism will always be opposed in principle to the Catholic Church. And this opposition, as a recent pastoral letter of the Dutch Reformed Church expressed it, is "for the sake of the gospel and conscience," in the sense Luther and the other reformers understood the gospel and the conscience of man.

From the very beginning there were in the main types of Protestantism important differences in christology and in the concepts of the church and the sacraments. Moreover in the course of the centuries profound contrasts have arisen, particularly in the dogmatic sphere, within the individual Protestant churches. An almost insuperable contrast is that between those who, acknowledging Christ as God and redeemer, accept the mysterious facts of salvation from the New Testament, and those who, denying the divinity of Christ, consider the facts of salvation mythological.

From the point of view of dogma and proclamation this contrast must be regarded as irreconcilable. Yet all Protestants do have something in common. But it would be incorrect to think that this common element which all Protestants share is something that has to do only with affection, for instance a solidarity in rejecting Rome, a feeling of antipathy against a common enemy, a similarity of policy, a common defense mech-

84

anism. It is true that this impression is sometimes given. But in reality the common basis of unity lies much deeper. It consists in a common vision of God, of man, of man's relationship to God, of man's encounter with God, of the nature and manner of Christian living, piety, prayer and services. All these concepts agree profoundly with the original vision and testimony of Luther.

Luther's original evangelic and Reformation testimony gives a real foundation for a further union and ecumenical consolidation of world Protestantism. We can therefore repeat what we have written in an earlier work:

Reformation Christians are more in agreement with one another than they know or realize. This truth is being discovered in the ecumenical movement. A person concentrating on the most profound characteristics of the Reformation concept of the Gospel must be struck by the reality of a fundamental unity, the awareness of which has often been lost in the turmoil of ecclesiastic and theological struggle.

The reader should keep these words in mind, particularly when later in this book we shall be writing again about Lutheranism and the other main types of world Protantism. The differences lie in the realms of theological development and ecclesiastic formulation of the original prophetic testimony of Luther and the other reformers. These differences are often found in connection with important religious, philosophical and cultural influences to which world Protestantism has been subject in the course of more than four centuries.

Melanchthon

Lutheranism as it actually appears in history is a creation not only of Luther but also of Melanchthon. The role of Melanchthon is sometimes regarded as being negative, without an underlying aim, reactionary and delaying. It is questionable whether such a judgment is based on sufficient historical insight. There are now indications of a growing understanding of the positive role played by Melanchthon in the history of the genesis of Lutheranism.

Philip Melanchthon (1497–1560) was born in the Palatinate of the Rhine. He was fourteen years younger than Luther and like Luther died at the age of 63. He studied at the universities of Heidelberg, where he was in contact with Thomism and the early developments of humanism, and Tübingen. This means that he was not subjected, as was Luther, to the influences of Ockhamism. Melanchthon also had great admiration for Erasmus and Agricola and at Tübingen developed into a convinced humanist. Even then he believed that the Hebrew text of the Old and the Greek text of the New Testament should be the only sources and norms for the teaching of the Church.

In 1518 Melanchthon was appointed professor of Greek at the University of Wittenberg. In his inaugural lecture, greatly admired by Luther, he spoke of the necessity of revising university teaching. He held that the then current textbooks with their conventional but partly antiquated contents should be discarded and that the students should be introduced to the original and authentic sources.

From that moment a firm friendship and mutual admiration developed between the two colleagues. Though Melanchthon possessed a well controlled, temperate and balanced nature the idea evidently never struck him that Luther's impetuous and passionate character might plead against the integrity and value of the latter's biblical convictions. Within a year Melanchthon was completely won over to Luther's vision of the gospel. Luther in turn owed much to the linguistic talents of his younger colleague.

Unlike Luther, Melanchthon was neither monk nor priest. He was a clear and acute intellectual in the humanistic sense of the word. There is not a trace of a religious crisis in his entire life. He arrived at his Reformation beliefs by means of a rational, scientific investigation of the sources. Though much younger than Luther he always maintained a certain independence from him. In 1519 he accompanied Luther on his trip to Leipzig for his discussion on religion with John Eck. After that Melanchthon followed Luther like a shadow. When in certain instances Luther's capacities were not sufficient Melanchthon came to his aid.

The early ordering of Luther's thoughts and the timely stabilization of the Lutheran doctrine would have been impossible without Melanchthon whose nature and talents enabled him to achieve accomplishments for which Luther lacked the necessary energy.

Melanchthon must unquestionably be regarded as the first dogmatician of the Reformation. If the major part of Luther's polemic writings appeared in 1520 they were followed no later than 1521 by the first systematic resumé of Luther's evangelic insights in the form of Melanchthon's *Loci Communes Rerum Theologicarum* (Basic Concepts of Theology). Melanchthon was then twenty-four years old. The *Loci Communes* presents the various elements of Luther's teaching on salvation in an orderly fashion and gives the first synopsis of what Luther had actually been preaching and teaching.

The disadvantage of this work is that it contains only those themes Luther was mainly occupied with in his teaching and activity: the connections between law and gospel, sin and grace, faith and justification, in other words the nucleus of the doctrine of salvation. In its treatment of the doctrine on God, the Trinity, the incarnation and christology Melanchthon's work was obviously incomplete, since the first discussions of the Reformation did not cover these theological problems.

Luther was greatly satisfied with this first work of his fellow reformer. Not only did he think that it should be preserved, he also thought it should be ecclesiastically canonized. Still, his work shows the first signs of an important change. Luther's prophetic testimony was transformed into a doctrine that was accounted for intellectually.

The existential, dynamic and paradoxical character of Luther's proclamation could not be reflected to its full advantage in such a stabilization and harmonization. While it is true that in the first publication of 1521 Melanchthon still shared Luther's anti-intellectualism and his aversion to Aristotle and the "sophists," this influence of Luther was quick in passing.

It can therefore be said that Melanchthon set the Reformation on the road that led it from the field of prophecy, piety and pastoral care to that of doctrine and theology, confession and church organization. He laid the foundations for the later Lutheran orthodoxy and its internal and external doctrinal polemics. From the moment that Luther's prophetic testimony was transformed into a doctrinal system Lutheranism became more contestable and vulnerable under attacks by Catholic doctrine and theology.

After 1521 Melanchthon himself experienced a development as a result of which he dissociated himself more and more from the irrationalism, exclusiveness and extremism of Luther. This development can best be characterized as a gradual re-discovery of intellectual, spiritual, religious and ecclesiastic values which were in danger of becoming lost in a one-sided interpretation and application of Luther's vision of faith. The humanism in Melanchthon came again to the fore and demanded a positive part in the construction of Lutheranism. In particular Melanchthon emphasized ever more strongly the positive value of a proper systematic thought and of all the truly human elements in man that have remained in spite of original sin.

The development which Melanchthon experienced led him to a twice repeated profound revision and modification of his *Loci Communes* (in 1535 and 1542). At a very early date he reversed his rejection of Aristotle and scholasticism which had so strongly marked his first publication and in 1527 he supervised a new publication of Aristotle's *Ethics*. In his revisions of the *Loci Communes* he made full use of Aristotelian terminology and thought. This resulted in a profound change in the manner in which Luther had envisaged faith. Luther's emphasis on justification by faith alone had been closely connected with the fact that for him the essence of the act of faith consisted in an existential capitulation of man to the living word of God that affected him in the totality of his existence.

Melanchthon on the other hand returned to the idea that the essence of the act of faith is an intellectual assent to a body of revealed truths. The necessary if not fatal consequence was that the real person no longer had a direct part in his justification. The justification by faith alone had acquired an intellectual and juridical character. In exchange for the intellectual act of faith God attributed to the believer the justice of Christ as a foreign, extrinsic justification that comes to man from without (doctrine of forensic justification). Luther's original meaning was therefore greatly weakened.

It is not surprising that in the long run Melanchthon could not be satisfied with such a completely juridical, forensic and almost mechanical theory of justification. Having devaluated the act of faith he now began to give greater emphasis to the necessity of good works to obtain eternal salvation. In other words he stressed man's cooperation in the achievement of his salvation. This is the teaching of synergism we will refer to later.

A second factor which contributed considerably to a gradual change of Melanchthon's theological insights was his irenic frame of mind. We can safely say that to the end of his life he kept hoping for a reconciliation between the Reformation party and the Catholic party, but no less did he spend his zeal in efforts to bring about an agreement between Lutherans and Calvinists. In his theology he tried as much as possible to bring extreme points of view closer together either by a "happier formulation" or by compromise. Distinct traces of these efforts can be found in the Augsburg Confession which for the greater part was his work—at least in its final redaction. The following documents also testify to this: a reconciliatory memorandum drafted in 1534 at the request of the King of France; another accommodating treatise of 1537 about the primacy of the pope, destined for the Council of Mantua which was announced but never held.

In 1540 and 1541 Melanchthon took part in the religious discussions of Worms and Ratisbon (between Melanchthon and Cardinal Contarini). In 1545 he wrote *Wittenberg Reformation* in deliberation with Luther and other theologians; it was destined for the Elector of Saxony. This document outlined very clearly and succinctly the farthest limits of a possible rapprochement between the Reformation party and the Catholic party. Finally there is the Confession of Saxony which Melanchthon composed in 1551 in preparation for his participation in the Council of Trent. However as a result of the insurrection of the Elector Maurice of Saxony and other Reformation princes against the emperor, Melanchthon did not take part in the Council of Trent. The insurrection, meanwhile, led to the religious peace of Augsburg in 1555.

Confessional writings

The confessional writings of Lutheranism do not have the binding and authoritative significance which is usually attributed to the confession in Calvinist churches. Apart from the minor and major catechisms of Luther the principal purpose of the confessions was to present as clearly as possible to the emperor and to the Catholic party which he supported a description of the views of the evangelic reform party. It was only after the deaths of Luther and Melanchthon that the need arose to fix the confession on behalf of the adherents of the Reformation who were experiencing internal differences of opinion about what must be believed.

The earliest and principal confession of Lutheranism is the Augsburg Confession, consisting of two different editions: the unaltered edition of 1530 and the altered one of 1540. It was composed in view of the Diet of Augsburg to be held in 1530, and was read there in Latin and afterward in German at the episcopal palace in the presence of Emperor Charles V.

It contains twenty-eight articles, of which articles 1 to 21 present a positive exposition of the Lutheran doctrine. The remaining articles have a negative character and are directed against abuses that had crept into the newly established church.

Although Melanchthon was the principal and final editor of these articles, thus greatly influencing their spirit and contents, he based their composition on the existing articles of Schwabach, Marburg and Torgau. The articles about the abuses are mainly based on those of Torgau. While composing these articles he also consulted other theologians and asked for Luther's judgment about them. Although Luther did not think that the work should proceed so cautiously he nevertheless had the greatest appreciation for Melanchthon's achievements.

The Augsburg Confession provoked a refutation by the Catholic party, which in turn was answered by a very extensive *Apology* composed by Melanchthon (1531). This *Apology* contained, properly speaking, Lutheran dogmatics. Special attention must be drawn to the very comprehensive article 20 of the Augsburg Confession on the relation between faith and good works, and to the comment on this article given in the *Apology*. Article 4 on justification should be interpreted in the light of these considerations.

Apart from the minor and major catechisms of 1529 the Schmalkalden articles of 1537 are the only contributions which Luther himself made to the confessional writings of Lutheranism. The Schmalkalden articles are actually one very extensive article. Luther had begun to write them at the instruction of the Elector of Saxony and with a view to the Council of Mantua convoked by Pope Paul III for May 1537. The Protestants had been invited to this council on condition that they should acknowledge the authority of the pope. The document which Luther composed was to be presented in 1537 at Schmalkalden to the members of the evangelic league of Schmalkalden for their signature. Sickness prevented Luther from being present. Instead of persuading the evangelic estates to attach their signature to Luther's concept, Melanchthon succeeded in having them subscribe to the Augsburg Confession and declare themselves in agreement with a hastily written treatise concerning the primacy of the pope. In this treatise he acknowledged the primacy of the pope, basing it however not on divine but on human right, and therefore not according to the sense of the text of Matthew 16:18: "And I say to you that you are Peter; and on this rock I shall build my Church."

After Luther's death in 1546 there was a growing conflict between the radical followers of Luther and the more moderate adherents of Melanchthon who were called Philippists. The gap between these factions was bridged only after Melanchthon's death in 1560. That the confessional unity of Lutheranism was saved has to be attributed mainly to one of Melanchthon's earlier disciples, Chemnitz, who enjoyed the close cooperation of other theologians.

As professor at the University of Wittenberg Chemnitz had started in 1553 with lectures on the *Loci* of Melanchthon. His work on the two natures of Christ dates from 1560. This work defended the Lutheran concepts of the hidden divinity in the incarnation and of the unity of the divine and human nature in Christ as opposed to the Calvinistic christology. It also opposed the efforts of Melanchthon to reach an agreement between the Lutheran and the Calvinist theology on the subjects of christology and the Lord's supper.

But if Chemnitz was opposed to the unionism of Melanchthon he also strongly opposed the latter's synergism. As the main instrument in arranging the *Formula Concordiae* of 1577 by which the two factions in the Lutheran church were united (article 2 against synergism; articles 7 and 8 against the unionism of Melanchthon), Chemnitz attained a theological victory over Melanchthon. But in a philosophical sense however it was Chemnitz who caused Melanchthon's intellectual stabilization to have a permanent influence on Lutheranism.

In 1580 the *Formula Concordiae* was incorporated into the *Book of Concordances* as the final confessional writing. The *Book of Concordances* appeared in Dresden on the occasion of the fiftieth anniversary of the Augsburg Confession. It is a collection of all the Lutheran confessional writings and is now accepted by practically all Lutheran churches as normative for the Lutheran teaching. The doctrinal development and stabilization of Lutheranism had therefore taken almost half a century.

Lutheran church formation

Like Reformed Protestantism and like Anglicanism, Lutheranism resulted in its own proper type of church formation. This does not mean that there is but one Lutheran church. The churches which developed from the Reformation movement have all organized themselves nationally into state or national churches, so that each type is represented by a number of independent churches.

The idea that the Catholic or universal Church, acknowledging the papacy, is built up from national churches does not have its origin in the Reformation. It goes back to the middle ages. Often there were conflicts between the pope or the bishops on the one hand and the princes on the other, because the latter also demanded a voice in the ecclesiastic affairs of their people. In his vision of the relations of the Christian and Christianity to the world Luther rejected any separation between the sacred and the profane, between the earthly and the spiritual, thus partially solving the difficulty. The prince was simply considered sovereign even in the religious and ecclesiastic life of the people.

The question then arises how the independent Lutheran church formation came about. Who brought it into being?

93

What were the influences and circumstances that played a role in it?

Luther is not the founder of the Lutheran church. Never for a moment did he think of founding a new church apart from and opposed to the Catholic Church. When his actions led him into conflict with Rome he considered himself the spokesman and leader of an evangelic reform party in the Church that opposed a papist party which was being used by Satan as his instrument in the destruction of the Church. He seriously thought that this was a question of a battle between two parties within the Catholic Church. Accordingly he asked to be heard by a general council, fully hoping and expecting that this would be a means in solving the conflict once and for all and that the truth of the gospel would be victorious. Accused of heresy he declared himself ready to revoke anything which could be proved contrary to the clear and distinct language of sacred Scripture. He was unaware that as far as the Catholic Church was concerned he had gone astray precisely in his scriptural principle and in his concept of ecclesiastic authority and of the Church in general. Only very gradually did it become clear to him that because of his activity a new church was arising apart from the Catholic Church.

Initially Luther even thought it possible that he might be declared in the right by the ecclesiastic authorities and even by the pope himself—who might have been misinformed about him. To Archbishop Albrecht of Mainz who had given Tetzel the task of preaching on indulgences, and to the bishop of Brandenburg in whose diocese Wittenberg was situated, Luther announced his intention to make his public defense in the form of his ninety-five theses, to be nailed to the door of the castle-church at Wittenberg. The bishop of Brandenburg at first did not reply but when rumor about the theses had spread all over Germany he was urged by Rome to advise Luther to drop the question entirely. It is certain that Luther originally considered obeying his bishop's wishes. However as a result of the actions of his opponents and following the disputations he became involved in at Heidelberg and Augsburg in 1518 and at Leipzig in 1519, it had become impossible for him to drop the matter.

Rather the events incited him and rumors about the conflict were spreading over a large part of Europe. Luther was no longer able to control events. Almost against his will he became more and more the exponent of a powerful movement the outcome of which he could not possibly have predicted. The most recent research on Luther has established that it was "the opposition which made Luther aware of the fundamental contrast that existed between his religious convictions and the teaching and customs of the Church" (MacKinnon I, 305). Meanwhile the Reformation movement could not be stopped. In Germany as well as in more distant countries separatist movements were under way.

Many of the diocesan and regular clergy were being won over to Luther's evangelic principles. The Dominican priest Bucer who attended the disputation of 1518 in Heidelberg became evangelic chaplain to Frederick of the Palatinate in 1521. Later, in 1524, together with Capito, former secretary and adviser to Albrecht, archbishop of Mainz, Bucer began to build up an evangelic community in Strasburg in a way which was quite independent of Luther's.

From the ranks of the apostate priests sprang an army of evangelic preachers which traveled all over Germany. In many of the imperial cities they founded communities according to evangelic principles, sometimes in direct consultation with Luther, sometimes quite independently. Protests from diocesan authorities were ignored. In any case some bishops also chose to join Luther. The first among them was George von Polentz, bishop of Samland, who openly declared his evangelic convictions in 1523 during a Christmas sermon in the cathedral of Königsberg. In the succeeding years he gradually introduced reforms in his diocese. Meanwhile a large part of the German

95

nobility had also made it known that they were in favor of Luther.

In order to gain a clear picture of the development and character of the Lutheran church it is necessary to realize the circumstances under which it was born and how much it was influenced by the ruling powers of the time.

The powers which could determine the outcome of Luther's reform movement were the power of the pope, the power of the emperor, but also the power of the princes. In a certain sense Luther became the plaything of clashing political interests— usually to Luther's advantage. It was usually a matter of a balance of power between the pope and the emperor and between the emperor and the princes, the emperor generally striving to maintain religious unity in his empire. Apart from a short period around the year 1527 when he himself was at war with the pope and his armies were plundering Rome, the emperor generally attempted to hinder if not destroy the Reformation movement.

Luther enjoyed the protection of Frederick the Wise, Elector of Saxony, a decisive factor in enabling the Reformation to hold its own and in the formation of a new church. Not to be overlooked as a contributing factor however is the fact that, in rapid succession, the princes began to declare themselves in favor of Luther.

Looking at it in retrospect it can be said that the year 1520 was the beginning of the formation of the new church. When Luther burned not only the papal bull of excommunication but also the law code of the Church, the *Codex Juris Canonici,* he made his final rejection of papal and episcopal jurisdictional powers and declared that these powers belonged to the princes.

It is true that it was not Luther's intention to place in the hands of the princes all the purely religious functions of the church such as preaching and the care of souls, the institution of divine services, the appointing of ministers, the drafting of a confession, the administration of the sacraments. But in a sense the prince had to take the place of the bishop of the diocese, particularly on the basis of the general priesthood of the faithful. For as actually happened in some instances, when the bishop refused to introduce in his diocese the reform dictated by evangelic principles, the prince would have to command the reform and provide the necessary protection in case of any resistance. When a bishop refused to follow instructions the prince had to take his place until orders from the church had regulated the relations of the prince, superintendents, consistories, preachers and people, and stated the duties and competencies of each. In this light it becomes clear that the success of the Reformation depended to a great extent on what side the princes joined, that of Luther or of the pope and the emperor.

The Lutheran national churches owe their existence to the attitude of the princes. In this respect they do not differ from the Anglican Church of England. Whenever a prince joined Luther and the Reformation, commanding that the gospel be preached and that the reforms be introduced, a Lutheran church actually arose. Luther personally protested sharply against this name. Originally, in Germany as elsewhere, people spoke of reformed or evangelic churches. The name Lutheran church began to be used only toward the end of the sixteenth century as a result of the theological controversies about the differences between Lutheran and Calvinist teachings.

By Lutheran churches must be understood those churches which regard Wittenberg as their place of birth, which consider their origin as primarily bound up with the teaching and activity of Luther (and Melanchthon), which acknowledge the *Book of Concordances* of 1580 as their confessional criterion, and which direct their institution and divine services according to the principles and tradition of the oldest Lutheran churches. However, as far as details are concerned, the Lutheran churches developed independently and according to the religious circumstances and needs of each country. Some churches changed very gradually and as it were unnoticed from a Catholic national church into a Lutheran one as a result of increasing reform.

97

It is obvious that the transition from a Catholic national church into a Lutheran one was accompanied by a great number of problems. The originally Catholic pastors had to be transformed into evangelic preachers. The introduction of the reforms was left to superintendents and visitors for the church. Frequently questions arose about matters of direction, distribution of tasks, nominations, changes in divine services. It was a matter of trial and error, the results of which are still in evidence in Sehling's edition of the numerous evangelic church ordinances of the sixteenth century.

Naturally it was the evangelic church of the Saxon electorate, to which Wittenberg belonged, which in its origin and development was most subjected to the influence of Luther. Until the death of the Elector Frederick in 1525 the reforms in Wittenberg and other Saxon cities were left to the private initiative of pastors who were in agreement with Luther's theses and evangelic directions. These original reforms often had to be improvised and sometimes went far beyond Luther's intentions, thus causing clashes and disagreements. It became necessary to undertake the organization of the church more centrally and purposefully. As long as Frederick was alive his clever policy of neutrality made any forceful and systematic action impossible.

But Frederick's significance for Luther and for the Reformation can hardly be overestimated. Luther could never have maintained himself against the force of his powerful opponents who were aiming at his destruction had he not enjoyed Frederick's protection from the very beginning. Yet no unanimous opinion has been reached about the motives of the Elector. They may have been mainly political; possibly he may have been concerned about the fame of his University of Wittenberg; but it is not improbable that Frederick was personally interested in Luther's ideas, though because of his character he required a great deal of time to shed the traditional and make a definitive choice in favor of Luther's vision. He certainly acted very cautiously, avoiding a personal meeting with Luther and not acting contrary to Catholic usages, though he closed an eye to the evangelic reforms. On his deathbed in 1524 he finally received communion under both species.

Since the Edict of Worms, which demanded his incarceration, Luther had been given the "Wartburg" as a hiding place by the Elector from May 1521 to March 1522. It was there that he began to prepare a German translation of the Bible for the evangelically minded people. After a correction of the first draft under the linguistic direction of Melanchthon the New Testament appeared in September 1522. The translation of the Old Testament progressed less quickly. It appeared in parts in 1523, 1524, 1532 and 1534. From then on the Lutheran churches in Germany had their complete Bible in the vernacular.

After the death of the Elector Frederick his successor John ordered the first regular visitation of the churches. In the years between 1521 and 1525 many priests had become convinced that the sacrificial character of the mass should be denied, that it was not permitted to celebrate private masses and accept stipends for them, that the blessed sacrament should not be adored, and that communion should be distributed under the two species of bread and wine.

In 1525 the question first arose how a person should be admitted to the evangelic office of preaching who had not received the sacrament of orders. That same year Luther himself had ordained George Rörer to the diaconate (assistant preacher) in the parish church of Wittenberg by the imposition of hands and a prayer composed for this purpose. It was however the normal course that evangelic preachers and pastors were former priests.

For the parishes that were in the process of evangelic reform Luther composed in 1526 a German mass so that the people should have a divine service in the vernacular. While the name of mass was being retained the divine service had nonetheless begun to get the character of a "service of the word" connected, if possible, with the celebration of the Lord's supper as a communion service.

As a result of the improvisory, uncertain and irregular situation there was an ever increasing number of complications. For this reason Luther toward the end of 1526 requested the new Elector John to undertake the reform systematically for all of the Saxon electorate and to found an evangelic church in the sense of a national church governed by the civil authorities. This action was therefore not based on the later Calvinist principle of community.

An extensive visitation of the churches was held in the Saxon electorate between 1527 and 1529. At the order of the elector Luther and the other theologians acted as visitors. The further application of the given directives was left to the superintendents. From this visitation of the churches resulted the electoral "Instruction" of 1527 and the "Church Ordinance of Wittenberg" of 1528.

In 1532 it appeared necessary to revise these two documents and to hold a second visitation of the churches. The final stabilization of the new evangelic church therefore came about only gradually and not without the necessary experiments, stagnations and revisions. The origin and development of other evangelic national churches took place in a similar manner. In the form of the Augsburg Confession of 1530 these churches had, in the meantime, acquired not only a liturgical and organizational norm and foundation, but also a confessional one.

The growth of Lutheranism in Germany

On Dec. 10, 1520 Luther had burned the papal bull which threatened him with excommunication should he refuse to stop his preaching and activity. At that time he also burned the ecclesiastic code of law. By Jan. 3, 1521 Luther and his adherents had in fact been excommunicated. At the Diet of Worms the emperor tried in vain to move Luther to revoke his teachings. The Edict of Worms of May 26, 1521 pronounced the civil ban on Luther, ordered also that he be taken prisoner and handed over, and prohibited throughout the empire the preaching of Luther's doctrine. On May 29, 1521 Luther's writings were solemnly and publicly burned in Worms.

This was not the end of the Lutheran movement. Rather it meant the beginning of the spread of Lutheranism. The Elector of Saxony kept Luther hidden at the Wartburg as "the squire Jörg" until March 1522. Meanwhile the number of imperial cities and princes who refused to put the Edict of Worms into execution was growing. The preaching and the spread of Lutheranism were increasing not only in Germany but also beyond its borders. At the same time there were a number of religious, political and social disturbances which, although Luther by no means intended them, were indirectly caused by him, such as the clashes between the nobility and the princes and the revolt of the peasants.

The Lutheran movement began to show some order only when the princes undertook its direction. The Elector of Saxony was followed in his declaration in favor of Luther by Philip of Hesse and Albrecht of Brandenburg. A number of imperial cities also followed, among them Nuremberg, Augsburg, Lübeck, Hamburg, Magdeburg and Frankfurt.

At the Diet of Nuremberg in 1524 it had become obvious that the Edict of Worms could not be put into execution. When the Diet resolved to have the religious question settled by means of a national council the emperor vetoed the resolution. In 1524 the Catholic estates of southern Germany formed the Ratisbon League for the destruction of heresy. In reply the evangelic princes founded the Gotha League in 1526. The ever-increasing tensions threatened the empire with civil war.

In 1526 the Diet of Spires adopted a more moderate attitude. It was resolved that each prince might interpret and apply the Edict of Worms as he thought best in conscience before God and before the emperor. The following Diet of 1529, again held in Spires, made another attempt to set bounds to the further spread of Lutheranism. Wherever Lutheranism had already been established religious freedom should be given to Catholics; in the other parts of Germany no measures were to be allowed against the Catholic religion. The evangelic estates filed protest against this resolution of the majority, thus acquiring the name protestants. By means of a solemn *protestatio* they declared that matters which had to do with man's conscience and God's honor could not be solved by a majority of votes.

At the Diet of Augsburg in 1530 the emperor, having heard the Augsburg Confession, allowed the Protestants a five month respite; should they continue to support Luther the Edict of Worms would be put into execution by force. Against this threat seven princes and eleven imperial cities formed the League of Schmalkalden. Because of his battle against the Turks the emperor was forced to abandon for the time being his plans to take action against the Protestants by force of arms.

Lutheranism meanwhile continued to spread in Germany. The imperial cities of Göttingen (1530), Lüneburg (1531), Bremen (1532) and Hanover (1534) declared themselves in favor of the Reformation. The year 1534 also saw the organization of the national churches of Würtemberg and Pomerania, while in 1536 the Wittenberg Concordia created closer bonds between the Zwingli-minded cities of southern Germany and the Lutherans. In Heidelberg and in the Palatinate Lutheranism gained a great deal of support, and in 1539 the national churches of the duchy of Saxony (bordering on the Saxon electorate which had been Lutheran from the beginning) and of the electorate of Brandenburg were founded. In 1547 the evangelic national church of the duchy of Mecklenburg was organized.

Some bishops, declaring their allegiance to the Reformation, reformed their dioceses according to Lutheran standards. Even the abbess of Quedlinburg and the abbot of Fulda adopted the Lutheran reforms. The archbishop of Cologne, Hermann von Wied, introduced a German communion service which was later incorporated in English into the Anglican *Book of Common Prayer*. The archbishop was unable to carry out his plans to

102

reform his entire archdiocese since the civil magistrate, together with the clergy and the emperor, caused his deposition in 1543.

The position of the evangelic principalities and the cities in the German empire reached a crisis as well as a final solution around the middle of the sixteenth century. Shortly after Luther's death in February 1546 the emperor, having concluded an armistice with the Turks and having gained victories over France and the duchy of Cleve, now had his hands free to reinstate the Catholic religion at all costs. When the emperor's proposition at the Diet of Ratisbon (1546) was rejected by the evangelic princes and cities he undertook the reconquest of the southern German cities. A decisive encounter between the emperor and the League of Schmalkalden took place in 1547 near Mühlberg and the Elector of Saxony and Philip of Hesse were taken captive. The emperor gained the victory and, sidestepping instructions from Rome, decided to put order back into the religious situation himself. To achieve his purpose he made a number of concessions (marriage of the clergy, sacrifice by the laity, abolition of abuses) to the people who favored the reform until the Council of Trent could make a final decision (Augsburg Moratorium of 1548).

However several politically unfavorable events forced the emperor to abandon his plans to reinstate the Catholic religion in Germany by force of arms. Among them were the rebellion of the evangelic princes under the leadership of Maurice of Saxony who by now had switched allegiance, the invasion of Lorraine by the French King Henry II, and the renewed advance of the Turks in Hungary. A religious peace was concluded at the Diet of Augsburg in 1555 which gave legal existence in the German empire to the evangelic principalities and cities according to the principle *cujus regio ejus et religio,* that is, in any given region the religion of the prince or magistrate would also be the religion of his people.

However the accord of Augsburg did not suffice to assure the permanence of religious peace. No political balance between

103

Protestants and Catholics had yet been achieved and increasing religious and political tensions in Europe ultimately led to a final struggle involving the Counter-reformation under Hapsburg protection. Germany, along with Bohemia, Denmark, Sweden and France, was involved in the Thirty Years' War which coincided with the last thirty years of the Eighty Years' War between the Republic of the United Netherlands and Spain. It was not until the Westphalian Peace of Osnabrück in 1648, which again coincided with the Peace of Munster, that lasting peace was assured for the evangelic states and cities which gained religious independence and a position of equality in the German empire, though still according to the principle *cujus regio ejus et religio*. Whoever could not or would not conform to the religion of the prince or magistrate had to settle elsewhere in an area where his own religion was the one legally recognized by the state. There was as yet no question of freedom of religion in the modern sense of the word. The struggle for freedom of religion between evangelics and Catholics was in most states followed by a struggle for freedom of religion by nonconformists and sectarians against the legal state churches, a struggle which many people sought to avoid by emigration to America.

The spread of Lutheranism throughout the world

Ever since the first few years of Luther's activity his teaching had found adherents in the various countries surrounding Germany. Numbers of foreign students who attended the University of Wittenberg returned to their own countries upon concluding their studies in order to proclaim the Lutheran teachings or to take an active part in the founding of a Lutheran church.

From a religious point of view a path had been cleared for Lutheranism in The Netherlands by the spirituality of the Brethren of the Common Life and by the teachings of Wessel Gansfort and the writings of Erasmus. Many people from The Netherlands who went to study at Wittenberg in the twenties undertook translations of Luther's writings and the spread of his doctrine after their return. Around 1525 Luther's writings were known all over the country, particularly in Antwerp, Dordrecht, Utrecht, Leiden, Amsterdam, Vere and in the central parts of the country, although they had also reached most of the cities in the east and north. Some people even had to pay for their Lutheran tendencies with their lives.

A flourishing Lutheran community existed in Antwerp and in the northern parts of The Netherlands there were efforts to introduce the Augsburg Confession as late as the second half of the sixteenth century. But the Calvinist influences were gaining strength. Some Lutheran communities owed their existence to influences from abroad and particularly to the settlement of Lutherans who later immigrated from other countries (seventeenth and eighteenth centuries).

In The Netherlands the Lutheran church was never a state church. The tasks of directing the church, which in other countries rested in the hands of prince or magistrate, were carried out by elders. The first Lutheran synod gathered in 1605 under the direction of the Lutheran community of Amsterdam. After the "French period" the Evangelical Lutheran Church, like the Dutch Reformed Church, obtained "general regulations for government" through the intervention of King William I. These regulations have undergone frequent revisions. In protest against the increasing rationalism and liberalism eight orthodox communities in The Netherlands united in 1791 on the basis of the Augsburg Confession and established the Restored Evangelical Lutheran Church. In 1952 the original evangelical and the restored groups were united. The Lutheran church in The Netherlands now numbers about 75,000 members.

Nowhere did Lutheranism acquire such a dominant place as in the Scandinavian countries, where it has now become practically the only form of Christianity. The Lutheran church has been the official state church in Sweden since 1529, in Denmark and Norway since 1536, in Iceland since 1554. In Finland, which then belonged to Sweden, a Lutheran state church arose under the rule of Gustave Wasa, King of Sweden from 1523. In 1527 Wasa confiscated all ecclesiastic properties, and promoted evangelic preaching. In 1529 he convoked a national synod to draft church regulations on the basis of which the Lutheran church in Sweden was constituted as the state church. As in the case of England the hierarchical structure of the church remained intact and ceremonies and customs which were not of themselves contrary to Lutheran teaching were preserved. In its external appearance the church in Sweden reminds one of the Catholic Church, as do other Lutheran churches elsewhere to greater or lesser extent. Its internal aspects however are penetrated throughout by the spirit and purpose of Luther and the Reformation.

The Swedish church even played an important role in warding off the same dangers that threatened the Reformation in Germany during the Thirty Years' War of 1618–1648.

After Gustave Adolf had first come to the aid of Protestantism in Poland he also involved himself in the German religious wars. He landed on the coast of the Baltic in 1631, gave battle near the river Lech, occupied Munich and Augsburg, and in 1632 won the battle of Lützen. Though he was killed in this battle he had in principle saved the position of Protestantism in Germany.

As early as 1520 King Christian II had invited Lutheran preachers from Germany to Denmark and his successors also promoted evangelic preaching among the people. In 1536 Christian III succeeded in suppressing a Catholic reaction. He invited the Wittenberg theologian Bugenhagen to draft church regulations and in 1537 introduced the Lutheran church as the state church of Denmark and Norway. The bishops whom Bugenhagen "consecrated" to their office are not in the apostolic succession.

106

In Finland the preaching of Lutheranism was supported by the Swedish king Gustave Wasa as well as by the bishop of Äbo, Erik Svensson. One of the first Lutheran preachers was Petrus Sarkilax who had returned from Wittenberg in 1523, but the principal reformer of Finland was Michael Agricola, who had also studied in Wittenberg. When in 1554 the Swedish king divided the diocese of Äbo, Michael Agricola became bishop of Äbo and Peter Justen who had also received his theological formation in Wittenberg became bishop of Viborg. For a number of the Finnish people evangelic preaching also meant their first contact with Christianity.

In the Baltic countries too the Lutheran doctrine had penetrated shortly after 1521, and in some places it had even led to iconoclasm. At the request of the bishop of Samland who had gone over to Lutheranism the Franciscan monk Briesmann, a graduate of Wittenberg, was sent to Copenhagen where in 1530 he composed the church regulations of Riga. In Latvia and Estonia the evangelic doctrine found many adherents among the populace. During the Polish occupation from 1562 to 1621 the Counter-reformation appeared to be gaining the upper hand, but the peace between Sweden and Poland yielded the Baltic countries to the domination of Sweden. By 1667 the Lutheran churches in these countries were definitively organized. Despite the many changes which the Baltic countries have undergone since the beginning of the eighteenth century the Lutheran churches there have been able to maintain themselves.

In Poland and Lithuania the rise of Lutheranism was at first delayed by King Sigismund I (1508–1548). Yet he was unable to prevent a spread of the Lutheran teachings in the larger cities and among the nobility. In 1525, as a result of an insurrection, the Catholic magistrate of Danzig had to make place for an evangelic magistrate. Sigismund II was more favorably disposed toward the Reformation but the Lutheran influence was being displaced by the Calvinism of Switzerland. In 1555 Lithuania opened its doors to Calvinist preaching, the influence of which however was restricted to higher circles and so did not reach the common people. The disagreements between the various Protestant confessions may possibly have contributed to this. During the reign of Sigismund III (1587–1632) Poland was largely reclaimed for the Catholic Church by the labor of the Jesuits.

In Bohemia and Moravia the chances for Lutheranism at first seemed quite favorable. The Lutheran preaching could here tie itself in with the nationalist popular movement which John Huss had created by his activities even though, from a biblical and theological point of view, his preaching had not been Lutheran in the proper sense of the word. Huss had mainly been opposed to ecclesiastic and social abuses. He had however rejected papal claims of authority and was a strong supporter of communion under both species (the lay chalice became the symbol of the Hussites). There was some connection therefore between the teachings of Luther and Huss.

John Huss was condemned as a heretic by the Council of Constance in 1415 and burned at the stake. But the Hussite movement was not thereby brought to an end, though a division into moderate and extremist parties did take place. Another division occurred in 1467 when the Bohemian-Moravian Brethren split apart. But the Hussites were able to maintain the ideal, particularly among the nobility, of a national church with valid ordinations and a Catholic liturgy, though without ties with Rome.

If even as early as the Diet of Worms in 1521 Luther had discovered that he agreed with Huss about papal authority, the Hussites in turn were, from the earliest beginning of Luther's activities, very favorably disposed toward his evangelic preaching. Yet in Bohemia and Moravia no Lutheran state church was ever founded. Not only did the kings remain loyal to the Catholic Church, so that the Reformation there could not possibly take a course similar to that in the Scandinavian countries, but the Lutherans were also faced with the opposition of the nationally minded Brethren whose aim was to preserve religious independence from German Lutheranism. Moreover Calvinist influences also made themselves felt.

After the battle of Mühlberg in 1547, in which the evangelic princes were defeated by the emperor, King Ferdinand of Bohemia took up the cause of the Counter-reformation. During the persecutions from 1548 to 1552 the Bohemian Brethren especially suffered. Some sought permanent refuge in Prussia and Poland although a number of them returned after 1552. For about half a century both the Lutheran church and the reorganized church of Brethren enjoyed a period of prosperity. After the battle near the White Mountain in 1621 and the massacre of Prague, the Catholic Church in Bohemia and Moravia was restored. Moravian Brethren who had taken refuge in Saxony founded the settlement of Herrnhut there in 1727.

In Hungary also the Lutheran doctrine spread at an early date. An attempt by the king to suppress the Lutheran movement led to a rebellion in 1526 and in 1545 the evangelic church of Transylvania (eastern Hungary) was founded, under the guidance of John Honter, on the basis of the Augsburg Confession. A year later the Catholic king was forced to permit the establishment of an evangelic church in western Hungary.

It did not take long for Swiss Protestantism to gain a number of adherents, particularly in western Hungary. As in Bohemia the German inhabitants were generally in favor of Lutheranism, while the native population preferred their own form, or at least some form of Protestantism other than the Lutheran.

In the second part of the sixteenth century the Counter-reformation began in Hungary. The restoration of the Catholic Church was accompanied by bloody persecutions and rebellions which continued for more than a century. Then in the early eighteenth century there followed for the Reformed and Lutheran churches a period of relative freedom of religion. Since 1848 Protestants have enjoyed complete legal equality with Catholics. Finally some remnants of Lutheranism continued to exist in Austria and in the northwestern regions of what is now Yugoslavia. And as a result of emigration Lutheran communities and churches also began to rise, from the middle of the seventeenth century on, in other continents, particularly in the United States of America.

The two standard American works on Lutheranism are Neve-Albeck's *History of the Lutheran Church in America* 1934, and Wentz' *The Lutheran Church in American History* 1933. Since Lutherans from various countries brought with them their own religious and ecclesiastic traditions a great variety of American Lutheran churches developed. This variety, though it often caused friction and separations, also gave rise to efforts at reunion.

The total number of Lutherans in the United States and Canada (particularly Pennsylvania, Iowa, Missouri, Illinois and Kitchener) is nearly six million. These are divided into three main church bodies: The National Lutheran Council, composed of the Lutheran Church in America and the American Lutheran Church; the Synodical Conference, composed of the Lutheran Church-Missouri Synod and the Synod of Evangelical Lutheran Churches; and the "independent" church bodies: the Church of Lutheran Confession, the Apostolic Lutheran Church of America, the Church of the Lutheran Brethren and the Eielsen Synod.

In spite of this great variety there is in our day a development toward a world Lutheranism. The Lutheran World Convention, founded in 1923 in Eisenach, developed in 1947 into the Lutheran World Federation to which about two-thirds of all Lutherans have subscribed. The total number of Lutherans in the world is estimated at almost seventy-three million. Like the World Council of Churches the Lutheran World Federation has its center in Geneva.

2

Reformed Protestantism

By Reformed Protestantism we understand that type of Protestantism which has its origin in the Swiss Reformation and in particular—though not exclusively—in the preaching, theology and activity of John Calvin (1509–1564). Reformed Protestantism is not merely a different form of Lutheranism. It is neither an offshoot of Lutheranism nor of the German movement. It has its own proper origins and its own native soil: Switzerland and France. It owes its development to the character, life, activity and teaching of its own reformers. It is true that at some time during their religious development these reformers were in touch with Luther's writings, but by then they were already on the path to a new understanding of the Bible, the gospel and—perhaps rather unconsciously—on the path to a new vision of the nature of faith and the Church.

All reformers have in some degree been influenced by Luther, though they were able to maintain a certain independence of him. Their acquaintance with Luther was for them rather a confirmation of what they themselves had already discovered in sacred Scripture, and it meant a final, decisive thrust to pursue the direction of the Reformation movement. It is incorrect to suppose that the Swiss reformers, including Calvin, were merely humanists and that their acquaintance with Luther only opened their eyes to the Reformation's "rediscovery" of the gospel.

It must be admitted however that none of the other reformers experienced a serious and personal crisis similar to Luther's. The course of their development was certainly less catastrophic. Though they ultimately acknowledged Luther's doctrine of salvation to be in agreement with sacred Scripture they were actually more concerned with the purity of divine faith and adoration and with a renewal of piety and Christian life on a biblical basis. The origin of Reformed Protestantism lies not in an interior crisis in the lives of the reformers who initiated it but in the biblical humanism of the early sixteenth century.

Biblical humanism

Biblical humanism accounts for the origin of what is called the *principium formale* of Protestantism, that is, the basic principle which shapes a religious conviction into a typically Protestant conviction. This basic principle is that sacred Scripture is the unique source of knowledge of revealed truth and that it contains everything that must be believed for salvation. Therefore, in relation to God or to a person's own salvation, no one can be asked to believe or do anything not literally contained in sacred Scripture.

This basic principle most certainly does not have Luther as its only intellectual author. Although not all humanists arrived at the extreme consequences of their new evaluation of the literal text of the Bible, they all did want to return to the original facts and data as expressed in the most ancient and authentic sources.

At the beginning of the sixteenth century this idea was widespread over a large part of Europe in the circles of the *devotio moderna* and of biblical humanism, and was particularly centered around figures such as Rudolf Agricola, Wessel Gansfort, Desiderius Erasmus, Thomas More, John Colet, John Fisher, Faber Stapulensis, Wimpfeling and Thomas Wyttenbach. Even Luther felt so closely related to these circles that in 1522 he published a new edition of a work of Gansfort, remarking in the preface that if he had read Gansfort earlier his own enemies might have thought that he had borrowed all of his doctrine from him, since the ideas of the two reformers corresponded in so many ways. As we noted in the preceding chapter Luther's vision of the gospel did not stem from a biblical humanism. Still it did not go by unnoticed. It is certain for example that prior to 1517, in the preparation of his lectures on the Psalms and the Epistle to the Romans, Luther made abundant use of the commentaries by Faber Stapulensis (Lefèvre d'Etaples).

Faber Stapulensis had introduced humanism into France from Italy. Under the influence of Erasmus (who had been led to a more Christian humanism in England by John Colet) he had begun to devote himself to the study of the New Testament according to its basic text. Until 1521 he was appointed professor at the Collège de France in Paris. After this he was vicar to the bishop of Meaux. Later, suspected of having Lutheran tendencies, he was forced to take refuge at the court of the learned, humanistic and Reformation-minded sister of the French king, Margaret of Orleans. Faber Stapulensis wrote commentaries on the Psalms (the copy which Luther used, filled with marginal notes, is still extant), on the epistles of Paul (1512) and on the gospels (1525). In 1530 he published his own French translation of the entire Bible.

Luther was also heavily indebted to the Greek edition of the New Testament Erasmus had published in Basel in 1515 and 1516. At first Luther put great trust in Erasmus, calling him in a letter dated in 1519 "our ornament and our hope." This is all the more remarkable since Luther, according to his recently discovered lectures, even at that time was explaining the sacred Scriptures in typically Reformation fashion. And it is evident from a letter he wrote to Zwingli that Erasmus was seriously convinced even in 1523 that he himself had all along been teaching what Luther was teaching.

113

Traces of the imminent separation betweeen the humanists who remained within the Catholic Church and those who sided with the Reformation were apparent for the first time in 1523. It was in this year that relations were severed between Erasmus and Zwingli on the grounds that the Zurich reformer had provided a haven for the Lutheran Von Hutten.

Erasmus' notion that his teachings were basically identical to Luther's appeared to be quite illusory when Luther published *On the Enslaved Will* in 1525. This was an answer, filled with cutting sarcasm, to Erasmus' *Discourse on Free Will*. These well known polemics between Luther and Erasmus on the freedom of man—or the lack of it—in his relations with God manifested the wide gap which lay between the humanists' and the reformers' understanding of sacred Scripture and the real nature of Christian faith. However this disparity should not lead us to deny or diminish the role played by biblical humanism in the origin and development of Reformed Protestantism.

Rise of the Swiss Reformation

At the root of the Swiss Reformation lies the biblical humanism of the University of Basle, where Thomas Wyttenbach was lecturing in the early sixteenth century. He taught his students to study the content of the Bible in an unprejudiced and exact manner. One of his students was Huldrych Zwingli (1484–1531), later the reformer of Zurich. After attending the humanistically oriented University of Vienna Zwingli continued his academic studies in Basle from 1502 to 1506. Zwingli is indebted to Wyttenbach for his conviction that the labor required in the study of the Bible can be done in a meaningful and responsible manner and that preaching and pastoral care have immense potential as long as they are based on the riches of sacred Scripture.

In the winter of 1515–1516 Erasmus was working in Basle on his edition of the Greek text of the New Testament. He was assisted by Oecolampadius, the reformer of Basle. A visit Zwingli paid to Erasmus during this period provided Zwingli with new stimulus to read the New Testament in the original language and to study it on the basic text.

Meanwhile biblical humanism was spreading from Basle in two directions: toward Zurich and toward Berne and Geneva. In 1507 Wyttenbach had returned to Biel, his birthplace, where he became a pastor. In 1515 he accepted a pastorate in Berne where he won Haller to his humanist ideals until the latter succeeded him as pastor in 1518.

Independent of Luther's activity in Germany the years 1518 and 1519 had decisive significance in the genesis of the Swiss Reformation. During this time Oecolampadius in Basle, Haller in Berne and Zwingli in Zurich where he had become a pastor in 1519 began their biblical preaching. They decided to draw the material for their sermons not only from the Sunday gospel but from all of sacred Scripture. Thus the biblical-humanist movement prepared the way for the Swiss Reformation, from Basle to Berne to Geneva and from Zurich to all of eastern Switzerland.

In the meantime Oecolampadius had, at the end of 1518, left Basle to take up his appointment as cathedral preacher in Augsburg where he was won over to the Lutheran Reformation. Still in many respects he preserved a theological independence of Luther. After some peregrinations he returned to Basle in 1522 and the following year began to deliver biblical addresses to the burghers of Basle. In 1523 he was also appointed professor at the University of Basle by the magistrate of the city. He also returned to the task of pastoral care and took the major part in introducing the Reformation there.

As early as 1519 Luther's writings had been published and distributed over all of Switzerland by the famous printers and publishers of Basle. It was in this year also that Haller and Zwingli first became acquainted with the content of Luther's teachings but they too remained to a great extent independent of Luther.

In 1525 Farel, Calvin's predecessor and compatriot, came to Switzerland from France via Basle. Farel had studied in Paris where he was subjected to the humanist influence of Faber Stapulensis. He had followed Stapulensis to Meaux where the latter, as vicar general of the humanist-minded bishop of Meaux, became the center of a circle of biblical humanists. Farel may here have come into contact with some of Luther's writings and he certainly did in 1525 in Strasbourg and Basle. Although it was in Basle that Oecolampadius won Farel over for the Swiss Reformation, the latter also labored for the cause of the Reformation in many places in western Switzerland, particularly in Geneva.

Ten years after Farel's arrival in Basle Calvin made this city his first Swiss residence. Here Calvin wrote the text for the first publication of the *Institutio Christianae Religionis.* This work appeared in 1536, the year when after a trip to Italy and France Calvin passed through Geneva, where he was detained by Farel and quite against his will made into the actual reformer of the city.

Meanwhile the increasing tension between Catholics and reformers had led to civil war. The Catholics gained a victory in the battle of Kappel (1531) in which Zwingli was killed. Since several cities returned to the Catholic Church the center of the Reformation movement was transferred to western Switzerland, first to Berne and then in 1536 to Geneva. Farel introduced the Reformation in this city in 1532 and a year later began to collaborate with Viret on a program for the formation of a church. This program was finally accomplished by Calvin in 1536.

Oecolampadius had died in 1531, the year of Zwingli's death, so Calvin never personally knew the first pioneers of the Reformation movement in Switzerland. Haller died in Berne in 1536.

Zwingli and the Reformation

We have noted that the beginnings of Zwingli's Reformation activities took place in 1519 when he became pastor in Zurich. On that occasion he decided to devote a great amount of care and attention to the task of preaching. Thus he conceived the plan of preaching on one complete book of the Bible after another and to deliver biblical sermons not only on Sundays but also on weekdays.

From 1519 to 1525 Zwingli preached from the New Testament. He had begun with the Gospel according to Matthew in order to present to the faithful a complete and well rounded picture of the life and teaching of Christ. Next he chose the Acts of the Apostles so as to give the faithful an idea of the primitive Church. After this he preached on some of the epistles of Paul (Galatians, Timothy and Hebrews) and on the Gospel according to Luke. After 1525 he also preached on books of the Old Testament.

It is clear that Zwingli's one purpose here was to have the faithful entrusted to his care obtain a better knowledge of Christ from holy Scripture. He was certainly not motivated by the evil intentions of starting an anti-ecclesiastic movement, of creating confusion or of causing a schism. It is true of course that he gave the first impulse to the Reformation movement he willy-nilly became the leader of before he realized what was happening, but it was a movement born of an unprejudiced and continual listening to the testimony of sacred Scripture. Difficulties with the ecclesiastic authorities loomed suddenly and unexpectedly. Zwingli as well as the magistrate of Zurich and a large section of the faithful was even then firmly convinced that his position was in full agreement with the testimony and intentions of sacred Scripture.

The question may be asked how far this course of events had been influenced by Luther's writings. It is certain that from the end of 1518 on Zwingli had personally read some of Luther's writings and that in his enthusiasm he also had others read them. But prior to his acquaintance with Luther's writing, according to Köhler, Zwingli manifested nothing but "pure Renaissance," and since the Reformation began to show itself only after Zwingli's reading of Luther, Zwingli thus inherited the Reformation from the German reformer. This one-sided, premature view Köhler himself has revoked in his biography of Zwingli.

It may likewise be asked whether there was question of a sudden conversion in the case of Zwingli. He did experience a crisis in the autumn of 1519 when during a pestilence he was afflicted and near death. The so-called Song of Pestilence, regarded by many as the manifesto of Zwingli's conversion, does not contain a line which could not also have been written by a Catholic. In a pamphlet about Zwingli and Calvin, Lang summarizes the contents of the Song of Pestilence as follows:

He wants to attach himself to God, and serve him alone. At the same time his conscience has been penetrated by the knowledge of what sin is. Sin became for him the sting of death; hence his fear of the temptations of the devil, against which he calls upon God and Christ for grace and redemption. With all this, the religious experience which is at the heart of the Reformation entered Zwingli's life.

According to Lang, Zwingli had not yet found the word that brings redemption. "There was no question yet of the forgiveness of sin and of the imputation of Christ's reconciliation. Neither had any connection been established between the notion of justification and the 'activity of God alone.' "

The above statement seems to imply that Zwingli, a priest who had enjoyed a Thomistic and humanistic formation, knew nothing of man's personal relationship with God, of the real nature of sin, of forgiveness, grace and redemption, and of man's participation in Christ's reconciliation since he had never explicitly expressed any of these concepts. Moreover Lang seems to imply that Zwingli would not even have been in a position to express them had he not received the gospel from Luther.

From this and similar statements it is impossible to gain a correct view of what took place during the Reformation and to form a correct judgment of the meaning, significance and possible legitimacy of the Reformation without a study, based on the best available sources, of both the Catholic and the Reformation teachings and theologies. It happens not infrequently that some of the original Catholic notions of the reformers are regarded as typically Protestant and anti-Roman by Protestant historians.

In this respect the most recent research on Zwingli has made important contributions. It is now established that Zwingli's dependence on Luther was not as considerable as has been previously supposed. It could not really be otherwise. For why should it have been impossible for men like Zwingli, who had dedicated themselves for years to a devoted and unprejudiced study of sacred Scripture, to discover independently of Luther the same gospel? If they had to depend on Luther then how is the clarity of sacred Scripture to be explained? The Catholic Church teaches that the individual believer needs the living teaching authority of the Church in order to understand sacred Scripture correctly and according to its true meaning and content. But viewed from the standpoint of the Reformation it can hardly be maintained that a person should need Luther to discover the gospel. This would mean that the teaching authority of the Church must be replaced by the teaching authority of Luther.

Even on internal grounds one must not accentuate too strongly any possible dependence of Zwingli on Luther. After 1519 Zwingli continued peacefully with the execution of his plan concerning preaching. If he had been suddenly converted by Luther he would no doubt have discontinued his treatment of the Gospel according to Matthew and immediately transferred to preaching on those passages of the Pauline epistles best suited to demonstrate what the nucleus was of Luther's testimony of faith. But Zwingli's preaching was mainly socio-ethical. In none of his writings does Zwingli appeal to Luther. His first mention of the latter's name is in his commentary on the sixty-seven theses of 1523 and even then he does so only to emphasize that he neither is nor intends to be a Lutheran, and that he has independently arrived at the decision to preach nothing but the pure word of God:

Who was it that inspired me to preach the gospel and to preach one evangelist from beginning to end? Has Luther done this? I began to preach even before I had ever heard Luther's name mentioned, and for that purpose I began to study Greek ten years before so that I might learn the teaching of Christ in its sources. Whether I have succeeded I leave to others to judge; in any case it was not Luther who directed me in all this; his name remained unknown to me for two years after I had begun to adhere exclusively to the text of Scripture. Even now I do not want to bear Luther's name. Therefore I do not wish to be called Lutheran by the papists, for I have learned Christ's teaching not from Luther but from the very word of God itself.

It is true that Zwingli's writings have in their content and design such a distinctly personal form and character that a direct and exclusive influence by Luther should be regarded as unacceptable. As we have just pointed out Zwingli's preaching was primarily of a socio-ethical nature and originally even had effects similar to Luther's teaching. For example the chapter of the minster (Grossmünster) decided to spend the founded stipends —donated so that the *Salve Regina* would be chanted at regular times—for charitable purposes by granting them to the municipal hospital in favor of the sick who had no financial resources. Also, when in the spring of 1521 Zurich was the only confederate which abstained from voting on an alliance with France, Zwingli considered this step as the first and direct result of his evangelic preaching.

The first friction with the pope did not originate with matters of faith but with the refusal to supply troops. Zwingli had convinced the people of Zurich that it was contrary to the spirit of the gospel to leave some useful labor undone in order to hire oneself as a mercenary to the highest bidder and to live from plunder and booty. Besides, Zwingli's pacifism was by no means based on the commandment "You will not kill." Zwingli, himself a born soldier, considered it perfectly legitimate to wage war in defense of the freedom of religion for here not booty but the honor of God and the conservation of religion were at stake.

In 1522 occurred the first conflict with the bishop of Constance in whose diocese Zurich was situated. This conflict resulted from a violation of the law of fasting by some inhabitants of Zurich and in their defense Zwingli produced his first Reformation writing—on the free choice and use of food. He followed this up with a more general apology wherein he points out that sacred Scripture is the one and only criterion by which judgments must be formed whether or not some particular fact is in agreement with Scripture.

What occupied Zwingli was not so much the question of personal assurance of salvation as the question of the general welfare and of a view of life according to the gospel. In particular he considered the celibacy prescribed for all priests as a danger to a manner of life pleasing to God. Putting this theory into practice he submitted to the bishop of Constance a proposal, signed by ten priests as cosignatories, that the priestly celibacy be abolished. Prior to this he himself entered into a secret marriage with a widow, the mother of three children. Shortly after, on Oct. 10, 1522, he publicly renounced all his ecclesiastic dignities and functions and at the order of the municipal magistrate accepted the office of preacher of the city. Zwingli did not regard this office as the continuation of his priesthood and attached no value to an ordination by the imposition of hands.

On the subject of the sacraments Zwingli set his own course from the very beginning. He totally rejected the idea that it was possible for the sacraments to confer grace. He would have nothing to do with any sort of identification of human words and actions with those of God. The Bible itself was not the word of

121

God but a human witness to this word. Baptism did not effect a supernatural change in man but was the sign of God's covenant with the believer. The Lord's supper too was a symbolic meal of the faithful which strengthened their unity of love with one another and with Christ. Bread and wine in the Lord's supper signified the body and blood of Christ only insofar as they are Christ's assurance to the faithful that out of love for them he died on the cross for them.

As we have seen, the real break between Zwingli and the Church took place in October 1522. To justify his activity and teaching he formulated sixty-seven theses as the starting point of a public disputation to which he invited the magistrate, the bishop and the clergy of the diocese as well as representatives of the Swiss cantons and of the burghers of Zurich.

The disputation took place on Jan. 23, 1523 in the council chamber of the city hall. The bishop of Constance was represented by a delegation under the leadership of vicar general Faber. As with most disputations however the outcome was predetermined. The Zurich council and burghers were in favor of Zwingli and paid little attention to the bishop's delegation. The day ended with the announcement of a proclamation whereby the magistrate of the city delegated Zwingli to continue preaching the gospel according to sacred Scripture and according to whatever inspirations the Holy Spirit might give him.

Zwingli's Reformation ideas were of a highly biblical character. He wanted to have the Bible speak for itself, with as simple and practical an explanation of the text as possible, and with no interpolation of *a priori* Church dogmatics. His first thesis accordingly read: "Anyone who says that the gospel is void if it does not have the confirmation of the Church is in error and scorns God."

In his second thesis Zwingli formulated the principal content of the gospel as follows: "The sum total of the gospel is that our Lord Christ Jesus, the true Son of God, has announced to us the will of his heavenly Father, and by his innocence has redeemed us from death and reconciled us to God."

On the basis of these two fundamental theses is built the entire complex of the sixty-seven theses:

3 Therefore, Christ is the only way to salvation for all men who have ever lived, now live, or will live.

4 Whoever looks for or indicates another way is in error; more than that, he is a murderer of souls and a thief.

5 Therefore, all those are in error who equate or give precedence to any other teaching than the gospel. They do not even know what the gospel is.

14 Therefore, all Christians must zealously see to it that only the gospel of Christ is preached in all places.

15 For our salvation is based on our belief in the gospel; our damnation on our disbelief. For all truth is clearly contained in the gospel.

16 The gospel tells us that the teachings and institutions of men are of no avail unto salvation.

Zwingli's theses also contain the first accusations of idolatry in connection with the sacrament of penance:

50 No one but God forgives sins through Christ Jesus, his son, our Lord, alone.

51 Whoever attributes this to a creature deprives God of his honor, rendering it to someone who is not God. To do this is pure idolatry.

Here we are confronted with the concern, typical of Reformed Protestantism, about the honor of God and with the abhorrence of anything resembling idolatry and the divinization of man. This concern appears in Zwingli for the first time in 1523, the year when Calvin as a "Roman" boy of 14 years old was sent to Paris to study.

Whatever the causes that gave Zwingli as a priest his ideas concerning the sacrament of penance, it is obvious that he lacked a sound knowledge of the teaching and intention of the Church in this respect. Time and again modern Catholics are struck by the fact that the reformers reacted more against the misunderstandings which the people and they themselves had of Catholic teaching, than against the true teaching of the Catholic Church. Lortz is correct in saying that one of the principal causes of the Reformation lay in the fact that the Church was no longer viewed as the Mystical Body of Christ, that the Church was no longer really operative in the life of the faithful, and that the Church was no longer consciously and in good faith accepted as the bearer of revealed truth.

The break between Zurich and Rome was an accomplished fact by 1523. The priests were subjected to a reschooling; from Catholic priests they were transformed into Reformation preachers and excused from the obligation of celibacy.

However the magistrate was quite tolerant in his execution of the program of Reformation, although during Holy Week of 1525 the mass was definitively abolished; on Holy Thursday evening the Lord's supper was celebrated according to Reformation standards. But anyone who retained the former beliefs was allowed to continue his residence in the city and carry out his religious duties elsewhere. Up to 1528 a person could even be a member of the council without abandoning the "old faith."

To promote the spread of a proper knowledge of the Bible an hour of "prophecy" was held each day beginning in July 1525. Preachers would first read among themselves some part of sacred Scripture in the original language. This was followed by a discussion. Then the meeting, held in the minster, was concluded by a sermon for the people.

Meanwhile some Anabaptist manifestations had been held in Zurich which among other things protested the tolerant position of the magistrate toward the former beliefs. From 1525 to 1527 the magistrate gradually began to take stronger steps against the Anabaptist propaganda and finally ordered the execution of Felix Manz.

The growing opposition between Zurich and the cantons which had remained Catholic resulted in the formation of a separate confederacy by the latter. There was an increasing danger of civil war. Beginning with the disputation of Berne in January 1528 the more moderate cantons of Berne, Basle, Schaffhausen and Appenzell shifted and joined in with Zurich. Whereas up to that time the mass had continued to be offered along with evangelic preaching these cities now followed Zurich in the abolition of the mass. Sacred images, statues and altars were removed, education and ecclesiastic life were reorganized, and in imitation of Zurich even the "prophecy" was introduced.

After many clashes Zurich declared war on the Catholic cantons in 1529. A decisive encounter took place in the battle of Kappel after Berne had vainly attempted to prevent an armed conflict. In this battle, fought on the night of Oct. 11, Zwingli was killed. Subsequently, especially in eastern Switzerland, many towns returned to the Catholic Church. Although the Reformation persisted in Zurich the center of the Reformation movement shifted to western Switzerland, at first to Berne and then in 1536 to Geneva.

In Zurich, five years prior to the arrival of Calvin, Zwingli was succeeded by Bullinger (1504–1575), who outlived Calvin by ten years.

Bullinger had received his education from the Brethren of the Common Life in Emmerich. Like Zwingli he began as a biblical humanist and admirer of Erasmus. In Germany he became acquainted with the first Reformation writings of Luther and Melanchthon. Upon his return to Switzerland he settled in Kappel as a teacher and preacher, established contacts with Zwingli and after the latter's death was appointed preacher of the minster and elected leader of the Reformation movement in Zurich. He became the actual organizer of the Reformed community in Zurich, just as Calvin was the organizer of the Geneva community. In some respects, for example in his teaching on the Lord's supper, Bullinger was closer to Luther than to Zwingli, but in other respects he was closer to Calvin.

In 1549 Bullinger and Calvin succeeded in establishing a

125

union between the Zwinglian east and the Calvinist west on the basis of the *Consensus Tigurinus*. It was in Geneva and under Calvin's direction that the foundation of a reform church took the shape in which it spread over a large part of western Europe. Therefore we will now limit our considerations to Calvin and Geneva.

Calvin and the Reformation

In Catholic circles Calvin was a less controversial figure than Luther. It was generally supposed that Calvin adopted Luther's ideas, applied them drastically and elaborated them in a systematic form. He was therefore not considered responsible for the conflict with the Church and its disastrous consequences.

But this picture is far too simple and one-sided. Calvin experienced his own personal religious development and like Zwingli was well on the way toward a new vision of the gospel and the religious life of the church long before he had heard about Luther. Calvin was moreover a very cautious, almost timid person. On the one hand he had an open mind, was acquainted with the most diverse philosophies (Thomist, Ockhamist, humanist) and was influenced by various professors and friends. In his period of reformation he studied the ideas of Luther, Bucer and Melanchthon as well as those of Farel, Viret and other Swiss reformers. But he was also able to maintain a high degree of spiritual independence, owing to his clear, acute and balanced mind. Once he had arrived at full maturity this independent character often led to a certain obstinacy and to a strikingly authoritarian if not haughty attitude, as witnessed for example in his connections with the magistrate of Geneva.

If Luther found his devil's advocate in Cochlaeus, Calvin found him in Bolsec, a former Carmelite monk who later became a medical doctor. Bolsec was undeniably in favor of the Reformation but in Geneva he became involved in a theological battle with Calvin and as a result was exiled from the city.

In 1577 Bolsec published a biography of Calvin based more on slander than truth, thereby presenting a completely false picture of Calvin. As in the case of Luther this picture, inherited by subsequent historians, is in need of a basic revision.

Research on Calvin properly got under way only upon the appearance of the extensive, richly illustrated biography by Doumergue in seven volumes (1899–1917). But Doumergue lacked even the most elementary knowledge of the Catholic Church and thus painted the significance of Calvin against a background of crass prejudice against and misunderstanding of Catholicism. Moreover the intensive examination of the sources conducted during the past twenty-five years has proved his picture of Calvin to be untenable in many respects.

A more recent, somewhat debatable summary of the present situation of Calvin research can be found in the work of the Strasburg professor Wendel (*Calvin, sources et évolution de sa pensée religieuse* 1950). The Calvin monographs which have appeared in the past few years are certainly as valuable as the great number of Luther monographs. The most important titles on Calvin can be found in the bibliography of Wendel's book.

The question about the sources of Calvin's theology is so extensive that, in the words of Wendel, no one has yet had sufficient courage and patience to undertake the gigantic labor necessary to arrive at a scientifically warranted picture of the development, continuity and content of Calvin's theological thought.

As a result of the Protestant revival in our age research into the Reformation has received a powerful stimulus. Not since the Reformation itself have such intensive efforts been made to penetrate into its essence, although a comprehensive understanding is still wanting.

Calvin arrived at his Protestant convictions in a manner different from Luther and Zwingli so in many respects his beliefs and theology have their own characteristics and structure.

127

John Calvin (1509–1564) was born in Noyons in northern France. Little is known about his youth. When the Reformation was in full swing in Germany and the surrounding countries Calvin, a youth of fourteen and the son of the lay secretary of the bishop of Noyons, was, like a good Catholic boy, destined to become a member of the clergy. He already enjoyed certain ecclesiastic benefices which made his studies possible and so was sent to Paris to study Latin, philosophy and theology.

The spiritual climate of Paris was much more capricious and precarious than in Erfurt. High scholasticism was still flourishing there although besides Thomism the universities also taught Ockhamism and humanism. The influence of Faber Stapulensis was still making itself felt but it seems that Calvin (in contrast to Farel, his later collaborator in Geneva) was not subjected to it. After his arrival in Paris Calvin established residence in the Collège de la Marche and there is no doubt that in this college he felt the influence of Cordier. According to the spirit of Christ and the gospel this progressive pedagogue tried to impart to his students a love of study by means of tact, understanding and mildness instead of fear and strict discipline. Love, not fear, is at the heart of the gospel. Therefore love and not threats or punishment should be the basis of a Christian education. In Catholic Paris before the Reformation such principles were expounded as: *Doce pueros Christum diligere, Christum spirare, Christum in ore habere*—teach the children to love Christ, to breath forth Christ, to have Christ on their lips.

Yet Cordier's influence must not be exaggerated for Calvin soon moved to the Collège de Montaigu where he remained until 1528, the year he changed his studies and moved to Orleans. In the Collège de Montaigu Thomism was still very much alive. It is remarkable that whenever Protestant theologians with a good grasp of Thomism become involved in modern Calvin research there has been frequent reference to the Thomistic tendencies in Calvin's theology. At the same time Calvin also studied under a master who defended nominalism and Ockhamism, but this was only one among the various influences Calvin underwent. Moreover at this time he also became acquainted with the Fathers of the Church, particularly Augustine. Therefore—even apart from his well balanced character—there was for Calvin far less danger of losing his spiritual equilibrium than there was for Luther at Erfurt where practically only Ockhamism prevailed.

Wendel thinks that up to 1530 there are no traces in Calvin that point to the direction of the Reformation. Still the year 1528 was a decisive year in his life and many have regarded it as the actual year of his—possibly unconscious—conversion to the Reformation. If there is question here of a religious crisis it is peculiar that, as in the case of Luther, it made itself known only when Calvin had his secular studies rewarded with the degree of master of arts. Abandoning his original plans to study theology in preparation for the priesthood, Calvin now switched to the study of law and moved from Paris to Orleans.

In his biography of Calvin (1564) Theodore Beza, Calvin's successor in Geneva, attributes this change to two causes: to the wishes of Calvin's father who, like Luther's father, considered the prospects of a law career more remunerative, but also to the influence of Calvin's cousin Olivetanus. As a result of this last influence he is supposed to have "got a taste for the pure religion, and to have begun breaking connections with the papist superstitions."

Wendel underestimates the value of this evidence. Apparently he wants to reserve the conversion for the moment of the open and decisive break with Rome in 1533. He attaches very little significance to anything that took place in Calvin's life prior to this time, labeling it nothing but pure humanism.

Such considerations, possibly inspired by an *a priori* theological point of view, seem too external. To determine the proper character of Calvin's Reformation convictions it is necessary to establish where and when the most important interior decisions in his life took place. In this connection full value must be given to brief, chance remarks which throw a surprising light on the hidden interior development.

It is a pity therefore that Calvin, in the preface to his commentary on the Book of Psalms (1557) speaks of a "sudden conversion to docility and obedience" without mentioning the time of the incident. Though Wendel tries to link this passage to Calvin's conversion in 1533 there is much to be said for the opinion of others (Doumergue, Pannier, P. Barth) that the passage refers to the interior change which took place in Calvin's life in 1528 or 1529.

In any case both the passage from Beza's biography and the one in Calvin's commentary on the Psalms mention "some taste of the true religion" and "some taste and understanding of true piety." Neither Beza nor Calvin himself describe his conversion as a sudden conviction of the assurance of salvation, reconciliation and forgiveness although, of course, Calvin did not deny any of these. Instead there is question of obedience and docility that caused him to make a radical break with any form of idolatry and superstition and thenceforth rightly to serve and adore the living God alone. The living God himself had taken possession of Calvin's heart. In this connection Strohl speaks of an *"emprise de Dieu"* and an *"expérience du Dieu vivant,"* a being captivated in an encounter with the living God. The question is where and how Calvin learned to know the living God, where and how he suddenly became aware of his confrontation with the typically Old Testament dilemma: to serve false gods or the living God. It certainly did not result from reading Luther's writings; rather from reading sacred Scripture and in particular the Old Testament, so close to the heart of Calvin and the Calvinists.

We should not yield to the desire to transform Calvin into a Lutheran. His conversion is rooted in biblical humanism by constant reading of the Bible. His conversion does not begin with certain texts from the epistles of Paul but with the prophetic Old Testament witness of the living God. Basically Calvin's conversion was, in his own awareness and conviction, a conversion from the service of false gods to the service of the living God, a conversion to true religion and piety.

Purity of religion and divine praise, the principal concern of the Old Testament prophets, was the main characteristic of Calvin's conversion and has been preserved as such by the Calvinist Reformation. Much more than Wendel supposes is this profound conversion connected with the influence of Olivetanus, the translator of the Hebrew Old Testament into French (Calvin renewed his contacts with Olivetanus in 1536 in Geneva where the latter had arrived in 1531 after a three-year period of exile in Strasburg). As Beza attests, Calvin's decision to change his course of studies was closely related to his conversion. Calvin's later acquaintance with Luther's writings may have been influential enough to supply the final motive for Calvin's definitive break with the papacy and the Church of Rome, but it certainly was not the all important and decisive factor. Rather this lay in his direct confrontation with the divine witness of sacred Scripture.

In Orleans Calvin met a philologist from Wurtemberg, Melchior Wolmar, a convinced supporter of Luther and stepfather of Theodore Beza (then nine years old). Personal ties were therefore established between the two future reformers as early as 1528 and Beza would remember Calvin from his pre-Reformation period of development.

Calvin acquired his knowledge of Greek from Wolmar, who must also have spoken to him about Luther. He probably had Calvin read some of Luther's writings and may have told him about the Marburg disputation between Luther and Zwingli in 1529. But since Calvin does not mention Wolmar's name in any of his works Wendel concludes that there is no foundation to the frequently suggested hypothesis that Wolmar perhaps played an important part in Calvin's conversion to the Reformation.

Such an argument from silence is very weak however. Since Calvin seldom wrote about himself and since a writer can have memories of persons who influenced his life profoundly without ever mentioning their names in any of his writings, great care must be exercised in the use or acceptance of such an argument.

We may therefore assume that in Orleans Calvin was perhaps for the first time in his life confronted with Luther's new vision of faith through the intervention of Wolmar. But it was in line with Calvin's character to absorb and digest these new impressions slowly. There is no reason to suppose that Calvin's lively interest in the ideals of humanism are proof that a profound interior religious process was at work in the direction of a final option in favor of the Reformation. On the contrary a profound interior process of growth and development may have been taking place long before external actions and activities gave reason to suspect its presence.

In 1529 Calvin left Orleans in order to continue, according to Wendel, his law studies in Bourges under the direction of the renowned lawyer Alciat. However it must be borne in mind that although the law faculty of Orleans was famous for its large number of competently occupied chairs, Wolmar in 1529 had been invited by Margaret of Navarre to establish himself in Bourges. This latter fact may well be connected with Calvin's change of universities, the more so since the subsequent course of events makes it evident that he was becoming increasingly engaged in the study of Greek and Hebrew. Most likely this preference for the study of languages cannot be explained by purely humanist interests but by a long-felt need to be able to read the Old Testament in Hebrew and the New Testament in Greek. For this reason Calvin considered himself dependent on Wolmar and therefore moved with him to Bourges.

That the study of law was not really Calvin's option becomes clear moreover at the death of his father in May 1531. Immediately after this he abandoned his studies and returned to Paris to devote himself to the study of classics and Hebrew.

In 1532 Calvin's first writing appeared: a commentary on the

De Clementia of the Stoic philosopher Seneca. According to Wendel biographies of Calvin have paid too little attention to the influence of this philosopher on the practical thought of Calvin. The implication is that the humanist ideals gave a lasting shape to his mind which Calvin was unable to shed even after his conversion to the Reformation, just as he was unable to rid himself of his Ockhamist formation. Whether this is true or not it is certain that, apart from his reading of the Stoics, Calvin was also occupied with the study of Hebrew and a cursory reading of the entire Old Testament. Why Wendel does not stress this latter point is not clear.

Unlike Wendel both Doumergue and Pannier do not consider the years immediately following his father's death as the years in which Calvin's humanism reached full maturity. Rather they consider them as that actual period of crisis when he unconsciously began to turn in favor of the Reformation: "During this period there occurred in him a religious development that came to a sudden stop. In 1533 he composed for his friend Nicolas Cop, rector of the University of Paris, a famous speech which Cop delivered on Nov. 1, 1533" (Doumergue).

Pannier identifies the period of 1531–1533 as a period of "intellectual and spiritual liberation" and "an ascent to truth." During this period Calvin read once again the entire Scripture in the new French translation Olivetanus was then preparing.

And even if Wendel is correct in affirming that not Calvin but Cop wrote his speech of 1533 the fact remains that Calvin was evidently quite in agreement with the purpose and content of the speech, that both he and Cop were suspected of Lutheran heresy, that he had to go into hiding, and that he soon after went into exile via Strasburg to Basle.

The final words of Cop's speech refer to Luther and his supporters and followers: "Heretics, impostors, deceivers, cursed men, these are the names which the world and the good-for-nothings give to those who exert themselves in all sincerity to have the gospel penetrate the hearts of the faithful. . . . Only

133

to God do we owe service; for love of him we must suffer and sustain everything. . . . In heaven we shall triumph forever. Amen."

Here too there is question of the pure and simple gospel, of the exclusive service of God and of the docility to follow, to obey and if necessary to suffer and to sustain. This is the attitude toward God and his word which from 1528 onward was peculiar to Calvin's religious frame of mind. This attitude suddenly became public on Nov. 1, 1533 just as Luther's long dormant attitude had become public on Nov. 1, 1517.

But obviously this was not the end of Calvin's development as a reformer. In 1534 he met for the first time two Strasburg reformers: Bucer, a former Dominican priest won over to the Reformation by Luther during the Heidelberg disputation of 1518, and Capito, former secretary and adviser of Archbishop Albrecht of Mainz. Here, for the first time, Calvin found a Reformation community with its own ecclesiastic order and liturgy. Although these acquaintances were only casual Calvin continued them in an exchange of letters. From the very first there was a perfect harmony between Calvin and Bucer which must, among other things, be attributed to the fact that both had received a Thomistic formation.

From Strasburg Calvin continued to Basle where he again encountered a community that in many respects had its own character. Here he made the first draft of what was to become his principal work, his *Institutes of the Christian Religion.* As far as the division of contents in this first publication (1536) was concerned it was similar to Luther's *Minor Catechism.* But in its extent and thoroughness it can be compared to Luther's *Major Catechism* of 1529, although Calvin was probably not familiar with this work at the time. Later, in Strasburg and Geneva, Calvin radically changed and recast his *Institutes,* partly because of contemporary polemics. The final publication appeared in 1559. The earlier editions of 1539, 1543, 1550 and 1559 appeared in French translations in 1541, 1545, 1551 and 1560 respectively.

When after a brief sojourn in Italy and France Calvin passed through Geneva in 1536, he was almost drastically forced by Farel to stay there and undertake the direction of the reformed community. This happened in July 1536, the same month that Erasmus died in Basle at the home of the publisher Frobenius.

Although the spirit of humanism would remain operative for some time after the death of Erasmus, nonetheless the period of biblical humanism had in a sense come to an end, only to leave as its legacy a particular type of Protestantism: the Reformed Protestantism of the continent and the Anglicanism of England. In Geneva Calvin became the founder, organizer and theologian of this Reformed Protestantism.

For the time being however Calvin was only a budding reformer. His first sojourn in Geneva (1536–1538) was from an ecclesiastico-political point of view a failure. Calvin's first efforts were too much of a montanistic and dictatorial nature. By means of strict measures he wanted to transform the community into a community of perfect Christians, into a sort of realization of God's kingdom on earth.

The magistrate was increasingly hesitant toward Calvin's suggestions. Here again it was a matter of the relation between *polis* and *ekklêsia*, between state and church. The magistrate was unwilling to relinquish his control of public morals and ethics in favor of an ecclesiastic disciplinary authority. Moreover the populace was quite recalcitrant, particularly when asked to subscribe to such a confession as the one summarized in the *Institutes*.

Added to all this was the fact that the first doctrinal differences began to appear. Caroli accused Calvin and Farel of Arianism. At first the synods of Lausanne and Berne showed some reluctance but eventually declared Caroli to be in the wrong. The synod of Berne in 1537 was visited by the Strasburg reformers Bucer and Capito. Even at this early date Calvin's idea of the Lord's supper appeared in agreement with Bucer's.

Calvin's implacable attitude toward Caroli however had caused a great deal of dissatisfaction in Berne. Moreover Berne disapproved of the drastic manner in which Calvin was reforming the liturgy in Geneva. When the new magistrate of Geneva was elected in 1538 he chose the side of Berne; Calvin, Farel and a few other preachers were dismissed from office and exiled from the city.

Calvin's first activity had failed because of his lack of knowledge of human nature and experience and his abundance of self-confidence and rigorism.

Calvin in Strasburg
Martin Bucer

Calvin no doubt went to Strasburg because his outlook was so similar to those of Bucer and Capito. He stayed in this city for three years (1538–1541), a period of considerable importance for his further development. Particularly under the influence of Bucer he matured here into the reformer of the stature he achieved after his return to Geneva. Despite the attempts of Holl, Noesgen and the later efforts of P. Barth to prove the contrary, Wendel too acknowledges the great significance of Bucer's influence on Calvin and the future Reformed Protestantism. This influence has also been defended by Pannier, Courvoisier, Strohl, Pauck and others.

In Strasburg Calvin transformed his *Institutes* into an entirely new book which shows distinct traces of Bucer's influence. Calvin also participated in the religious discussions of Frankfurt (1539), Hagenau (1540), Worms (1540) and Ratisbon (1541). He also met Melanchthon personally and came to have great admiration for him.

In this way there developed in Calvin's mind that open, irenic and ecumenical attitude subsequently peculiar to him. Because of this attitude Calvin, after his return to Geneva, became the man par excellence to act as liaison between Calvinists, Lutherans, Zwinglians and Anglicans. "No doubt," says Pauck, "it was in Strasburg that Calvin became familiar with the notion of a universal Protestantism, a cause to which he gave his untiring labors in the last years of his life" (*The Heritage of the Reformation* 1950, 82).

Unfortunately the ecumenical spirit Calvin owed to Bucer and shared with Bucer and Melanchthon went with these reformers to their graves. From time to time this spirit revived in such solitary figures as Hugo Grotius, and in the Church of England, whose struggle against puritanism and sectarianism was basically a struggle toward a Reformed but at the same time universal and ecumenical Christendom.

Martin Bucer was one of the most remarkable figures among the sixteenth century reformers. He is the actual link between evangelic (Lutheran) and Reformed (Calvinist) Protestantism on the one hand and between these two and Anglican Protestantism on the other.

The intensive Reformation research of our own days stresses the roles Strasburg and Bucer played in the rise and development of Reformed Christianity. Even as early as 1900 Huber had prepared a publication of the Strasburg liturgical ordinances in the age of the Reformation. Ficker, who discovered Luther's lectures on the Epistle to the Romans, has also written several studies about Bucer and the Reformation in Strasburg. Doumergue, Seeberg, Lang and in later years Eells, Pannier and Courvoisier occupied themselves with Bucer's influence on Calvin. Nor has the profound influence Bucer had on the character and form of the Church in England and Anglicanism been neglected (see Hopf, *Martin Bucer and the English Reformation* 1946).

Martin Bucer (1491–1551) was a little younger than Luther and almost twenty years older than Calvin. In his native Schlettstadt, at the age of fifteen, he had entered the Dominican order. From 1517 on he studied Greek at Heidelberg where the following year he was won over to the Reformation by Luther. He

137

also had great admiration for Erasmus and in 1520 established contact with several Reformation-minded persons, such as Capito. The latter too had been won over for the Reformation but at an early date adopted his own strikingly undogmatic views. He disapproved of Luther's uncontrolled rage and activity against the Anabaptists.

In 1523 Bucer and Capito settled in Strasburg and became close collaborators. Bucer was the actual, Capito the official leader of the Reformed community in Strasburg. After Capito's death in 1541 Bucer assumed the direction entirely. When in 1549 he refused to submit to the conditions of the moratorium of the Diet of Augsburg (1548) he went into exile in England.

Bucer and Capito retained a great deal of religious and spiritual independence in regard to Luther. On the Reformed community of Strasburg they bestowed a distinct organizational, liturgical and doctrinal nature the significance of which is being recognized in our own ecumenical times. But it is questionable whether the stabilized positions brought about by the orthodoxy of the Reformation and the theology of the Counter-reformation are actually and respectively based on a biblical and on an authentically Catholic proclamation of faith. And it is quite possible that the most valuable contributions to a solution of the ecumenical problem will be made by those sixteenth century theologians who in an age of polemics were counted among the least because of their careful and often very professional attitudes.

Bucer was undeniably the most ecumenical of all reformers. Courvoisier considers him the first precursor of the modern ecumenical movement: "Someone who studies Bucer's activities in the ecclesiastico-political realm cannot fail to see that his ideas have been adopted anew in Stockholm and particularly in Lausanne, though as far as I know his name has never been mentioned in this connection" (*La notion d'église chez Bucer*, 148).

Pannier has done much to refute a premonition especially prevalent among Lutheran historians, namely that it was not until he arrived at Strasburg that Calvin became a Lutheran. Pannier contends that if Calvin must somehow have a label it should state that during his stay in Strasburg Calvin became in certain respects a "Bucerian." But it is not correct to attribute a person's conviction directly to someone's influence—unless of course one wants to consider all reformers as followers of Luther. But this supposition is not historical and not ecumenical:

At all times and in all places [Calvin] was above all biblical, as were the first Protestants in the area around Meaux and elsewhere. He knows himself called *directly* by the Holy Spirit to build his faith *directly* on the rock of the word of God. This is by no means to deny the care and reverence with which Calvin, like Bucer, continued to study the tradition of the Fathers of the ancient Church and the opinions of his contemporary theologians (Pannier, *Calvin à Strasbourg*, 55).

Pannier approvingly cites a statement of Kampschulte, the nineteenth century Catholic biographer of Calvin:

Calvin's horizon was widened in Strasburg, his understanding deepened. These three years were necessary to make him the powerful reformer, the lawgiver, who upon his return to Geneva was able to withstand all the attacks made against him.

Bucer's influence on Calvin was not restricted to the ecumenical field but covered practically all of theology. For instance he widened Calvin's views on church organization and liturgy; moreover as organizer of the community of French refugees Calvin was able to consult Bucer regarding the formation of a church. Calvin became continually more aware of the basic principles all Christians share. In Strasburg as well as in the religious discussions we have mentioned he also learned to formulate the reform principles as clearly and sharply as possible and to distinguish them from those of the Lutherans, Zwinglians and Anabaptists.

Accordingly Calvin's esteem for Melanchthon appears not only in the exchange of correspondence between these two reformers but also in Calvin's translation of the *Loci Communes* into French. For this reason Hans Weber is quite correct when

139

in his work on Reformation, orthodoxy and rationalism he maintains against Niesel, Lang, and others that in his elaboration, presentation and application of the Reformation witness Calvin is more closely allied to Bucer and Melanchthon than to Luther. As will be seen in the following chapter the same can be said of the Anglican Reformation.

Calvin and Reformed Protestantism

After Calvin's departure from Geneva in 1538 the community in this city became the living example of disorder and furious ecclesiastic struggle. In the fall of 1540—after the followers of Calvin and Farel had also been sent into exile—a delegation was sent to Strasburg to persuade Calvin to return. Calvin certainly did not relish the idea of being the leader of the Geneva community. As long as possible he resisted the pressure brought to bear on him from all sides, even from Zurich and Basle. Only in September 1541 did he return to Geneva.

In Geneva, availing himself of the experience in church organization he had gained in Strasburg, Calvin concretized his now fully matured vision of the Church. It was here that he laid the foundations of the Reformed Protestantism of Geneva, France, The Netherlands, (West) Germany and Scotland, giving it its own confession and its own ecclesiastic organization.

Calvin was unable to realize completely his ecclesiological and liturgical ideals. It was no doubt his desire and intention to organize the Geneva community according to the pattern of Strasburg and to establish universal Christian rather than local Swiss criteria. For example he wanted to continue the succession in office by the imposition of hands, he wanted to have the sacred supper celebrated at least once a month if not every Sunday and he wanted to maintain the custom of receiving communion while kneeling down. In all this however he met with the resistance of the magistrate.

Beginning in 1528 Calvin personally kept himself open to

any and all Reformation influences while at the same time desiring to stay as much in agreement as possible with the faith of the undivided Church and the theology of the Church Fathers. His protest was directed against the ecclesiastic devotions and practices of the late middle ages. He emphasized that the sacred supper means for the faithful a real and true consuming of the body and blood of the Lord (see 214). It was Calvin's serious intention to lead Christians from the crisis of the Reformation to a universal, irenic and ecumenical Christendom which would conquer all differences of viewpoint among the reform-minded, and thus confess and live the full faith of the "catholic" church in all its purity.

Calvin resolutely rejected any and all heresies, from Docetism to Pelagianism, which had been condemned by the Church from the very beginning. How serious he was in his ideas about discipline is clear from the examples of Castellio who was forced to leave the city, of Gruet who was decapitated, of Bolsec who was banished, of Trolliet who was relieved from office, and of Servetus whom the magistrate condemned to be burned at the stake (Calvin had pleaded for decapitation). Moreover Berthelier and other leaders of the Libertine party were forced to flee the city in 1554 and Gentile was condemned to death although he saved his life by recanting his teachings.

Whatever we may now think about the persecution and capital punishment of heretics the ideas of Calvin, Beza, Bullinger and Melanchthon in this respect differed in no way from those of the members of the Roman inquisition. Heretics were considered murderers of the soul and deserved on that account a heavier punishment than murderers of the body. Shortly after Servetus' death Calvin wrote a "declaration" in which he defended capital punishment as a means of safeguarding the true faith against the loathsome heresies of Servetus. This writing was answered by Castellio in his *De haereticis an sint persequendi*. This debate initiated an endless series of writings which have appeared since the end of the seventeenth century on the subject of religious tolerance and freedom of conscience.

(The *monument expiatoire* erected in 1903 by "grateful sons of Calvin" on the spot of Servetus' execution missed its purpose in that there were liberals among those sons of Calvin who were more closely allied to the teachings of Servetus than Calvin's.)

After his return to Geneva Calvin had to wage a difficult battle with the magistrate as well as with a number of opponents and enemies before his position and influence were finally assured (c. 1555). The questions at stake were not only matters of doctrine and ecclesiastic discipline but also of defining the competencies of magistrate and church council, and of preserving the spiritual and religious autonomy of the community in its relation to the state.

Calvin's concern about safeguarding belief in the triune God as expressed in the oldest creeds of the Church did not make it impossible for him to labor wisely, and in true ecumenical spirit, for the establishment of a close unity among all the reform groups who confessed the ancient Christian faith in a trinitarian sense. He based this effort on the belief and common tradition of Christendom in its entirety. He knew how to distinguish between principles not subject to compromise and differences of opinion subject to discussion. This irenic and ecumenical frame of mind was neither sufficiently understood nor followed up by the magistrate of Geneva, by later puritanism or by post-Reformation orthodoxy.

Confession, church ordinances and liturgy

There are considerable differences between Luther and Calvin as far as their foundation and evaluation of church ordinances and liturgy are concerned.

Luther considered liturgy and church ordinances mainly practical matters requiring some attention for the sake of right order but which ordinary human insight could regulate. Existing customs, wishes and circumstances could certainly be taken into consideration. Pre-Reformation forms and institutions could if necessary be preserved provided they did not stand in the way of the effectiveness of the gospel.

Calvin on the other hand was convinced that sacred Scripture contained express and positive criteria and prescriptions to which right order in the church and the liturgy must correspond. In his organization of ecclesiastic life, the liturgy and arrangement of church buildings he did not consider the existing state of affairs but only data from Scripture. He strove after a church ordinance and liturgy "according to the Scriptures," emphasized that a strict ecclesiastic discipline be kept and saw in the church ordinance and liturgy a sort of confession. He gave much attention to the manner in which the true doctrine should be maintained, demanding—at least from the preachers—an explicit acceptance of the confession as expressed in his catechism. Church ordinance and liturgy were rooted in the confession.

Reformed Protestantism has always seen more of an inner connection between confession, church ordinance and liturgy than has Lutheran Protestantism. Also Reformed Protestantism has generally considered the confessional writings to have a binding rather than—as in Lutheranism—a merely normative force. On the other hand neither Calvin nor Reformed Protestantism in general ever attributed to the confession an absolute authority based on infallibility. The content of the ecclesiastic confession must always remain subject to verification with sacred Scripture. There is always the possibility that if necessary the confession can be clarified and revised, although this does not pertain to the competency of the individual believer or theologian but of a lawful consistory of the church that has accepted the confession in question.

Immediately after his return to Geneva in 1541 Calvin composed a church ordinance (*Ordonnances ecclésiastiques*), a liturgy (*La forme de prières et chants ecclésiastiques*) and a catechism. The Geneva catechism of 1541 is the oldest Reformed confessional writing.

In his desire to bring the people into closer contact with the Book of Psalms and to facilitate the singing of the psalms by the congregation during religious services Calvin had the psalms translated by Marot and Beza, while he had Bourgeois and others compose the proper musical accompaniment.

Since many communities in Switzerland and France asked Calvin for advice and chose his church ordinance as the basis for the organization of ecclesiastic life, Geneva was becoming an important center of Reformed Protestantism. In 1548 Calvin sent a manual to Somerset, the Protector of England and guardian of King Edward VI, a minor. This manual was to serve as a directive in the final establishment of the Reformation in the Church of England, which had been postponed until after the death of Henry VIII. Protestantism in east and west Switzerland was reunited by Calvin and Bullinger in 1549 on the basis of the *Consensus Tigurinus.*

During the reign of the Roman Catholic Queen Mary in England a community of English refugees was established in Geneva (1553–1558). One of the preachers of this community, John Knox, upon his return became the reformer of Scotland.

Meanwhile in 1555 Calvin had with the support of the foreign refugees gained a final victory over the Libertine party. Only then was Calvin's position for the first time fully acknowledged, accepted and supported by the magistrate. The foundation of an academy in 1559, with Calvin's future successor Beza as rector, attracted great numbers of theology students to Geneva from all parts of Europe.

Calvin died in 1563, two years after he had completed a last revision and expansion of his church ordinance. Although Geneva is the place from which Reformed Protestantism spread throughout France, The Netherlands, West Germany, Scotland (and in a sense England), to Bohemia, Hungary and Poland and finally, through emigration, to North and South America, it acquired its own personal character in each of these countries. Calvin can nowhere be considered as the sole founder; wherever it went Reformed Protestantism felt the influence of the reformers and the reform movements of the particular country. For this reason a reorientation based too exclusively on Calvin always results in an impoverishment of the specific and proper elements in the spiritual and religious heritage. This applies also to matters of doctrine and theology. Rather than being the creator of Reformed Protestantism Calvin is its most important representative.

Confessional writings

Prior to the definitive formation of the Reformed confession the years 1559 to 1566 were of decisive importance.

The *Confessio Gallicana* and the French church ordinance date from 1559. They were the first confession and church ordinance not pertaining to a local community, as in the case of Geneva, but rather to a developing national church and this in spite of the fact that the church was not only not recognized but even persecuted in its own country. They were composed during the first national synod of the Reformed communities in France, held in 1559 in Paris. Both had a considerable influence on the development and formation of Reformed Protestantism in other countries.

The Confession of Scotland dates from 1560 when the Scottish parliament declared itself in favor of the Reformation. The confession was composed by a commission of six theologians under the direction of John Knox and at the request of parliament.

In the same year of the final revision and expansion of the Geneva church ordinances (1561) the *Confessio Belgica* was drafted by Guido de Brès, who followed the *Confessio Gallicana*. The Belgian confession was dedicated to the "invincible King Philip, sovereign Lord" by the faithful of the southern part of The Netherlands who wished to live according to "the true

Reformation of the gospel of our Lord Jesus Christ." The fina text of this confession was later determined by the general synoc of Dordrecht (1618). Like the Dutch confession it is dividec into thirty-seven articles and is the most important of the *Three Formulas of Union* which together form the official basis of the Dutch Reformed Church and of the Reformed Churches in The Netherlands.

The *Church Ordinance of the Palatinate* dates from 1563. In order to emphasize the inner connection between faith, church ordinance and liturgy the Heidelberg Catechism and the liturgica formulas were incorporated into this church ordinance as integra parts.

The Heidelberg Catechism, composed by Olevianus and Ursinus by order of the elector of the Palatinate and with the cooperation of the theological faculty of Heidelberg, was acceptec by the synod of Heidelberg in 1562. The synod of Dordrech later adopted it as the second of the *Three Formulas of Union* (the third being the "Five Doctrinal Rules Against the Remon strants" of 1618).

The Swiss Confession (*Confessio Helvetica*) dates from 1566 The original draft was made by Bullinger, Zwingli's successor in Zurich, where it first appeared in May 1566. After a few changes had been made it was accepted as the basis of the fina reunion of the communities of east and west Switzerland, thus proving and realizing the possibility of a synthesis between Zwinglianism and Calvinism.

The *Three Formulas of Union* have been continued up to the present in the Dutch Reformed Church as well as in the Reformed Churches in The Netherlands. The manner in which these *Formulas* are accepted is very similar to the manner in which even now most Lutheran churches accept as their confes sional basis the Augsburg confession and the other confessiona writings included in the Book of Concordances of 1580. The Dor drecht Ordinances, built on the above Reformation ordinances was replaced in 1816 by the General Regulations introduced by order of King William I. After a struggle of more than a century the Dutch Reformed Church decided in 1950 to replace the Regulations by a new set of church ordinances and the liturgical formulas of Dordrecht were incorporated in a new *Book of Services*. A provisional draft has even appeared of a possible revised edition of the confession of the Dutch Reformed Church entitled *Foundations and Perspectives of Confession.*

In practically all Reformed churches in The Netherlands, Scotland, France and Germany there is a growing realization that new times demand new reforms. Without departing from the original principles there is a general movement toward a revision of confession, church ordinances and liturgy. In these attempts it is possible to discover definite influences of the theology of Karl Barth on the one hand and on the other the World Council of Churches and participation in ecumenical world conferences, although it is true that this latter influence is practical rather than theological.

The teaching of Reformed Protestantism

As we have mentioned earlier, in dealing with Reformed Protestantism the terms *hervormd* and *gereformeerd* are used as synonyms. These terms can be distinguished only by a study of the ecclesiastic situation which arose in The Netherlands during the nineteenth century as a result of separation and mutual distrust.

Reformed Protestantism agrees with the respective visions of Luther and world Protestantism in the following ways: the vision of the gospel, the nature and function of the act of faith, the salvific work of Christ and the one way of salvation for the Christian, the relation between man's sin and God's grace, justification by faith alone, sacred Scripture as the only source of man's knowledge of revelation, the three Reformation exclusives —through Scripture, grace and faith alone. All these are concerned with the most essential and profound core of the witness

147

of Luther and all Reformation Christianity. All the various forms, types, groups and orientations of world Protestantism have in this common Reformation witness a broad basis for a truly strong unity of faith.

Leaving aside the extreme forms of modernism and liberal Protestantism it is safe to say that the division in Protestantism is not nearly as extensive and deep as Catholics generally think. Because of the numerous divisions in the organization of Protestantism and because of the often incomprehensibly furious battles over details of doctrine many Protestants no longer have the awareness of their underlying unity, and many Catholics have impressions of hopeless confusion, contradiction and insecurity of faith. The more profound unity of faith linking all Protestants with one another and in a certain sense even with non-Protestants has now more than ever become manifest in the ecumenical movement.

The differences are frequently concerned more with the application of Reform principles than with the principles themselves since all Protestant churches and groups, at least in their intention, desire to retain the faith of the ancient Christian councils and Church Fathers, although this faith must always be tested against the content of Scripture and be complemented and deepened directly from within Scripture.

The most important differences lie in the realm of piety and in the field of individual and social ethics. In this connection it is best to speak of a difference in climate and accent.

The distance between the all holy God and sinful man, between the infinite creator and finite creatures is viewed and experienced differently in Lutheran and in Reformed Protestantism. In theology this difference manifests itself in the concept of the two natures in Christ as well as in the concept of the manner in which God, through the Holy Spirit, is acting in man and in the concept of the sacraments. Lutheranism sees the encounter between God and man as grounded in the mystery of the incarnation of God's Son. Calvinist Reformed Protestantism on the

148

other hand isolates this mystery so that it pertains only to Christ and emphasizes the distance between the believer and God. Man's relation to God and the atonement are experienced differently in Reformed Protestantism than in Lutheran or Anglican Protestantism.

Secondly there is a difference in the evaluation of natural life and the life in the world. Concerning the enjoyment of natural life the Calvinist is considerably more reserved than the Lutheran. With the Calvinist the conviction of being in the service of the living God at all times, in all things and places has resulted in a strong awareness of responsibility in regard to God's gifts of health, time, money and possessions. Life does not remind him so much of pleasure and advantage as of task and duty. More than the Lutheran does the Calvinist feel himself to be placed in the midst of life and the world with a positive God-given task with regard to material and spiritual culture, and with regard to social and political life. The Calvinist has a more consciously biblical concept of the church and divine service and is more concerned with safeguarding the independence of the church from the state than is the Lutheran. He respects and supports civil authority insofar and as long as it protects the true religion; he offers resistance to any civil authority that treads underfoot God's holy commandments. The Calvinist's relation to God's law also differs from the Lutheran's. And this leads us to the cardinal difference between the Reformed Protestant and the Lutheran teaching and practice.

The Reformation witness of Luther and Lutheranism concerning the gospel and man's salvation appears too isolated to the Calvinist. While Calvin and Reformed Protestantism agree with this witness they put it in a far wider, all embracing context. Reformed theology is less anthropological, more theological in the strict sense of the word than Lutheran theology. It is of course perfectly true that Luther was also concerned with God, just as Calvin was concerned with the salvation of man. But the accent is different; or rather, with Calvin the doctrine of

149

salvation is incorporated into and integrated with a biblical, predominantly Old Testament teaching about God. Reformed Protestantism includes the mystery of original sin and the salvation of man in the still more profound and inscrutable mysteries of God's sovereignty, God's self-sufficiency, God's eternal and irresistible decrees, and God's providence, predestination and election. These are secrets of God's being and acting which inspire the Calvinist with awe, fear, humility and awareness of sin. They put an unmistakably clear, indelible stamp on his whole religious life and practice—even on his physiognomy.

The Calvinist has a unique respect for God's word and God's law. For him these are not cold truths and moral precepts to which one listens calmly and which one either does or does not believe and practice. God's word and God's law are for him numinous realities before which he stands in fear and trembling. Faced with these realities he would lose all courage if he did not have Christ as Mediator.

It is true that for the Calvinist as well as for the Lutheran Christ's work and the message of the gospel are the only means of salvation for fallen man as sinner. But the glory and the consolation of the gospel in no wise detract from the holiness, the severity and the inexorable character of God's holy word and God's holy law. The truth that God is not to be trifled with applies equally to the person who believes in the gospel and who is saved by this faith and to the person who does not know the gospel or rejects it. The gospel must not be isolated from the totality of God's word. It does not abolish the law. Good works do not arise spontaneously from faith. Besides the promise of salvation there belongs to faith in the gospel the demand of holiness.

But Reformed teaching agrees with the Lutheran in that obedience and sanctification, pursued with all one's power, will never serve as the basis of justification. They can never be held up as merits or as a juridical basis for external salvation for this would mean that man's salvation would depend on his personal merit, and thus would no longer be a free gift. It would mean that God would be deprived of his honor and glory. Calvinism denies the Arminian contention that man can and must cooperate in the attainment of eternal salvation.

This is the Calvinism which is the principle and foundation of that Reformed teaching and theology wherein and above all there can be no question of the reality of the living God. Of course this reality is not denied by other Christians but the Reformed teaching and theology is, in every respect, a *witness* to God. It is a witness to the living God, the God who "has not failed to make himself known," who has acted in this world, who has intervened by his acts in the history of mankind, who revealed himself first to the elect of fallen humanity, then to the patriarchs and the chosen people of Israel and finally to the community of all true believers in Christ.

Sacred Scripture is the witness to God's self-revelation: "As I live, so says the Most High, he who is exalted, who has his throne in eternity, who is called the Holy One: I inhabit an exalted and holy sanctuary, but I live also in the contrite and humble spirit."

By speculative thought man may arrive at some notion of God, by his religious imagination he may arrive at some ideas of God, but the true and living God comes to encounter man in the word of sacred Scripture. Here it is a question not of intellectual considerations but of a real encounter. The Reformed teaching and theology are an orderly summary of the biblical witness to God. They do not form a logically constructed system even though in later Calvinist scholasticism reasoning occupies a more important place than Calvin intended. For in the Reformation of the Reformed-Calvinist type the Reformation witness has developed by way of an intellectual orthodoxy into a Reformed-Protestant rationalism which has been overcome only in our own age.

Primary in Reformed Protestantism is the "knowledge of the Lord," the "knowledge of God." This knowledge is not of an intellectual but of a personal nature. Just as men can come to know one another in daily intercourse so too can man come to know God if in his daily prayer and reading of the Bible he is ready to listen to God's word as it speaks to him directly and personally in sacred Scripture.

To believe is to acknowledge that the word of sacred Scripture is the personal word of God. However this notion must not be understood in an individualist sense for the testimony of sacred Scripture is preeminently of an historical and social nature. Sacred Scripture contains the history of God's chosen people, of the Church in the actual sense of the word. Scripture testifies to God's speaking and acting with his people as a whole and thereby with the individual. God reveals himself to his chosen ones in and through the history of his people. This history, essentially a history of salvation, culminates in the advent of Christ and his salvific work. Christ suffered, died and rose from the dead for God's chosen ones. Therefore the real core of the act of faith is the firm conviction, instilled in the heart of man by the Holy Spirit through the word of God, of truly belonging to God's chosen people and thus participating in all the fruits of the redeeming death and salvific work of Christ. There is no question of individualism in Calvin and Calvinism.

To the question "what is true faith?" the Heidelberg Catechism answers that genuine faith is not only the firm conviction of the truth of God's revealed word but also the firm trust that the Holy Spirit works in man's heart through the gospel; that not only to others but also to oneself has God gratuitously and only because of the merits of Christ granted forgiveness of sins, eternal justification and salvation (question 21).

This assurance of salvation however should not cause the believer to concentrate on himself and his own salvation. His "eye of faith" should continually be fixed on God or, as the Scottish Confession has it: "We confess and acknowledge one God to whom alone we must adhere, whom alone we must serve, whom alone we must adore, and in whom alone we must put our trust."

God's action in history has but one purpose: to select the true believers and children of God from fallen and damned humanity and to gather them into a holy people, consecrated and dedicated to God, belonging to him alone. This is a work of God's free grace and has as its purpose the eternal glorification of his name. Faith is ultimately nothing else than the firm assurance of belonging to God's chosen people. The true knowledge of God consists in the knowledge of having been purchased, as it were, by God (we have been bought at a great price, the price of the precious blood of Christ), of being his property, of belonging to him in time and eternity. Actually the knowledge of God consists in the knowledge and firm conviction of "being known by God," that is, of being chosen by God. Even in the doctrine of salvation God and not man is the beginning and the end, the first and the last, the principle and the goal: God is at the center of the whole of the doctrine, confession and theology.

The Reformed Christian does not arrive at faith in God by way of speculative thought. Faith is not based on the activity of the intellect but of the Holy Spirit. As the only means to lead man to faith the Holy Spirit uses "the two-edged sword of God's word" by which man is revealed to himself and by which he learns at the same time to know God in "his condescending love and fidelity." The lasting wonder of so much unmerited grace toward the sinner who has forfeited everything dominates the Calvinist's religious sentiments. His faith in God is aroused, nourished and specified by the testimony of sacred Scripture concerning "God's interventions" regarding Abraham and the patriarchs, Moses and the prophets, David and the kings, regarding the chosen people forever inclined to superstition and idolatry, and regarding the advent and work of Christ as the only mediator between God and man.

Reformed doctrine and theology emphasize the unity of God's action, the unity of the biblical testimony to God and to Christ,

153

the unity of the old and the new covenant, the unity of the Old and the New Testament.

The New Testament witness to Christ is not essentially new. It has not done away with the Old Testament witness to God. The Scripture Christ and the apostles and the ancient creeds refer to is always the Old Testament. It is even impossible to understand the New Testament witness to Christ apart from the witness to God of the Old Testament. The Old Testament witness to the one, true and living God retains its force for the Christian too. Neither in the confession, nor in preaching, nor in piety, nor in theology should the Old Testament be neglected or rated second to the New. The Reformed Christian considers it self-evident that preachers and theologians study and examine Scripture in the original languages (Hebrew and Greek) and that a scientifically schooled theologian have as profound a knowledge of Hebrew as of Greek. The Latin translation of the Vulgate is not very highly esteemed; translations into the vernacular are made from the original basic texts.

Sacred Scripture is called the only source wherein God's special revelation can be known not merely because of a theoretico-theological interest in the question how God can reveal himself to man, for this question is beyond man's competency. In his good pleasure God could have made himself known to man apart from any source of knowledge. The exclusiveness of the *sola Scriptura* is so emphasized in reverence for God's word —with which no human word can be equated. In comparison to the majestic holiness and the absolute, superhuman authenticity of the living, efficacious word of God any human word, however well intentioned, vanishes into nothingness:

No human writings, however saintly, may be put on a par with the divine Scripture; neither may tradition be put on a par with God's veracity and truth (for truth stands above all else); nor should this be done with the consensus of the majority, with antiquity, with succession of times or persons, with the councils, decrees, or decisions. For of themselves all men are deceivers and more vain than vanity itself (Dutch Confession of Faith, article 7).

Reformed Protestantism's faith in God implies a profound awareness of distance and contrast between the infinite, sovereign Creator and the finite, futile creature, between the absolutely holy God whose eyes cannot stand the sight of evil and man who is unholy, impure, conceived and born in sin, whose nature ever since original sin inclines to a hatred of God and neighbor.

The Old Testament appeals to the Reformed Christian, particularly when it calls man "a drop of water in the pail, a grain of dust in the scale," or when it acknowledges man to be "but dust and ashes." Reformed Protestantism has a certain appreciation of humanism as a cultural phenomenon and of the spiritual formation and erudition it has produced but it rejects on principle any idea of a natural nobility of soul and goodness of man. In religious matters and in its vision of life and the world it will have nothing to do with any efforts to make man and not God the cornerstone, to attribute any value or independence to man apart from God or in opposition to him, to replace the divine theonomy with human autonomy.

Of the various types of Protestantism the Reformed is most averse to any form of mysticism which holds that by prayer and meditation man can achieve some union with God. The prayer of the Reformed Christian is of a prophetic, not of a mystical nature. It is a struggle with God in order to obtain strength in temptation, submission in trial and faith in tribulations. It is active, not contemplative; existential, not speculative; dynamic, not static. Extremely conscious and attentive, it is seldom bound to a fixed form; sparing in words, it avoids needless repetition.

Reformed theology is also averse to any ontology which tends to lose sight of the essential distinction between the being of the creature and the being-totally-other of God. It rejects in particular the ontological concept of grace as a created gift of the Holy Spirit, as a reality of the supernatural order by which man

155

—having been supernaturalized and elevated to the level of existence above his nature—participates in the nature of God.

Consequently there is in Reformed theology no place for the contrast between nature and grace, as if a distinction could be made in man between what pertains to his human nature and what exceeds his nature: the grace of adoption as a child of God and participation in the divine nature. Man's nature is so far from being capable of any participation in and union with the divine nature that the term divinization, when applied to man, sounds like blasphemy to a Reformed Christian. For this reason Calvinism, more than Lutheranism, has difficulties in christology when confronted with the teaching of the twofold nature of Christ as propounded by the early Christian councils and the Fathers of the Church.

In Reformed theology it is not nature but sin that is contrasted to grace. Man's nature remained unchanged even after original sin, even after the redemption by Christ—in the sense that by original sin man did not lose supernatural grace; nor is he by faith and baptism adorned anew by infused supernatural grace. In Christ the faithful are united with God and with one another not by supernatural grace but by faith in God's grace (in the sense of unmerited loving kindness and favor) and by his forgiveness stemming from the all sufficient salvific work of Christ. Man's sin and guilt are contrasted with God's grace and forgiveness, which in no way depend on any work of man but exclusively on the work and merit of Christ.

In Reformed theology as well as in Lutheran theology, the concept that faith and baptism do not remove the radical corruption wrought in man by original sin is taken in an ethical, not an ontological sense. By the fall man rejected God and made himself the center of his own existence. This arrangement so sharply contradicts the purpose man was created for that the egoistic human being no longer corresponds to his true nature. If the Christian has difficulties with his faith this is because the believer, whether or not he is fully aware of it, for the rest of his life wants to continue living for himself alone and not for God or his neighbor. Whoever is not aware of this fact is the victim of vainglory and self-deception—qualities peculiar to the unconverted.

It is precisely by conversion, effected in the hearts of men by the Holy Spirit and by God's word alone, that the believer arrives at a true understanding and acknowledgment of how deeply he has fallen, how completely insignificant he is of himself because of his corrupted nature, and how little he is inclined to make true sacrifice. Reformed theology refuses to acknowledge any infused grace as the source of a higher and better life. Only in gratitude for God's incomprehensible kindness and favor and in profound reverence for God's holy Law does the Reformed Christian strive to lead a life that is pleasing to God and according to his commandments. But this "new life" is a life of obedience, of responsibility, a life in an ethical sense. It is not a life in an ontological and supernatural sense.

The above description reveals in part why Reformed theology absolutely rejects Catholics' veneration of Mary and the saints, their reverence toward the visible Church and the priest, any semblance of sacramental devotion, and Catholic teaching on the sacraments. And this rejection must also be explained against the background of the Reformed vision of the nature of sin on the part of man and grace on the part of God, against the denial of any supernatural grace by which man's nature is elevated, ennobled, renewed and restored and in a certain sense made divine.

The Catholic Christian is above all else concerned with the reception and preservation of the supernatural life of grace, normally imparted through the sacraments. The Reformed Christian on the other hand is concerned with the faith which the Holy Spirit imparts to man's heart by means of God's word. This of course does not mean that the word has no part to play in the religious and ecclesiastic life of the Catholic. Nor does it mean that the Reformed Christian does not believe in the work of the Holy Spirit or that he will have nothing to do with sacraments. But we must always bear in mind that in this connection the words faith, church, sacrament and grace are used in a different sense.

The Reformed Christian is convinced that it is the subjective act of faith which effects salvation and the common bond with God and other believers. This faith is aroused by consciously and personally hearing and accepting the word. The Catholic Christian is convinced that the reception of supernatural grace (which presupposes faith as its basis) is the actual cause of salvation and the common bond with God and other baptized Christians. Normally this grace is granted by means of the sacraments of the Church.

According to the Catholic Church therefore the common bond which unites Protestants and Catholics through baptism is a real bond of grace in an ontological sense, even in those instances where external communion of faith with the Church has been disrupted. There are still ecumenical possibilities and problems in this area which have not yet received sufficient attention. For here is found the cardinal difference in matters of faith between Catholics and Protestants, while on the other hand there is also found here a real basis for union and communion between both segments of Christianity.

Reformed and Catholic notions of the church

According to Reformed teaching the church is, as it were, born of the word, for the word awakens belief and belief links the individual believers through a common bond in the body of Christ. According to Catholic teaching the Church is established by the operation of the supernatural, divine grace which through the sacraments is infused into the souls of believers by the Holy Spirit. Within the Church the life of grace is bestowed, preserved and if necessary restored through the sacraments. Consequently

158

in Catholic teaching it is primarily grace which unites believers in the Mystical Body of Christ. Hence the important place the sacraments occupy in the life of the Church—possibly at the risk of neglecting somewhat the proclamation of the word.

In Catholic teaching the one and visible Church is not merely a community of faith; it is especially a supernatural community of grace in an ontological sense. Although according to Catholic teaching this community of grace can be recognized by its union with the Apostolic See, by the faith as preserved and handed on by the living magisterium and by the complete and active functioning of the sacramental life of grace, nonetheless all baptized Christians of whatever non-Catholic sect participate in the community of grace of the Catholic Church as long as they are in the state of grace. And God alone can judge or decide whether they are in the state of grace. That no baptized Christian is ever completely outside the Catholic Church is evident from the fact that, according to Catholic teaching, all baptized Christians are subject to the jurisdictional power of the pope and that a marriage between persons baptized outside the Catholic Church is indissoluble.

It is clear that Reformed teaching concerning the church, her offices and sacraments, her liturgy and discipline varies in many respects from Catholic teaching. Or rather, in its doctrine concerning the nature, task and functions of the church the Reformed teaching considers itself in this respect to be the Catholic teaching in its original formulation.

The principal sources from which to acquire an understanding of Reformed teaching concerning the church are the fourth book of Calvin's *Institutes* and the various Reformed catechisms, confessions and church ordinances (cf. 134 f).

But though these sources supply abundant material about church regulations, offices, authority, discipline and sacraments they supply very scant information about the nature of the church. Most confessions are limited to a compact definition or description. In this respect the Swiss Confession of 1566 is the most detailed.

While the church is often referred to as "a body" or "the body of Christ" there is no mention of the church as the Mystical Body of Christ. When the church is called the body of Christ it is done in imitation of Paul, particularly in connection with his letter to the Ephesians. Reformed theology, however, carefully remains within the limits of the biblical manner of speaking and does not go into any speculative considerations that might give more weight and content to this expression than is clearly contained in biblical imagery. This does not mean that the expression has no more than a purely figurative meaning. The Church as confessed in the creed is truly the body of Christ. The question is how Reformed theology understands "truly."

To the question "what is the Catholic Church?" the Geneva catechism of 1542 answers: "It is the community of believers destined and chosen by God for eternal life." Believers are those who make a sincere and genuine, personal and conscious act of faith in God and his word. These true believers coincide with God's elect who from all eternity have been predestined to beatitude. And just as in the objective order of salvation Christ died not for all men but only for the elect, so too in the subjective order of salvation it is only the elect who can posit a true (sincere and redeeming) act of faith. Only by the genuine act of faith are believers truly united to Christ and to one another in one body. Christ is the head of this body; the true believers, i.e. the elect, are the members.

For this reason there are in Calvinism and the Reformed confessions definitions of the church which give the impression that the real church as confessed in the creed is an invisible, hidden reality. This Church is strictly one and cannot be scattered or divided because, as Calvin states in his *Institutes*, "if there were to be two or three churches, Christ would be divided—and this is impossible." He continues:

Indeed, God's elect are all so united in Christ that just as they depend on one head, so too they grow, *as it were,* into one body, so that they are linked together as the members of one body; they have become *one*[1] in reality since they live together by one and the same faith, hope, and charity, and by the same spirit of God, called not only to the same inheritance of eternal life, but also to participate in the one God and Christ (*Institutes,* 4, 1, 2; emphasis added).

The fact that both the Reformed and the Catholic confessions and theologies use such words as community, unity, presence, participation, united in one body, etc. might give Catholics the impression that these realities are understood in the same sense that Catholic theology understands them. Such an impression however would be based on a misunderstanding of Reformed teaching. In this connection distinctions are all the more necessary since it is precisely here that the cardinal differences lie in the Catholic and Reformation notions of the manner whereby the revealed reality touches upon the life of man.

Calvin and Reformed Protestantism distinguish the objective work of redemption (once and for all in the fullness of time) and the subjective application of redemption to the believer in the here and now. For example in the seventeenth chapter of book 4 of the *Institutes* we read:

When he called himself the bread of life, he did not refer to the sacrament as some erroneously hold; he called himself this because he had been given to us as the bread of life by the Father, and because he also manifested himself as such when, having become a partaker in our human mortality, he made us into partakers of his divine immortality; when, offering himself as a sacrifice, he took our curse upon himself in order to bestow his blessing on us; when by his death he conquered and wiped out our death; when in his resurrection he raised to incorruptible glory this, our corruptible flesh which he had put on (para. 4).

All this, for all believers of all times and places, has taken place in the past. The efficient cause of salvation coincides with the actual salvific effect in that one event of the past, "in the full-

[1] Thus excluding the "as it were."

161

ness of time." What is taking place in the present in the life of the believer is something else:

> What remains is that all this be applied to us; this takes place not only through the gospel but also, and even more clearly, through the holy supper in which he offers himself to us with all he has, and in which we accept him by faith. The sacrament, therefore, does not bring it about that Christ begins to be the bread of life [in and through the reception of the sacrament]; but because it grants us the tasting of the bread it makes us feel the power of this bread by calling to mind that he has become the bread of life so that we should eat forever. For it is the pledge that all that Christ has done and suffered has happened to give us life (17, 5).

What happens in the present therefore is the application, i.e. that both the gospel and the sacrament pledge and assure us that what Christ did once and for all in the past applies to us now. Though we are more aware of this promise and assurance through the sacrament than through the gospel the effect is essentially the same. The sacrament does not effect something other than what the word effects. Gospel and sacrament both testify and assure the believer that here and now he truly participates in all that Christ has done in the past for the believers and elect, but only when and insofar as he truly believes. Subjectively therefore it is faith that effects the real participation in Christ. It is a real participation in the redemption Christ has prepared in the past by his cross and resurrection. But it is not a participation in an ontological sense, as though participation in God and in Christ were more than the combination of promise and faith. Without faith the sacrament is but an empty symbol.

Even when Calvin and the Reformed confessions declare emphatically that the reception of the holy supper is a true reception of the body and blood of the Lord unto eternal life, nonetheless the distance between the then and now is not abolished. The true and real communion with and participation in the body and blood of Christ consists in the believer participating in the fruits of Christ's suffering and death on the cross just as fully

162

as he is now eating the bread and drinking the wine. Therefore not only is there no transubstantiation in the elements of bread and wine: neither is there in the reception of communion any question of Christ coming into the soul of man supernaturally and ontologically and uniting him with God by a supernatural operation. The union with Christ is effected in and through the faith of the present moment, a faith in the full and real application to the true believer of the fruits of the salvific work of the past.

The distance between the actual event of the past and its application to man in the present is bridged objectively by the gospel and the sacrament, subjectively by the act of faith. By faith the Reformed Christian is *now* certain that he truly participates in the salvific act which Christ *then* accomplished. Neither in the proclamation of the word nor in the sacrament is there question of an event in the supernatural order of being. It is true that Christ is actively present in the proclamation as well as in the sacrament but in both instances it is a spiritual presence and activity by means of the word and the Spirit. The bond, the union, the communion and the participation are effected by the objective word and the subjective act of faith—not by a oneness with Christ in a supernatural sense, not by any infusing and imparting of a new reality that belongs to an order of being other than the natural.

According to Reformed theology the distance between the historical, actual salvation event of the past and its application in the present through the gospel and the sacraments is similar to that between the church as the community of true believers and elect whose names are known to God alone, and the church as a composite of certain regulations, offices, disciplines and authority. Reformed Protestantism therefore acknowledges both facets of the church but it is profoundly conscious of a strong tension between these two facets, and combines them only with great difficulty and with many qualifications.

There is lively awareness of this distance between the hidden reality of the chosen people of God and its visible manifestation in a church on earth. It is not a matter of the distinction and contrast Catholics see between the divine and the human within the Church as a visible and mysterious reality. Rather it is a question of the distinction and contrast between the visible church itself and the invisible, hidden reality of the church as the chosen people of God.

The finite cannot contain the infinite, time cannot absorb eternity, neither can man or earth possess God or heaven. According to Catholic teaching the essence of the mysteries of the faith: the incarnation, the Church, the eucharist and the sacraments, consists in their transformation by God into an inscrutable but very real possibility and reality. Reformed Protestantism, when faced with the mystery in this Catholic sense, comes to a dead stop. This the Catholic considers a hesitation, if not a refusal (an unequivocal refusal on religious grounds) to accept the full reality and significance of the mystery of the incarnation with all its implications and consequences in regard to the Church and her sacraments.

It is true that the visible church exists. It was willed by God and strengthened by the apostles. Bound to certain scriptural rules the true church is distinguished from other churches that do not correspond to the criteria of Scripture. But without the hidden community of God's elect (i.e. without the church in its strict sense) the church is nothing; it does not coincide with the church of the elect; it does not occupy a place higher than the word but is the humble and obedient servant and dispenser of the word; it is often in danger of infidelity to its vocation—even of going completely astray.

Often tensions and even contradictions arise between the visible manifestation and the invisible reality, between the "revealedness" and the hiddenness of the church. How then could a certain visible Church possibly dare assert without reservation that it is the one and only true Church and identify itself with the church of the creed? The church of the creed is the church as the community of the elect and alone is, in the full sense of the word, the body of Christ. The manner in which Catholics obediently accept the authority of the Church as divine authority, the manner in which they acknowledge the mystery with reverence, worship and adoration are, according to Reformed Protestants, symptoms of unlawful, dangerous steps in the direction of a divinization of man, of superstition and idolatry. They consider these presumptions as a sinful identification of creatures and humans with God, an identification they abhor.

As long as the Roman Church continues in this "guilt" Reformed Protestants look upon her as a disobedient church. The contrasts here are much more profound and fundamental than may be affirmed by false irenics. Among Catholics too there are some who attempt to interpret Reformed usage of the terms in an overly Catholic sense, thus contributing to that regrettable situation whereby the Church is no longer seen as it truly is. This is neither in the interests of truth nor an honest mutual understanding.

When Reformed confessions and theologies emphasize the visibility of the church this is not meant in the Catholic sense. As we said above the church of the creed is for them strictly the community of all believers and elect of God who in true faith are united to Christ as the head and to one another as the members of the body.

In the Geneva catechism the question "what does this word 'catholic' or 'universal' [as used in the apostles' creed] mean?" is answered: "This word serves to indicate that just as there is but one head of all believers, so too they must all be united in one body in such a manner that there are not many churches, but one only, which is spread over the entire world."

The hesitation of Reformed Protestants regarding the church of the creed is clearly expressed here. For from the words "they *must* all be united" it is evident that it is a question not of fact but of command and obligation. Union in one body must be realized so that there may be one church spread over the earth.

The last phrase indicates that it is a question of one visible church here on earth.

When the question is asked whether this Church can be seen and recognized or whether it can only be believed, the answer inclines once more toward the invisible church: "There is indeed a visible church of God which he has provided with certain marks of identification, but here [i.e. in the creed] there is really question of the gathering of those whom God has chosen to be saved, and this is not completely visible to the eye."

When in the various Reformed confessions one reads the articles defining the nature of the Church one gets the definite impression that the Reformed teaching is wavering between two opinions. The church which is believed is actually the invisible, hidden community of all the elect of all times. Yet the visibility of the church is not entirely discarded. In spite of the fact that there are many independently organized communities and churches this visible church is referred to in the singular. There is but one true church and it can be clearly distinguished from the erring church. When the confessions contrast the marks of identification of the true and the erring church the latter is clearly thought of as the Roman Church. On one occasion in the *Confessio Gallicana* it is even mentioned by name in this connection.

According to most confessions the three marks of the true church are: the preaching of the pure gospel, the administration of the sacraments according to the institution and intention of Christ (i.e. in accordance with what Scripture tells us, without human ceremonies or other additions), and the ecclesiastic discipline for the punishment of sinners.

From time to time this true church may be diminished to a small remnant of true believers who refuse to serve the gods of the times. But it must not without further ado be identified with one certain sect or church. For even the Reformed sects may at times fail to be the true church, even to the extent that they cannot be considered true churches. This accounts for the numerous divisions and efforts at restoration in Reformed Protestantism.

Neither should the true church be identified with the catholic or universal church. In contrast to Luther the *Confessio Scotica* mentions expressly that the universal church is the hidden community of all the elect (article 16) and that the true church is given the name "particular church" (article 18).

Finally the true believers and the elect should not be identified with the members of a definite visible church. For true children of God, i.e. the elect who in spite of theological errors still have true faith in God, are found even in churches which are in the most serious of errors, in fact even in the Roman Church. But at the same time even in the purest of churches many sanctimonious people are found who do not have true faith and who therefore do not belong to the community of the elect. Yet the confessions impose on everyone the duty of joining the true church. In this connection it seems that by true church is meant a definite church which can be pointed out. Great difficulties arise when in some nation or city there are several churches that claim to be the true church.

One of the marks of the true church is that she is persecuted by the erring church. The Dutch Confession characterizes the erring church in article 29 as follows:

The erring church arrogates to herself and her ordinances more power and authority than to the word of God, and refuses to subject herself to the yoke of Christ. She does not administer the sacraments as Christ has ordained in his word, but deals with them as she pleases; she follows man more than Christ; she persecutes those who live a life of holiness according to the word of God, and who admonish her for her defects, avarice and idolatries. These two churches are easily recognized and distinguished from one another.

Predestination and covenant

This brief exposition of the teaching of Reformed Protestantism would certainly be incomplete if no mention were made of the doctrine on predestination and the covenant.

Calvin describes predestination as follows:

We call predestination the eternal decree of God by which he has determined for himself what he wished to happen to any person. For not all are created under identical conditions. Some are predestined to eternal life, others to eternal damnation. Therefore, according as each is created for the one purpose or the other we say that he has been predestined to life or to death (*Institutes*, 3, 21, 5).

It must be admitted that Calvin approaches the subject of predestination with the greatest care and trepidation. The severe and even irrational character of later rationalist theology is certainly not in line with Calvin's intention. Calvin's *Institutes* is moreover a modest and reverent attempt carefully to order and summarize the divine testimony of sacred Scripture. Calvin would have nothing to do with any human addition to or detraction from the clear testimony of Scripture. He was convinced that his description of predestination reflected as precisely as possible what Scripture has to say on the subject.

Calvin's treatment of the mystery of predestination is on all sides hedged by precautions: scriptural testimony on this subject is to be strictly observed; the mystery should be examined not out of curiosity but out of a desire for salvation; no attempts should be made to clarify and explain the mystery; above all it should be approached with great reverence and humility; an "understanding" of the mystery can be achieved only by a true believer and only for a true believer can the mystery of predestination (as the unshakable foundation of beatitude) be a source of consolation, just as for an unbeliever it is a source of despair and scandal. Those who run the danger of approaching this mystery with temerity and irreverence are admonished by Calvin as follows:

When delving into the mystery of predestination they should first of all remember that they are penetrating into the mysteries of divine wisdom. Whoever does this frivolously and impudently will obtain nothing wherewith to satisfy his curiosity since he enters a labyrinth from which he will find no exit. For it is not fitting that man should without impunity investigate something which the Lord wished to keep concealed within himself. It is unfitting that he should search the exalted wisdom of God of which God himself desired that it should be adored, not understood, so that even through this hidden wisdom he might arouse man's admiration. Any hidden aspects of his will which he wanted to make known to us he has revealed through his Word [i.e. we should not think that we could have achieved an understanding of them by our own intelligence]. And he has decreed that whatever he foresaw to be in our interest and advantage should be revealed (*Institutes*, 3, 21, 1).

Predestination, whether to eternal life or to eternal death, is above all a hidden fact we must leave untouched. We must honor and adore it. The proud man who (as a consequence of the fall) desires to be God wishes to determine his own lot and effect his own eternal salvation. He must be converted. When faced with predestination, revealed as fact and as mystery, he must acknowledge that before God he is absolutely nothing and can do nothing but surrender to God for better or for worse, submit himself unconditionally to his holy will. The mystery of predestination must humble a man, make him small in his own eyes, make him abstain from any self-glorification, make him realize that he has no claim whatsoever to reconciliation with God and to eternal salvation:

For when Scripture mentions predestination its intention is not that, with growing pride, we should unashamedly and rashly attempt to search into God's inaccessible mysteries, but rather that we should humbly learn to fear and tremble before his judgment, and ask for mercy. Believers should have this alone in mind (*Institutes*, 3, 23, 12).

The capitulation before the mystery of predestination is one of the most essential elements in the true act of faith. It is one of the most important traits of real faith in God, in God's word and in the gospel. At the same time this capitulation causes in the true believer the miracle whereby, owing to the faith effected in his heart by the Holy Spirit through God's word, he becomes absolutely certain of being personally predestined to eternal life. In no way can this certitude be established by any proofs. In fact any such attempt would rather be a sign of disbelief and distrust in God's word and promise. If a Reformed believer were asked to supply proof for his conviction of belonging to the predestined elect of God he might as well be asked to put an end to his faith.

While it is true that faith includes an acknowledgment and acceptance of the salvific character of Christ's death and resurrection, the certainty of salvation is ultimately based on God's eternal and unchangeable promise of a life of which the believer, precisely because he believes, is absolutely assured. His human limitations may subject a believer to doubts and temptations but rising from these doubts and failures he will forever call upon the unwavering fidelity of God who will never relinquish a work he has once begun, and who will never revoke his eternal decrees.

God's eternal decree is "irresistible," his election unchangeable. If someone has from all eternity been predestined to eternal salvation it is impossible that he should lose his faith or defect. Positing a true act of faith is the same as being an elect of God; to be an elect of God means to have the assurance of final perseverance. This is the doctrine of the perseverance of the saints—the word saints being used in the sense of true believers.

The one and only basis for divine predestination and election is God's mercy, in the sense of God's free choice. The mystery of predestination keeps intact God's absolute and exclusive honor and glory as well as God's complete freedom in his relations with created and fallen mankind. To think that God should have any obligation to predestine a person to eternal salvation because of merit he foresaw is to deprive predestination of its very essence. The motive, basis or cause of predestination lies neither in God's foreknowledge nor in the merits of man.

On the other hand predestination does not mean that God takes away man's responsibility. Just as the damned are responsible for their deeds and are therefore justly punished for their sins and disbelief so also do the elect retain their responsibility. In fact the true act of faith creates full responsibility. True faith is expressed in serious, persevering efforts at sanctification and in a sincere joy and pleasure in the law of the Lord. True faith is manifested in a holy manner of life. This manner of life however may never be considered as the basis of election, though some hold that it is a sign of election.

Difficulties arise when it comes to the relation between predestination as the eternal decree of God and its actual effect or application in time in the form of election, vocation, covenant, promise, baptism, regeneration and membership in the church. Among Reformed Protestants this subject has at times led to serious differences of opinion. We will discuss this in the section on the Reformed Churches in The Netherlands.

Finally we must say a few words about the Reformed teaching on the covenant. The origin of this teaching, now an important part of Reformed theology, was Zurich rather than Geneva. In the chapters of the *Institutes* which deal with predestination and election Calvin scarcely mentions the covenant. The same applies to the chapter on baptism. Baptism is referred to as "a sign of initiation by which we are accepted into the membership of the church, so that, incorporated into Christ, we are counted among God's children" (*Institutes*, 4, 15, 1). Only when there is question of infant baptism does Calvin call baptism one of the signs of the covenant with God. It is a covenant, for the child belongs only if it is born of parents who are believers, just as circumcision was for the Jews the sign of the covenant God made with Abraham and his descendants. However the covenant does not occupy a dominant place in Calvin's theology, as it does in the theology of the Zurich reformers Zwingli, Bullinger and Jud. The latter places his minor catechism entirely in the framework of the "Covenant of God with us." Bullinger's collection of sermons, *Decades,* is likewise entirely inspired by the idea of a covenant.

The theology of the covenant does not stem from pre-Reformation, Catholic theology but is based on sacred Scripture, in particular on the salvation history of the old Testament which makes frequent mention of an agreement or covenant of God with man.

Covenant theology distinguishes between a covenant of work and a covenant of grace. Before the fall man, living in the state of justice, lived according to God's will and intention but did not yet possess eternal life, and was therefore able to betray his calling. He was being tested by the command not to eat of the "tree of knowledge of good and evil" in order to see whether he would obey God in all things. By his complete and unconditional obedience man himself had to merit eternal beatitude. Consequently before the fall eternal beatitude was based on the merits of good works. When man transgressed the command he himself broke the covenant of work once and for all.

In his never failing fidelity God replaced this covenant of work by his covenant of grace with man. The covenant of grace is based on the perfect work which Christ has accomplished once for all. Christ alone has fulfilled the original demand of the covenant of work. Because of the fall no man is able to restore the union with God and merit eternal beatitude by means of good works. But Christ has done this once and for all. He has done this for all those who belong to the covenant of grace of the Old and the New Testament. Between the covenant of the Old and the New there is no essential difference. They merely represent two different phases in salvation history. Actually God's covenant with Abraham and his descendants (the old covenant with the chosen people of Israel) was the beginning of the new and eternal covenant of God with the chosen people of God, the Church, a covenant sealed in the blood of Christ.

To this covenant of grace belong all those who under the old covenant were expecting the Christ and those who under the new covenant believe in Christ's advent and who are looking forward to his second coming. But a distinction is made here

172

between adults and children. By the mere fact that they are born from parents who are believers children belong to the covenant of grace; adults who were born outside the covenant of grace are accepted into it by true and sincere faith in Christ. Just as under the old covenant circumcision was the sign of the covenant so now is baptism the sign of the new covenant of grace. For this reason children, even when born from believing parents, should be baptized soon after birth if the mother can be present at the baptismal ceremony to answer, together with the father, the baptismal questions asked in the midst of the community. Infant baptism is based therefore on the consideration that baptism is the sign of the covenant of grace. Accordingly it is usual at a Reformed baptismal ceremony that the following verse of Psalm 105 be sung:

> Remember the wonders that he has done,
> His portents, and the judgments of his mouth,
> O descendants of Abraham, his servant,
> Children of Jacob, his chosen!
> He is the Lord, our God;
> His judgments are in all the earth.
> He remembers his covenant forever,
> The word he has commanded to a thousand generations;
> The covenant he made with Abraham,
> And his oath to Isaac.

Covenant theology has also given rise to a number of theological differences of opinion and ecclesiastic disagreements.

In Reformed Protestantism as well as in Lutheran Protestantism theology has, since the end of the sixteenth century, gradually taken on a more intellectual, scholastic and finally a rationalist character. Particularly was the first part of the seventeenth century a period of polemics. From this period dates the furious struggle between the Gomarists and Arminians (Counter-remonstrants and Remonstrants) over the final establishment of the Reformed Church of the Republic of the United Netherlands during the first general Synod of 1618 in Dordrecht.

The Dutch Reformed Church
(3.4 million members)

The Dutch Reformed Church in the Kingdom of the Netherlands was reorganized under this name in 1816, according to the *General Regulations* supplied by King William I. It is the continuation of the national church organization which came about in The Netherlands during the sixteenth century Reformation.

The church organization in question is of a distinctly Reformed-Calvinist structure and confession. As early as the second half of the sixteenth century some Dutch communities of refugees had united (Wesel 1568, Emden 1571). In accordance with the church ordinances of Emden, the provincial synod of the churches of Holland and Zeeland (Dordrecht 1574), as well as the national synods of Dordrecht (1578) and Middleburg (1581), efforts were made to establish a national Reformed church. In 1618–1619, a full century after Luther's first appearance, this church was finally established under the auspices of the states general and on the occasion of the national synod of Dordrecht. It was based on the *Dordrecht Church Ordinances* and the *Three Formulas of Union* (cf. 146).

The name Reformed Church which we have been using first appears in the second half of the eighteenth century. Until the time of the French domination the plural was used, either as Reformed Churches or Reformed Churches of Christ, since the national church organization was considered a national union of local churches or communities.

The Dordrecht synod is based on the conviction that in the New Testament the early apostolic church emphasized the personal character and independence of each local church (the church of Jerusalem, of Antioch, of Corinth, etc.). Therefore the synod considers its church ordinances as strictly in accord as possible with the demands of sacred Scripture. Along with Calvin it is convinced that the threefold partition of the ecclesiastic office into the offices of *episkopos* (overseer or bishop), *presbyteroi* (elders) and *diakonoi* (deacons or servers) is applied in the New Testament to the local church only.

The presbyterial institution of the church is based on this conviction. The local church is governed by a council consisting of elders (chosen by the church) and the preacher or overseer (called by the church). The latter leads the church, also called community or congregation, and thus is also the president of the council. His task is to proclaim the word of God, to administer the sacraments and, with the assistance of the elders, to exercise the pastoral care of souls. The elders are the confessional conscience of the church. They see to it that the teaching of the preacher and the members of his congregation remain orthodox; they also exercise ecclesiastic discipline. It has been remarked that the elder is the pawn with which Calvin checkmated the pope. Finally the deacon looks after the care of the poor.

A difficult problem is the precise relation between the local church and the church in its entirety. It continues to harass Reformed Protestantism and has often led to conflicts and even separations. The principal source of the tension between the church in its entirety and the local community lies in the fact that from the very beginning there existed two different notions of the church among the Reformed. There are those who attribute great importance to the unity of the church organization. They tend to regard the church as a state church, or at least a national church, to which all baptized people of the nation ought to belong. Others emphasize the autonomy of the local church. Montanistically they refuse to see the church as a church for all of the baptized, but as a community of "saints," i.e. of truly chosen ones and sincere believers. According to them the local church is a church in the fullness of being and so it does not need other churches for its own completion. A necessary consequence of this position however is that the local church can hardly attribute higher authority to the church union, and cannot permit other churches to mingle in its own affairs. Hence

175

arises the question of the authority of the so-called major meetings over the minor meetings (in sequence: the great or national synod, provincial synods, territorial meetings, church councils).

Although the unity of the Dutch Reformed Church rests on a jointly accepted confessional and church organization basis it must primarily be seen as a national church union, as a union of churches that belong to the same state or nation.

For a proper understanding of the character of the Dutch Reformed Church it is also necessary to distinguish its official appearance from the actual religious position of the various groups the members of the Dutch Reformed Church can be divided into.

It is true that the establishment of the national church union at the synod of Dordrecht (1618–1619) was a victory for Calvinism but it certainly did not mean that from then on all the church members were of one mind and spirit. The Reformation movement in The Netherlands dates from the early part of the sixteenth century and from the very beginning it presented a multiple image. Long before the arrival of Calvinism various types and forms of religiousness had arisen, traces of which can even now be found in the Dutch Reformed Church.

In a highly instructive work on the confessional development of the Reformation in The Netherlands, Lindeboom analyzes the various tendencies of reform that have made a permanent contribution to the complicated character of Reformed Protestantism in The Netherlands. Apart from the aftereffects of the earliest stages of Lutheranism and of the Mennonite–Baptist tendencies, Dutch Protestantism is also rooted in biblical humanism and in a typically Dutch Reformation movement.

This latter tendency is usually referred to as a sacramentarian movement and is related to Zwingli's concept of the Reformation; it may even have influenced Zwingli himself. It is best characterized as a way of thinking averse to any supernatural sacramentarianism, ceremonies and too heavy a stress on ecclesiastic authority and action. Such aversion is practically native to the Dutch, particularly those of the northern regions. As a result the original typically Dutch tendencies of the Reformation emphasized apostolic simplicity, personal belief, a non-dogmatic conception of the gospel and a faith that is neither more nor less than confidence.

In the Dutch Reformed Church the interior of churches and religious services were until recently characterized by great simplicity. The service consisted of an hour-long sermon, a very free form of prayer, readings from Scripture and the singing of some psalm verses or hymns. This was due more to the after-effects of the sixteenth century Dutch Reformation than to the influence of Calvinism.

It was not until the second half of the sixteenth century that Calvinism began to penetrate gradually, starting in the southern regions of the country, only to find a widespread and disorganized reform movement that differed in many respects from Calvinism. From a Calvinist point of view one could regard Guido de Brès, composer of the *Confessio Belgica,* as the principal reformer-martyr of The Netherlands.

The national synod of Dordrecht, convoked by the states general, was ordered to undertake a Dutch translation of the Bible. Until the time of the French domination and in a way even until the middle of the last century the state governed the church. In the Republic of the United Netherlands the states general had the right to convoke a national synod, the states provincial to convoke a provincial synod. To the states general also fell the decision whether resolutions of the synod should be put into execution or not.

Warned by the clash between Remonstrants and Counter-remonstrants the states general let two centuries pass after the synod of Dordrecht without convoking a national synod. If any of the states provincial put the resolutions of the synod of Dordrecht into execution it was done only in part and with hesitation.

Once the Dutch Reformed Church was established there arose —apart from the offshoots—two distinct types of reformers: the strict observants and the tolerants. Initially the first type was heavily represented among the preachers and theologians, the second type among the regents. This accounts for the fact that Catholics and other dissidents could continue to exist in the life of the nation. Besides, at the time of the synod of Dordrecht the majority of the people was still Catholic.

In the centuries that followed the synod of Dordrecht the differences between the official teaching of the Reformed Church and the religious ideas of many of its members gradually became more acute. As a result of internal and external influences several new visions of faith developed, as well as new types of piety and practice. These new types, directions, tendencies and modalities all succeeded in acquiring their own *raison d'être* within the church. Consequently the Dutch Reformed Church of the nineteenth and early twentieth centuries presented to outsiders a bewildering picture of the most divergent and contrasting beliefs, though somewhat camouflaged by a strict unity of church organization and liturgy.

Reactions against the rationalist superficiality and modernist hollowness of the faith led to a new Reformation revival within the church on the one hand and to critical divisions on the other. The Reformed Churches in The Netherlands arose from the latter. Furious battles developed within the Dutch Reformed Church. Around the beginning of the twentieth century five main directions had developed, each organized into a league or union with its own publication: the Reformed within the Dutch Reformed Church, the confessionals, the ethico-irenic proponents, the evangelics and the moderns (later the liberals).

The Reformed and the confessional groups had a distinctly Calvinist-Reformed character. The representatives of the ethical groups were influenced mainly by German Lutheranism, also by German pietism or English Methodism, also by Kierkegaard. They and the evangelics and the liberals had undergone the

178

theologico-philosophical influence of neo-Kantianism and/or Hegelianism. Among the Dutch Reformed Protestants therefore one can find the numerous Reformation ideas described earlier in this chapter, not to mention a more Lutheran vision of Christian life and belief, or an orthodox Reformation or a modern-liberal point of view.

As a result of the spread of the Swiss theology of Barth and Brunner and the awakening of a renewed Reformation consciousness the ethical group has practically disappeared in recent years, in The Netherlands and in other countries. Ethical Protestantism was based on some serious misconceptions of the real essence of the Reformation (see Bouyer, *The Spirit and Forms of Protestantism* 1956). The evangelic trend has also ceased to exist.

The struggle among the various groups during the past hundred years has led to repeated attempts to arrive at a *modus vivendi*. The aim was a coexistence in which each group would retain its own peculiar point of view. But many of the Reformed were not satisfied with this. They wanted a Dutch Reformed Church with a positive confession, a national church conscious of its Reformation character.

Their efforts, which reached a high point during the last ten years prior to World War II, resulted in two different proposals and drafts for a new church ordinance. Both proposals were rejected by the general synod.

When during the German occupation of The Netherlands the totalitarian regime attacked the freedom of the church the Dutch Reformed Church was aroused from its conventional lethargy. The purely administrative general synod of thirteen members resigned of its own accord, thus giving the church an opportunity to elect a truly representative and competent general synod. The new synod consisted of forty-five members and twelve advisers and had its first meeting in Amsterdam on Oct. 31, 1945. It resolved to draft a new church ordinance, to study the confession and to revise the liturgy.

179

The new church ordinance of the Dutch Reformed Church was put into effect on May 1, 1951. The provisional results of the study of the confession were expressed in the *Foundations and Perspectives of the Confession* 1949 and in the *Pastoral Letter of the General Synod of the Dutch Reformed Church Concerning the Roman Catholic Church* 1950. In the revised liturgy classical texts and prayers were incorporated from the early Christian, pre-Reformation churches and from the churches of the Reformation. It was presented to the church in 1955 in the form of the *Book of Services of the Dutch Reformed Church.* The draft contains "the various orders of service, formulas for baptism, the supper, marriage, etc. as also prayers in the sequence of the ecclesiastic year, morning and evening prayers, prayers for the family, grace at table, and prayers for children." This revision of the liturgy, and at the same time an expansion, should be seen as the fruit and final stabilization of the liturgical movement in the Dutch Reformed Church. In 1938 the revision of the liturgy had been preceded by the introduction of a new collection of hymns the first ninety-five of which were ordered according to the ecclesiastic year. It is also an expression of ecumenism since a good number of hymns were taken over from Lutheran, Anglican and free churches, and even from the Catholic Church (among others an arrangement of the *Adoro te devote*).

If one reviews the events of the past few years he must conclude that for the time being the Dutch Reformed Church will continue to be primarily a Calvinist-Reformed church, but certainly not exclusively so. For it will officially have a general Reformation and ecumenical character. Swiss theology and the ecumenical movement have not passed unnoticed. The Dutch Reformed Church consciously orients itself to world Protestantism and takes its membership in the World Council of Churches seriously. This is particularly evident from its attitude on society. But in view of the motley composition of the Dutch Reformed Church it is obvious that not all individual members and congregations can easily approve this official course of events.

It cannot be said that these recent developments indicate a rapprochement toward the Catholic Church. The new church ordinance of 1951 declares emphatically that "the Dutch Reformed Church continues to uphold the Reformational character of the nation and the people" (article 8, para. 4). From the ordinance concerning the apostolate it appears that the church considers itself called henceforth also to extend its apostolate to the members of the Roman Catholic Church since they are regarded to be among the number of those who lack "the right understanding of the gospel" (article 34).

The Reformed churches in the The Netherlands (700,000 members)

The Reformed Churches in The Netherlands arose as a result of the protest of Calvinist orthodoxy against the ecclesiastic and religious situation in the Dutch Reformed Church during the nineteenth century. In 1834 this protest led to the Separation under the leadership of Hendrik de Cock, and in 1886 to the Indictment under the leadership of Abraham Kuyper.

Those communities of the Separation which did not unite in 1892 with those of the Indictment formed the Christian Reformed Churches, now numbering 60,000 members. Like the Reformed Churches it follows the Church Ordinance of Dordrecht and the *Three Formulas of Union.*

It is not easy for outsiders to arrive at a proper understanding of what unites and separates the Reformed churches. All who do not belong to the Dutch Reformed Church are able to accept in principle the official Reformed confessional writings. In this they all agree with one another, in contrast to large segments within the Dutch Reformed Church that are more under the influence of Lutheranism, Methodism or even Anglicanism, or to those who adhere to liberal Protestantism. All reject the Swiss

181

theology which has so strongly influenced the Dutch Reformed Church.

The differences between the branches of the Reformed Churches in The Netherlands are connected with a number of theological questions which have arisen within the limits of the strictly Calvinist realm of faith and thought, and which therefore are often beyond the spiritual horizon of the major part of the members of the Dutch Reformed Church. These questions concern the manner in which the relation must be understood between baptism and regeneration, covenant and predestination, the visible church and the church as the community of the elect.

There are moreover considerable differences of spirituality and mentality. Notable is the contrast between an ecclesiastico-doctrinal type which principally if not exclusively follows the objective word of God, and a pietistic type which places great emphasis on the personal experience of "God's work with the soul" and on the personal knowledge of belonging to those "who are known by God."

In some communities much attention is given to the external signs of election: a special gift to render witness, a special gift of prayer, special mystical experiences, a pious way of life. This stress on personal piety and on the special charismatic gifts sometimes takes on a Montanist character whereby one looks down upon the large mass of arid souls, led by blind leaders who do not correctly dispense the word of God. One either dissociates oneself from the mass to form a small, select flock of "saints," or extra-ecclesiastic meetings are called under the direction of a "practitioner" or an independent community is formed. Apart from the Reformed within the Dutch Reformed Church and apart from the various Reformed church unions there are independent and old-Reformed communities having no connections with any church and on principle opposed to any ecumenical effort.

We will now limit ourselves to the Reformed Churches in The Netherlands. These churches owe their existence to the activity of Abraham Kuyper and to the Indictment of 1886, although in 1892 some of the churches of the Separation of 1834 joined these churches.

The theological development in the Reformed Churches runs from Kuyper via Bavinck to Berkouwer, the creators of the neo-Calvinist theology in The Netherlands—the theology of the Free University of Amsterdam. Initially this theology was directed particularly against the ethical and liberal theology in the Dutch Reformed Church. Because of the new religious situation this theology has, in the person of Berkouwer, also turned against the Swiss theology of Barth and Brunner and Catholic theology. Between Barth and Berkouwer however there has been a certain rapprochement. The contrast between Reformed theology and Swiss theology stems from different concepts of inspiration and authority in sacred Scripture. The contrast between Reformed and Catholic theology concerns the authority of Scripture and Church.

In 1926 a disagreement within the Reformed Churches on the extent of inspiration in the Bible and on whether or not scientific biblical criticism should be permitted led to rebellion by Geelkerken and his followers. The result was the organization of the Reformed Churches in The Netherlands in Restored Union. These churches, attracted to new problems, also showed great interest in the ecumenical movement. The Restored Union (thirty-three communities) was accepted into the Dutch Reformed Church in 1946.

The same objections which in 1892 had prevented some parts of the Separation from joining the Reformed Churches in The Netherlands soon made themselves felt among the groups mentioned above. One of the principal points of discussion was whether or not a baptized child should be considered regenerated. The decision of the synod of Utrecht in 1905 never satisfied the Reformed, the decision that "according to the confession of our churches the seed of the covenant must, because of God's promise, be considered as regenerated and sanctified in Christ unless during their adult years they manifest the contrary by their way of life or teachings."

This decision evoked a number of questions which, in the course of the years, have been dealt with by various synods. At the synod of Sneek in 1939—continued in Utrecht in 1942—several decisions were made which, if not "infallible," were considered binding for preachers and professors in their preaching and theological tasks.

The objectors denied that synodal decisions are contained in the "confession of our churches." They agreed with the "synodals" that baptism must be regarded as a sign of the convenant, but they disagreed that baptism must also be regarded as "the bath of regeneration and renewal by the Holy Spirit" (Titus 3, 5). Baptism is therefore the sign and pledge of an efficacious operation of grace by which the baptized child must be considered regenerated. The objectors on the other hand maintain that regeneration must not be placed outside consciousness, but that it coincides with the first personal conscious act of faith. The act of faith together with regeneration is the fruit of the operation of the Holy Spirit in the truly chosen children of God. Not all the baptized are among the elect, though they do belong to the covenant; and only the elect are regenerated. Because of this the objectors found it impossible to consider baptized children regenerated simply on the basis of the covenant and baptism, even though such consideration be grounded in a "judgment of love."

The difference can be further specified. The synodals emphasize the visibility and the full reality of the church, the sacraments of baptism and supper, and the covenant. At no price will they see these visible manifestations of God's grace as empty signs by which man is, as it were, deceived since there is no hidden reality corresponding to them. The objectors on the other hand refuse to see these visible signs as guarantees of election and regeneration. They point out that according to sacred Scrip-

184

ture many of those who belonged to the old covenant fell into idolatry and were lost.

According to the objectors the covenant is only an offer of God's promise of salvation. Salvation and regeneration are realized only in and through the positing of a sincere, personal and living act of faith. Only a member of the elect is able to posit such an act of faith, through the operation of the Holy Spirit, thus actually accepting salvation from God's hand. Both faith and regeneration are the work of the Holy Spirit as a realization in time of God's eternal, hidden and gratuitous predestination and election.

The objectors carefully maintain the distance between the church as a visible organization and the church as the visible community of God's elect, between the sacrament of baptism as the seal of God's promise and regeneration as the fruit of the gratuitous operation of the Holy Spirit, between the convenant as the offer and salvation as the realization of God's promise.

Under the leadership of Schilder the objectors refused to conform to the synodal decisions. In this they appealed to article 31 of the church ordinance which appears to declare such decisions as "firm and binding unless they are proven to be contrary to God's word." The synodals however contend that this appeal is based on a false interpretation of article 31.

Consequently the conflict was transferred from the realm of theology to that of church law. Questions arose which had frequently caused difficulties among Reformed of other countries— for example questions on the nature and extent of Reformed church law or the relation between office and authority.

After an extensive exchange of letters and discussions between Schilder and the synod the former was removed from office in 1944. Shortly after the objectors published an Act of Liberation and Return. They insisted on their appeal to article 31 and formed a new, "liberated" church union—liberated from the synodal church which had degenerated through unlawful hierarchical claims of authority—and returned to a church union in accordance with the intentions of the Dordrecht church ordinance and the original Reformed notion of the church. The Reformed Churches in The Netherlands now includes more than 250 communities (churches), with a total of about 100,000 members.

Reformed Protestantism in other countries

The only country where, from the second half of the sixteenth century on, Reformed Protestantism occupied a place similar to that in The Netherlands is Scotland. Scottish Protestantism however has had more success in preserving its original character. It is more balanced, less inclined to extremes, less puritanical, but also less influenced by modernism. The interior of the church and the liturgy are more in accordance with the liturgical principles of Strasburg and with the liturgical insights and intentions which Calvin had been unable to realize in Geneva. Finally Scottish Presbyterian Protestantism has in the course of this century achieved a unity Reformed Protestantism in The Netherlands has yet to match.

In 1560 the nobility and the people of Scotland opted for the Reformation in spite of the fact that Mary Stuart remained a Catholic. In 1567 the queen fled to England only to be imprisoned and beheaded there. Since 1559 the Reformation movement had been directed by John Knox who, in Geneva, had become a staunch supporter of Calvin.

The Scottish parliament officially ruled in 1560 to introduce the Reformation and to establish a Scottish national church on Reformed principles. The confession of this church is contained in the *Confessio Scottica,* its church ordinance in the *Book of Discipline;* both date from 1560. Its liturgy is contained in the *Book of Common Order* of 1564, not to be confused with the Anglican *Book of Common Prayer.* The Scottish Church, not impeded by any division such as that in the cantons of Switzerland or the provinces of The Netherlands, from the beginning placed great emphasis on the unity of the Church, not on the plurality of the churches of which it is composed. The presbyterial institution of the church has found its clearest expression in the Scottish Church. The few Scottish communities in The Netherlands are part of the Dutch Reformed Church.

The Scottish Church experienced a very difficult period of struggle and persecution from 1603, when England and Scotland were united under the Stuart monarchy, until 1688, when the last Stuart was put to flight and when Prince William III of The Netherlands assumed the throne of England and Scotland. A short respite had been enjoyed only during the years of the English Commonwealth, from 1649 to 1660.

The Stuarts were ill disposed toward the Scottish Church and tried to force the Anglican structure and liturgy on the Church of Scotland. This strongly resembled the manner in which, from 1640 to 1660, Cromwell's Long Parliament tried to replace the Anglican church structure and liturgy of the Church of England with a presbyterial or congregationalist one. Under the Stuarts Scotland was the scene of many rebellions and persecutions, particularly in the years 1660 to 1688. But since 1688 the Scottish Church has officially been acknowledged as the state church. The Anglican Church continued to exist in Scotland as a small but autonomous minority church.

Peace had hardly been established when disagreements arose within the Scottish Church which ultimately led to separation. In this connection it was not so much a question of doctrine and theology as of the authority of the church and religious practices. The following free churches arose: in 1733 the Secession Church, in 1752 the Relief Church and finally in 1843 the Free Church of Scotland. The latter was the fruit of a powerful evangelic revival protesting the soft and superficial spirit of the times. It was related to the revival in The Netherlands of the past century and, as far as origin, spirit and aim were concerned, it was even akin to the Anglican Oxford movement. It differed from the revival in The Netherlands in that from the very beginning efforts were made to arrive at reunion. As early as 1847 the churches which had arisen in 1733 and 1752 were united into the United Presbyterian Church. In 1900 this Church was reunited with the Free Church of Scotland (United Free Church). And in 1929 this combined church was finally reunited to the original state church, so that the Presbyterian Church of Scotland now includes practically all the Reformed of Scotland. Its membership is about three million, with more than a million communicants. The confessional basis of the reunited Scottish Church is the Westminster Confession.

In 1929 a new *Book of Common Order* was completed and eleven years later revised to its present size, form and content. The Anglican Church in Scotland, which in many respects went through its own development and which is independent of the Anglican Church of England, introduced in 1929 a revision of the *Book of Common Prayer,* usually referred to as the *Scottish Prayer Book.* It is worthwhile to compare these two church books with one another and with the *Book of Services* of the Dutch Reformed Church, and with the new liturgy of the Reformed Church of France.

The Scottish Church is quite interested in Swiss theology and in the ecumenical movement. In this respect it is similar not so much to the Reformed churches in The Netherlands as it is to the Dutch Reformed Church, the Reformed churches of Switzerland, France and Germany, and the presbyterianism and congregationalism of England, the United States, Canada and South India. The various members of Reformed churches in The Netherlands represent a type of Reformed Protestantism for which the Dutch national character seems to possess a special affinity. It is practically absent in all other parts of the world except among the Reformed of Dutch ancestry in South Africa and the United States (Michigan), and in countries where Reformed communities have been established by the missionary activity of the Reformed churches.

Reformed Protestantism in England, in its protest against

188

Anglicanism, has acquired two main forms: a presbyterian and a congregationalist. Through emigration and colonization these found their way to the United States and to the various parts of the former British Empire.

Switzerland, the country where Reformed Protestantism was born, has since the Reformation been divided into Catholic and Protestant cantons. As a result of the Battle of Kappel in 1531, and because of the Counter-reformation of the late sixteenth century, many cantons returned to the Catholic Church. The division of cantons is the reason why Switzerland has no national Reformed church. In each of the five principal centers of Reformation—Zurich, Geneva, Berne, Basle and Schaffhausen —types of Reformed Protestantism developed peculiar to each center. Except in Geneva each of these types favored extreme national churches. Musculus in Berne and particularly Gualter in Zurich waged heavy battles against the church ordinance of Geneva, mostly because this ordinance attributed to the consistory, in matters ecclesiastic, an authority and disciplinary law independent of and opposed to the authority and rights of the magistrate. Church council and city council were set in opposition to one another. Musculus and Gualter maintained that judicial and governmental matters within the church should come under the competency of the magistrate. The Anglican principles concerning the relation between church and state, principles which are at the basis of the struggle against puritanism, have their origin partly in the Swiss ideas on this subject.

A certain measure of confessional unity was expressed in the *Consensus Tigurinus* 1549, in the *Confessio Helvetica* 1566, which is based on the theology of Bullinger, and in the *Formula Consensus* 1675. With the latter Swiss orthodoxy reached its high point. As in Germany and The Netherlands so also in Switzerland was Reformed Protestantism influenced by several new movements and by the spirit of the enlightenment, French liberalism and German idealism. Even the famous theological

189

faculty of the academy founded in Geneva during Calvin's lifetime did not escape the superficial spirit of the time.

However early in the nineteenth century a powerful evangelic revival took place, partly as a result of the activity of Scottish preachers. The resistance of the liberal cantons caused serious clashes and eventually some schisms as well as the rise of the free churches. One of the best known Swiss champions of complete separation of church and state was Alexander Vinet (1797–1847), who can also be considered one of the fathers of the ethical trend in The Netherlands. The entire nineteenth century was characterized in Switzerland as well as in other countries by a fierce struggle of trends which began to subside only toward the end of that agitated century. A solution toward unity progressed faster in Switzerland than in The Netherlands.

In 1920 the Swiss Evangelical Church Union was organized, to which belong the canton churches, the free churches of French Switzerland and the episcopal Methodist church. At this time the rise of the Swiss theology of Barth (Basle) and Brunner (Zurich) also took place. This theology rapidly gained influence not only in the Swiss Reformed churches but also in others as far away as America and Japan. The general secretariat of the World Council of Churches, founded in 1948, has its see in Geneva. The number of Reformed Protestants in Switzerland amounts to two and a half million.

In France circumstances seemed at first quite favorable to the establishment of a national Reformed church. But after the unfavorable outcome of the religious wars waged between 1562 and 1593 (St. Bartholomew's Night, 1572), and particularly after the abolition of the Edict of Nantes which had, for about a century, guaranteed a certain amount of freedom of religion for the Reformed, many Protestants left the country. The group that remained was acknowledged by the state in 1802. The struggle between orthodoxy and modernism also made itself felt in France and led to schism. Complete reunion was achieved only in 1938. This reunion also included the Methodists. The first complete liturgical *Book of Services* was published in 1955. The present Reformed Church of France numbers 350,000 members.

In Germany about 10 per cent of the Protestants belong to the Reformed type. The rise and expansion of Calvinism in the second half of the sixteenth century led to a violent struggle with the Lutherans and in some instances the prince or the municipal magistrate replaced Lutheranism by Reformed Protestantism; in others they tried to force a fusion of Calvinists and Lutherans. However these forcible attempts at union were never popular. The most outstanding example is the *Unierte Kirche* (United Church) which arose as a result of the Union of Prussia in 1817, whereby Frederick III united Lutherans and Reformed in one church. The political catastrophe of 1918 resulted in a separation of church and state.

Since that time events followed a rapid course. In 1922 the German Evangelical Church Union was established which united Lutheran and Reformed churches. Under the influence of Barth (Bekenntniskirche) Lutherans and Reformed Protestants took part in the struggle against National Socialism and the "German Christians." After World War II, in 1948, the Evangelical Church of Germany was organized as a federation of Lutheran and Reformed Churches, but not without confessional difficulties. The advantage is that this is a voluntary association strongly supported by the ecumenical efforts of our own day. The federated churches have a total membership of more than forty million persons, of whom four million are Reformed Protestants.

During the sixteenth century some Reformed churches also arose in Hungary (since 1918 divided into Hungarian and Rumanian groups), in Czechoslovakia and in Lithuania, all of which have so far been able to maintain themselves as minority churches despite difficult circumstances. The Hungarian-Rumanian church numbers about three million members and is the only Reformed church with an episcopal structure.

The total number of Reformed Protestants as described in this chapter is estimated at fifty million.

3

Anglican Protestantism

Is Anglicanism Protestant?

Anglicanism is the most debated form of Christianity. It is judged in a variety of ways not only by outsiders and spectators but also by the Anglicans themselves. Continental notions about the origin and character of Anglicanism generally leave much to be desired. Even for a person who has spent a great part of his life in the world of Anglicanism it is not easy to disentangle the knot of misunderstanding about Anglicanism.

A first point of discussion is whether Anglicanism should be considered part of Protestantism. In many of its expressions, particularly among those who are called Anglo-Catholics, Anglicanism shows striking points of resemblance to Catholicism. Today we can even find Anglican churches in which the interior differs in no way from that of a Roman Catholic church, Anglican churches in which the Lord's supper is again considered the sacrifice of the mass, in which the priest wears Catholic vestments, and in which practically all the Roman Catholic devotions, such as benediction of the blessed sacrament, devotions to Mary and the saints, the recitation of the rosary and veneration of the Sacred Heart have been introduced. However by far the majority of Anglicans finds all this just as strange as does a Dutch Protestant. In any case whatever judgment may be formed of Anglo-Catholicism from the viewpoint of the Catholic Church the official conduct of the Anglican churches should not be measured by Anglo-Catholic criteria. For this would *a priori* render a proper understanding of the activities of these churches impossible. As opposed to the Anglo-Catholic Anglicans there are many other Anglicans whose vision of the nature of Christian religion, the Church, the sacraments and the gospel is typically Protestant. As a result of their insular formation many Anglicans scarcely know how much of the Reformation heritage they share in their faith, thought and actions.

It may be true that Anglicans generally do not like to be called Protestant and that Anglicanism as it presents itself today should not simply be considered a part of Protestantism, but nonetheless there is a type of Protestantism which, according to its nature and origin, cannot be called Lutheran or Reformed but must be called Anglican.

On the Catholic as well as on the Protestant side there is a fairly recent widespread opinion that Anglicanism is closer to the Catholic Church than to the Reformation. This notion had its origin in the nineteenth century Oxford movement, which was a catholicizing revival. It has left permanent traces in the total picture of Anglicanism today but in the form it has assumed in later Anglo-Catholicism it has remained a foreign and isolated element in the world of Anglican churches.

As a result of the lively activity and propaganda displayed by Anglo-Catholicism for almost a century many people have come in contact with Anglicanism by way of Anglo-Catholicism, for example by reading the Anglo-Catholic *Church Times*. Consequently many of these people have the impression that Anglicanism belongs in principle to the Catholic type of Christianity and that it has been influenced by the sixteenth century Reformation and Protestantism only accidentally and superficially.

Such a neo-Anglican vision is untenable. It is contrary to the historical facts, at least if all the facts, documents and data are taken into consideration. The neo-Anglican vision is based on a one-sided, arbitrary interpretation of the ecclesiastic and religious events which took place during the troubled and confused reign of Henry VIII. It also disregards the distinct Reformation characteristics of Anglican sermons and writings of the sixteenth century. Moreover it is based on serious misconceptions of the deepest essence of the Reformation and of the real content, purport and intention of the teaching and theology of the Catholic Church.

In the formation of an unbiased judgment about the origin and character of Anglicanism, consideration should be given not only the neo-Anglican vision as expressed for example in Carpenter's recent work *The Church in England 597–1688*, 1954, but also to the Reformation and Catholic points of view as presented in such works as Rupp's *Studies in the Making of English Protestant Tradition* 1949 and Hughes' three-volume *The Reformation in England* 1954.

The notion of many Reformed Protestants that Anglicanism was never really reform-minded and thoroughly Protestant is, like the neo-Anglican vision, based on a one-sided judgment which, in this instance, sees the situation only from the puritan viewpoint. But as is evident from classical sixteenth century Anglican theology it is impossible to explain the struggle between Anglicanism and puritanism under Elizabeth I as a secret nostalgia for the Roman church, or as an attempt to arrive at a compromise without principle.

The struggle between Anglicanism and puritanism was based on the common foundation of the sixteenth century Reformation. From the actions of Whitgift, the great champion of the Establishment, and from the works of Hooker, Jewel and other founders of classical Anglican theology it is quite evident that these bishops were in principle on the side of the Reformation on the continent. Their acceptance of the basic principles of the Reformation however did not mean that they were also in full agreement with the Calvinist-puritan ideas about the authority of the church, ecclesiastic discipline and liturgy.

If the Anglican Reformation ran a different course from that of the Lutheran and the Reformed this must be attributed not to aftereffects of Roman Catholic influences, but rather to certain typically English circumstances, to certain traits in the English national character and to the practical, humanistic character of the English religiousness.

In an investigation into the origin of Anglicanism as a type of Christianity it is not the period of transition under Henry VIII or Edward VI that deserves most attention, but the period under Elizabeth I. Ecclesiastic and religious confusion during the former period was too widespread and too many unfavorable extraneous circumstances made themselves felt for the Church of England to assert itself sufficiently.

The rise and development of Anglicanism was influenced by the king, the archbishop of Canterbury, the convocations of Canterbury and York (consisting of a House of Bishops and a House of Clergy), and by the parliament (consisting of a House of Lords and a House of Commons). The collaboration between these various authorities in laying down regulations concerning ecclesiastic and religious matters shows a changing picture in the course of history, a collaboration marked by frequent serious clashes. Under the tyrannical reign of Henry VIII the convocations as well as parliament lacked all freedom of movement. It is for this reason that the character of Anglicanism should not be judged by official measures by the authorities but by the content of the *Book of Common Prayer* and the thirty-nine articles. And these should be interpreted as the bishops and theologians always interpreted them and as the clergy and the people generally understood and practiced them. Nor should any judgment about Anglicanism be influenced by one-sided manifestations of certain extremist groups in the Anglican churches.

During the sixteenth and seventeenth centuries the Tudors and Stuarts tried to impose on the Church of England as strict a uniformity as possible (Acts of Uniformity). In spite of these efforts Anglicanism, under the influence of the most varied—if

195

not contradictory—opinions about the church and Christianity, has gone through a number of different stages. In fact Anglicanism's search for a definitive form and content has never quite come to an end. The Anglican Church of England has always been the scene of clashing opinions and interpretations.

The Anglican Reformation never reached a static position where nothing could be changed or revoked. It has always preserved a certain openness to the Catholic and the Reformation interpretations of Christian faith. It has taken seriously the principle *reformanda quia reformata:* the church must forever be reformed because its name is reformed. For this reason Anglicanism more than any other form of Christianity has a dynamic, not a static character: even to the extent that the Anglican churches of our own day appear ready to sacrifice their own independence and identity if it is a matter of reuniting Christianity. This could be called Reformation Catholicity or Catholic Protestantism.

The fact that the Reformation developed differently in the Anglican churches and in the Lutheran and Reformed is, as we have already remarked, also connected with certain traits in the English national character. This is particularly marked by an extraordinary combination of social consciousness and consciousness of individuality. An Englishman does not like to come into conflict with the society to which he belongs, but still less does he like to sacrifice his own individuality. This easily leads to the development of an official or public, and a private or hidden world of thought, to both of which an Englishman can do justice without much trouble. This applies to the realm of religion as well. As long as he enjoys a certain amount of personal freedom and no force is brought to bear on his conscience he will, if at all possible, conform to what is official and prescribed. But at the same time he will go his own way in his personal life and in the smaller or greater circle of persons who are similarly minded. Consequently from the very start Anglicanism shows in the members of the various Anglican churches a much greater variety and contrast of viewpoints, interpretations and forms of practice than would be deduced from official instructions and decisions.

Finally all of this is also connected with the practical and humanist character of English religiousness. Anglicanism, as its own proper type and form of Reformed Christianity, has always had a remarkably moderate, controlled, wise, balanced and culti-vated character. The typically Anglican mentality and manner of speech and action gives an important and aristocratic im-pression. The English idea of the Christian gentleman stems from Anglicanism. The Benedictine sense of order, style, tradi-tion and docility, as well as the humanist sense of erudition and honesty, and the humanist respect for sources, facts and argu-ments live on in Anglicanism, even when they plead in favor of a possible opponent. By nature Anglicanism has a wide vision. Moreover it has great reverence for what has grown slowly, what has been tried, what is generally accepted, in short for tradition (not to be confused with the Catholic concept of tradition).

The bishops who laid the foundations of Anglicanism during the time of Elizabeth were not striving for an unprincipled com-promise between Romanism and Protestantism. As is clear from their writings they knew quite well what they wanted. They were in principle reform-minded and precisely for this reason they battled puritanism, in which they saw a suspiciously one-sided interpretation of the original aims of the reformers. When they battled puritanism they were concerned about protecting the church against premature and shortsighted abolition and against disorder and liturgical dissoluteness. In their letters there is not a trace of Roman sympathies. It is true that they rejected the church ordinance of Geneva but at the same time they maintained close relations with the Reformed churches of Berne and Zurich. Like the latter two the founders of the establishment considered the church to be the people. According to them the church was not a community apart from the community of the people. Consequently the authority of the magistrate or the prince extended to ecclesiastic as well as to civil matters. As far as the episcopal institution of the church, the liturgy and the sacraments were concerned it is out of the question that the Anglican bishops of the time included anything of a Roman Catholic origin. Elizabeth I and her bishops had no other aim than to give the Reformation movement in England its own austere form and style. More than did Lutheran and Reformed Protestantism Anglicanism succeeded in realizing the universal Christian and ecumenical ideals of the reformers.

It cannot be denied that in the course of time the vision of the true nature of the Reformation and of Protestantism has for many Anglicans been clouded. As a result of the battle against puritanism, sectarianism and a movement for independence many Anglicans have more and more come to see Protestantism as a negative, destructive force which lacks the respect due to age-old Christian tradition and community values. No doubt the rise of a pietistic subjectivism and liberal individualism within the Lutheran and Reformed churches also influenced the development of this view of Protestantism. Finally, as we remarked earlier in this section, Anglo-Catholicism has succeeded in wiping out the last traces of an awareness of being related to the Reformation.

There are symptoms that many Anglicans of our own day are once again becoming conscious of the fact that Anglicanism as a form of Christianity is rooted not only in Christian antiquity but also in the Reformation of the sixteenth century. Partly as a result of the general revival of a Reformation consciousness among Protestants, and partly as a result of their own ecumenical contacts, the Anglicans are well on the way toward a rediscovery and re-evaluation of the heritage of the Reformation. In their relations with Protestant churches they are no longer prepared to take into account the objections and protests of Anglo-Catholics; at least they do not take them into account in the same measure as before. A favorable factor is that in Protestant churches there is a growing ecclesiastic and liturgical awareness. In proportion as these churches put more emphasis on Catholicity the Anglicans will have fewer objections against being called Reformed or Protestant.

There is a growing conviction that the Anglican churches have always been basically Reformation churches and that therefore there is a greater prospect of a possible reunion with the free churches which had severed themselves from Anglicanism and with other Reformation churches, rather than with the churches belonging to the "Catholic group."

Finally it does not appear to have been a mistake for the Anglican Church in the United States to call itself Protestant. Neither is it a mistake that the King of England at his coronation must solemnly declare to "do all that is in my power to maintain the Protestant Reformed religion in the United Kingdom, as established by law." It follows then that we should not only speak of an Anglican type of Protestantism but must even regard Anglicanism as one of the three main types of Protestantism.

Henry VIII and Anglicanism

A second question about which there is a wide variety of opinion and a great deal of misunderstanding is the relation between Henry VIII and the Church of England. Since there are so many different aspects to this complicated question it is not easy to evaluate correctly all the relevant facts and to present a clear, objective picture of the part played by the king in the rise of Anglicanism.

In the first two chapters of this book we have seen that in the rise and development of the Reformation in the Lutheran and Reformed countries there were always two factors at work: a religious and a political factor. The Reformation movement everywhere was in itself a movement of a purely religious character. But nowhere would it have had a chance to succeed without the support of the secular authorities: the prince, the municipal magistrate and possibly even parliament. It is often difficult to determine whether the decision of the princes to introduce the Reformation was based on religious or political grounds. In any case the success or failure of the Reformation was everywhere dependent on the attitude and the decision of the secular authorities.

Moreover wherever the Reformation was introduced and developed it was always preceded by a transitional period of searching, tension and insecurity. Often when the prince or magistrate had decided to introduce the Reformation there was a good deal of resistance by that part of the clergy and population which wanted to remain true to the established faith. There were also frequent theological disagreements or frictions between the secular and the new ecclesiastic authorities.

In all these respects the course of events in England was similar to that in other countries. In England the rise of the Reformation led to the formation of the Church of England as an independent national church, and of Anglicanism as a separate type of Reformed Christianity. The religious and political factors played their part in England too. For the moment we will restrict our attention to the political aspect, viz. to the part played by the king in the formation of the Anglican-Reformed Church of England. Subsequent sections will deal with the religious aspect.

The part played by Henry VIII consisted first of all in that like the princes or magistrates of other countries he prepared the way for the rise and development of the Reformation. Through his conflict and ultimate break with Rome he indirectly and even somewhat unwillingly supplied more room and freedom for the Reformation movement already begun in England. But he contributed scarcely anything to the form and content of Anglicanism. Rather he thwarted as much as possible the renewal of the Church of England according to the principles of the Reformation. An essential difference between the course of events in England and in other Protestant countries lay in the tyrannical manner Henry VIII, even after his break with Rome, continually interfered in the life of the Church of England, not to mention the fanatical manner in which he executed not only Thomas More, John Fisher and many others who remained true to the pope and the Catholic faith, but also numerous Anabaptists, Sacramentarians (who denied the real presence of Christ in the sacrament of the altar) and others suspected of Lutheran heresies.

Henry VIII apparently had no other intention than to solve his personal conflict with the pope by making the Church of England a national church independent of Rome, but Roman in doctrine, structure and liturgy. Some bishops undoubtedly shared this viewpoint of the king and considered the break with the pope and the royal supremacy over the church in this sense. However Cranmer, archbishop of Canterbury since the final break with Rome in 1533, together with such bishops as Latimer, Ridley and Hooper had quite different intentions. Long before the break with Rome they were in their hearts dedicated to the teachings and principles of the Reformation. But because of the attitude of the king they had to proceed cautiously and were unable to realize their plans of reform while the king was still living. Consequently the real foundation of the Church of England was not laid under Henry VIII but—at least provisionally—under his successor Edward VI, who governed under a lord protector of England, and definitively only during the reign of Elizabeth I. While Henry VIII was still alive the tension between him and the Anglican bishops who wanted to put their Reformation ideas into practice was quite similar to the tension between him and the pope prior to 1533.

In the light of these facts it is almost comical to hear Henry VIII called the founder of the Church of England. The popular opinion that he was the intellectual author of Anglicanism must therefore be rejected as a superficial if not misleading oversimplification.

However the fact remains that the break with Rome was in

itself a much more radical break with the original Catholic faith than Henry apparently suspected. In this sense the birth of the new Anglican Church of England coincides with the break with Rome. But when the Church of England is considered in its real essence an Anglican-Reformation church it cannot be said to have resulted from the marital problems and the tyranny of Henry VIII. Rather we must say that in this sense the Church of England originated from the religious efforts and beliefs of the sixteenth century Reformation.

It is of course generally known that the break between Henry VIII and the pope and Henry's desire for full supremancy over the Church of England were intimately connected with the tragic results of his marriage to Catherine of Aragon. But as we noted above when it is a matter of understanding, characterizing and judging Anglicanism as a separate type of Reformed Christianity the marital question can be safely left out of consideration. However since it was the indirect occasion of the rise of Anglicanism it is necessary to have a balanced view of the development of this marital conflict.

In 1509, the year of his coronation, at the age of eighteen, Henry VIII married Catherine of Aragon, his senior by six years. She was the widow of Henry's brother Arthur, who had died in 1502, and to whom Catherine had been married only four months. Henry's marriage to Catherine was initially a happy one even though it had been arranged at the express will of his father Henry VII who, after Arthur's death, had announced Henry's engagement to Catherine. At the time Henry was only twelve years old.

According to the canon law of the Catholic Church a man is not allowed to marry the wife of his deceased brother. In Henry's case however Pope Julius II had granted a dispensation from this impediment. Prior to this such dispensation had been granted only sporadically, if ever.

Henry's marriage was a source of disappointment to him since all male children either were stillborn or died shortly after birth. Only one daughter lived, the later Queen Mary Tudor. It was evident that there was no hope of a male heir to the throne. And difficult as it is to read into the hearts of kings the emotions and motives that guided Henry VIII in his marital conflict will never be known.

If it is beyond doubt that a marriage between baptized persons has been concluded validly and that it has been consummated such marriage is indissoluble under any circumstances. Consequently there could be no question of having Henry's marriage to Catherine dissolved by the pope. Henry was well aware of this. Therefore it is obvious that when in 1527 he raised the question of his marriage Henry did not want to have it dissolved, but rather to have it declared invalid. There was never any question of divorce.

The question whether the Pope actually had the power to grant the dispensation from his original marriage impediment and whether, therefore, his marriage to Catherine was invalid seems to have first occurred to Henry VIII, possibly under the influence of his advisers, when none of his sons lived after birth. The king seems to have considered this as a punishment for his transgression of God's express prohibition in the Book of Leviticus (18:16; see 20:21) to marry the wife of a deceased brother, a deed called an abomination in God's sight. The sincerity of this religious motivation should not *a priori* be doubted. Henry was by nature very religiously inclined, he detested heresies and he was personally interested in theological questions. However it cannot be denied that, partly under Wolsey's influence, his moral character declined as the years passed.

In 1527 the king petitioned Pope Clement VII to declare his marriage invalid. The case proceeded very slowly and the decision was pending for seven years. During this time the king, prompted by his advisers, gradually arrived at the conviction that a solution had to be forced by taking matters into his own hands. When one studies the tangle of facts, intrigues and circumstances connected with this marital tragedy one finds that it is hardly fair to put all the blame on Henry alone. There was the role Cardinal Wolsey played, the promises and advice received by the king and the statements by (partially bribed) juridical faculties of practically all the famous universities in Europe.

Meanwhile the king had developed a growing resistance to the papal claims of jurisdiction over the entire Church, including the Church in England, and as a result he began to think of appropriating to himself the exclusive and complete supremacy of the Church over his subjects. The gradual realization of his plans and ideas took another five years of negotiations with the pope. During these negotiations the chasm between England and Rome grew wider and a series of legal measures were taken by which both parliament and the convocations were increasingly forced to allow themselves to be used as mere instruments of the king.

Early in 1529 Henry sent Gardiner, jurist and later bishop of Winchester, to Rome with the threat that the king would relinquish his obedience to the pope if the latter did not expedite the marriage process. The critical moment arrived when Cardinal Campeggio, as president of the English court of justice which dealt with the process, suspended the deliberations for three months. This decision was partly due to an appeal by the queen and her cousin Charles V to the papal court of law in Rome. The adjournment and transfer of the process resulted in the fall of Wolsey, who decided to dedicate himself henceforth to the government of his archdiocese of York. He died on his way to London in 1530, accused of treason. Thomas More had succeeded him in 1529 as lord chancellor of England.

In November 1529 Henry convoked the parliament later to be known as the Reformation Parliament. For the next seven years this parliament met to legislate a number of anticlerical laws which at the same time also defined and assured the king's position as supreme head of the Church in England.

In the mid 1530s the nobility of England sent a letter to the pope defending Henry's standpoint. The answer to this letter is the principal document for a proper knowledge of the claims and arguments of Rome. An English translation of this letter is given in Hughes' *The Reformation in England* (I, 378).

In 1531, under heavy pressure from the king, the convocations of Canterbury and York acknowledged Henry's supremacy over the Church of England, though in a mitigated form suggested by John Fisher. This was followed in May 1532 by the submission of the clergy, legally defined in 1534 in the Act of Submission. This submission meant in fact the rejection of papal jurisdiction in England, the surrender of all ecclesiastic law to the judgment of a royal commission appointed for that purpose, and the renunciation of the right to legislate independently of the king's approval. The submission caused Thomas More to resign as chancellor of England.

The great turning point however came only in August 1532 after the death of Warham, archbishop of Canterbury. It was the king's wish that Cranmer should succeed him. The pope gave his approbation to this choice by appointing Cranmer the archbishop of Canterbury, not realizing that in Germany Cranmer had been completely won over to the Reformation, and that he had married. Before taking the oath of obedience to the pope, Cranmer took another oath by which he declared that the oath of obedience to the pope was to be valid only insofar as it was not contrary to God's command and the interest of the king.

Shortly after his consecration as archbishop of Canterbury early in 1533 Cranmer, in complete disregard for the process still under way in Rome, declared Henry's marriage to Catherine to have been null and void from the very beginning. Though aware of the fact that Henry had secretly married Anne Boleyn he seriously admonished the king to abstain thenceforth from marital relations with Catherine, the wife of his deceased brother, since this would be contrary to God's express prohibition.

On July 4, 1533 Cranmer and the bishops who had cooperated in the declaration of nullity were excommunicated by the pope. The king was threatened with excommunication if by Sept. 4 he did not acknowledge and take back Catherine as his lawful spouse. For the time being however this excommunication was not put into effect.

Pope Clement VII seems to have hesitated until the very last moment, perhaps hoping for an unforeseen solution, perhaps for fear of what would happen to the Church in England if he should push Henry to the utmost limits. The final decision came on March 23, 1534. In a consistory of twenty-two cardinals the pope declared valid Henry's marriage to Catherine. The king responded to this decision with a prescription for the entire clergy in their forthcoming Easter sermons to condemn the arrogant claims of the pope. This was the beginning of a large scale antipapist propaganda by word and writing all over England. One of these writings was *The Glasse of the Truthe,* possibly written by Henry himself in collaboration with one or more bishops.

The clergy was enjoined to make clear to the people the distinction between the unassailable law of God and the relative character of purely human prescriptions and decisions, such as those by the pope. The Reformation in England therefore also had the nature of a crisis on authority. Once again, as in the early days of Luther, the papal authority was at stake. It was a question of the biblical teaching on the relation between human and divine authority. It was a question of the exclusive binding power of sacred Scripture over man's conscience.

Meanwhile the king had enjoined parliament to enact five laws with the intent of eliminating completely any possible remnants of papal influence in England. Most important were the Act of Submission and the Act of Succession. The latter excluded the succession of Princess Mary in favor of the offspring of the marriage with Anne Boleyn. On April 13 Thomas More and John Fisher refused to take the oath of allegiance to Anne Boleyn's progeny and consequently were imprisoned in the Tower. In 1535 they were executed because of their refusal to

accept the Act of Supremacy wherein the king was legally proclaimed "the only supreme head on earth of the Church of England called *Anglicana Ecclesia.*" John Fisher was decapitated on
June 22, 1535, Thomas More on July 6, 1535. The Anglican
historian Carpenter calls Thomas More "the man who was possibly the best Christian in a thousand years" (*The Church in
England,* 226).

By the Bull of Aug. 30, 1535 Henry VIII was excommunicated by Pope Paul III. The reason given was "that in a shame-
ful manner he has promulgated laws threatening his subjects
with terrible tortures, even with capital punishment, if they do
not accept certain propositions which are heretical and schis-
matic, among others, that the bishop of Rome is not the head of
the Church taking the place of Christ, but that the king himself
is the supreme head of the English Church."

In the meantime the king had appointed Thomas Cromwell
vicar general in ecclesiastic affairs; his primary duty was to enforce observance of the law of supremacy throughout the
country. For this purpose Cromwell appointed four official
visitors. During the next four years he exercised a veritable reign
of terror in the church and was responsible for the royal in-
junctions against monks and clergymen which ended in the con-
fiscation of church properties and the abolition of monasteries.
In northern England this led to serious protests and rebellions
(the Pilgrimage of Grace) which were smothered in blood in
1537. More than two hundred leaders of the movement were
executed.

The royal supremacy of Henry VIII over the Church in England belongs to one of the darkest pages of the history of the
English people. It gives us a glimpse of the despotic actions of
the king but says nothing of the character of Anglicanism as a
form of Christianity. The title supreme head practically disappeared with the death of Henry VIII. The relations between
church and state were finally settled under Elizabeth I. The
principles which guided the Church of England in its relations

207

with the state are of a typically Swiss-Reformed character. They originated largely in Berne and Zurich. Actually the state church is not one of the essential marks of Anglicanism. Even if we leave aside the opinions expressed within the Church of England in favor of a separation of church and state it is certain that none of the other autonomous Anglican churches belonging to the Anglican communion is a state church. The relation between religion and politics has been thoroughly changed in the course of the past century. Therefore in our discussion of Anglicanism the political factor will be considered only when warranted.

The prelude to the Reformation in England

The earliest antecedents of the English Reformation and of a separate Anglican type of Christianity lie in the distant past of the English people.

The foundation of the Church in England in 597 by Augustine, the first archbishop of Canterbury, had been preceded by a period of Celtic Christianity. In its insular isolation this had developed quite independently and had left permanent traces in the religiousness of the British segment of the population. But the Anglosaxon Church also developed in many respects in an independent manner in keeping with the English national character.

With the conquest of England in 1066 by William of Normandy a period of tensions and conflicts between church and state began (notably the murder of Thomas à Becket in the cathedral of Canterbury in 1170). In these conflicts some of the bishops even at that time had sided with the king. The *Statute of Praemunire* of 1354, by which English ecclesiastic courts of law were forbidden to appeal to a foreign (read: papal) court of law, was only the beginning of a long series of legal stipulations for obstructing papal jurisdiction in England.

John Wycliffe had in the last years of his life called a power ful evangelic movement into existence, mainly through his preaching, his writing and his English translation of the Bible. Of considerable historical and theological importance is Wycliffe's 1378 treatise on the Church. A great student of Augustine of Hippo, Wycliffe based his ecclesiology on him. This work exercised great influence on John Huss and already contained all the principles of the sixteenth century Reformation theory of the church.

After Wycliffe's death in 1384 the evangelic movement continued in some parts of England. Itinerant preachers, called Lollards, held open air religious meetings, preached against practically all ecclesiastic ceremonies and practices and considered the reading and preaching of the Bible the most important thing in religion. They also promoted the spread of Wycliffe's translation of the Bible, criticized ecclesiastic and social abuses and attempted to persuade the people to a simple, personal piety and evangelic way of life.

Even after Henry VIII had ascended the throne the bishops were busy suppressing the activities of this movement, and many of its supporters ended their lives at the stake. Therefore both before and after the sixteenth century Reformation there existed in England a "Protestant underworld" whose motto was no popery. This is true even of the Anglican Church of England after the Reformation. This church should not be judged exclusively by its official pronouncements; account should also be taken of what the people commonly hold. The typically Protestant religious mentality has not only found refuge in the later free churches but also lives on within a large portion of Anglicans. This Protestant undercurrent, much more powerful in the Anglican churches than is commonly accepted, finds its earliest origins in the pre-Reformation, anti-Roman movements. Even in the late middle ages a certain anti-Rome tendency was an undeniable trait of the English national character. Not even the most avant-garde "catholic" convictions can lead an Anglican to acknowledge the pope and to become Roman.

In the first years of the sixteenth century processes against heretics by one bishop or another were common fare. The number of accused sometimes amounted to more than ten or twenty at a time, and in one instance there were even hundreds of them. In 1506 forty-five appeared before the bishop of Lincoln; in 1510 forty before the bishop of London; in 1511 forty-six before Warham, archbishop of Canterbury; in 1517 thirty-seven before the bishop of London; and in 1521 three hundred and forty-two before the bishop of Lincoln. Each of the processes resulted in a number of condemnations to the stake; most of the accused were forced to abjure their heresies. The process papers of each case showed that in several sections of England, in the areas around London, in Kent, in the Cotswolds and in the Chiltern Hills, even before the beginning of the Reformation on the continent, "typically Protestant" ideas were circulating. Examples of such ideas are that the pope is not the successor of Peter; that the papal claim of jurisdiction over the entire Church is unfounded; that the pope is the antichrist; that veneration of the saints and adoration of the blessed sacrament are idolatrous; that priests are servants of idolatry; that pilgrimages, fasts and penances are nonscriptural, human inventions; that there are only two sacraments; that purgatory does not exist; that religious services should be held in the vernacular; and that likewise people should pray in the vernacular. All the above "typically Protestant" opinions and objections were circulating in England even before anyone had ever heard of Luther.

Rumors about Luther's activities were not slow to reach England and were soon followed by a flood of Reform writings. Even as early as 1521 at the White Horse Inn in Cambridge, regular secret meetings were held in which a circle of theologians and students would discuss the new Reformation teachings spreading on the continent. The later archbishop of Canterbury, Cranmer also belonged to this group. Initiates used to call the inn Germany. When rumor had it that Lutheran heresies were making the rounds at the University of Oxford Warham, then archbishop of Canterbury, insisted in 1525 that a visitation of the university be held. Between 1527 and Warham's death in 1533 hundreds of people were accused of heresy, among them many priests and monks. Eleven were condemned to be burned at the stake. The best known of these first martyrs of Lutheranism in England was the priest Thomas Bilney of Norwich who had won the later Anglican bishop and preacher Latimer over to Lutheran doctrines.

In spite of the fact that until 1533 Henry VIII and the bishops continued to take steps against heresy many priests and theologians were building the foundations for the future Anglo-Reformation Church of England. Many of them took refuge in Germany where they obtained firsthand knowledge of Lutheranism. Apart from their own writings they also forwarded works by Luther and Melanchthon and other German and Swiss reformers to England. The bishops frequently published lists of forbidden books. Around 1530 Thomas More wrote that the titles of condemned books were so numerous that they could fill a volume and that it would take a week to add them up. Many books arrived in England by way of The Netherlands and were supplied by the Dutch printing presses. At unseasonable hours, hidden among all sorts of cargo, they were regularly brought into the country through the numerous ports on the east coast of England. In his book about the Reformation in England Hughes states that these Lutheran and other Reformation writings were the first bestsellers the English market had ever known.

The most important English propagandist for the Reformation was William Tyndale who was originally professor of dogmatic theology at the seminary in Oxford. He started an evangelic campaign in Gloucestershire in 1521. He took refuge in Germany in 1524, visited Luther at Wittenberg, and in Cologne and Worms worked on an English translation of the New Testament. This appeared in 1525 in octavo and quarto format, the latter edition of which is well supplied with explanatory notes. In Worms Tyndale had come in contact with Zwingli's Reformation ideas so that with Tyndale's New Testament translation and other writings Zwinglianism was introduced into England. In his abusive language against the pope and in his railings against the papist superstitions, idolatries and extortions Tyndale surpassed all other reformers (Tyndale's *Doctrinal Treatises,* ed. Parker Society, 32, 1848).

Tyndale's *The Obedience of a Christian and How Christian Rulers Ought to Govern* made a deep impression on Henry VIII. It had appeared in 1528 and reached the king in the course of the following year. It undoubtedly stimulated the estrangement between the king and the pope and also supplied the king with arguments and formulations in his efforts at complete supremacy over the Church in England. Thomas More devoted several writings to the refutation of Tyndale's tenets. In 1536 Tyndale was condemned and executed as a heretic in Antwerp where he had spent the last years of his life.

Cranmer: the course is provisionally set

With the consecration of Thomas Cranmer (1489–1556) as archbishop of Canterbury on March 30, 1533 begins the actual history of the Church of England as a new, independent and national church, the mother church of all those churches that would later form the Anglican community. The break with Rome became final upon the excommunication of Cranmer on July 4, 1533, followed by the excommunication of Henry VIII on Aug. 30, 1535. These were the years when Calvin openly declared himself in favor of the Reformation, fled to Basle and wrote the first edition of his *Institutes.*

Neither the king nor the archbishop paid any attention to the bulls of excommunication. Of Cranmer it is said that even from 1525 on he used to pray daily for the overthrow of the papal authority in the Church.

However enough has been said here about the political, national and juridical aspects of the Reformation in England. We can now limit ourselves to the study of the religious aspects of Anglicanism in its rise and development.

From a religious point of view the period from 1533 until Henry's death in 1547 was transitional, filled with confusion and arbitrariness, tensions and uncertainties. The period that followed (1547–1553) under the reign of Edward VI was more sharply delineated. In these years a course was set in a definite reform direction but, as a result of the Catholic reaction under Mary Tudor, this was only provisional. In this brief phase of development Cranmer's influence reached its high point. It was the most Protestant period in the history of the Church in England. The subsequent five years saw the Catholic reaction under Mary Tudor's reign and only after this could there be question of a definitive course in a moderate Anglican direction. From 1533 to 1558 opinions and tendencies varied so widely that during this initial period, even more than in our day, the much praised and much maligned Anglican comprehensiveness reigned supreme.

Cranmer had spent a good part of his life (1503–1530) at the University of Cambridge where, after his graduation as a doctor of theology, he lectured on that subject. From the very start he was a strong supporter of biblical humanism. From 1521 on he belonged to the reform-minded group which held its clandestine meetings at the White Horse Inn. He left Cambridge in 1530, was discovered by the king as a welcome counselor in his marital problems and was sent on several missions to the courts of German princes. In Germany he was completely won over to the teachings of Luther. He also entered into his second marriage in Germany; his first wife had died in or about 1525, only a year after their marriage. Cranmer must therefore be regarded as a man who had accepted the Lutheran reform principles from pure conviction.

He was not alone in this respect. In one form or another the reform principles were also hailed by Latimer, Ridley and Hooper. Latimer was bishop of Worcester from 1535 to 1539

213

during the reign of Henry VIII; Ridley was bishop of Rochester and London from 1547 to 1553 during the reign of Edward VI; Hooper was bishop of Gloucester and Worcester from 1551 to 1553, also during the reign of Edward VI. However the official attitude to the reform principles was for the time being rather unsettled. If Gardiner, bishop of Winchester, spent the last years of Edward's reign in prison because he had opposed the introduction of the Reformation in the Church of England, Cranmer, Latimer, Ridley and Hooper ended their lives at the stake because they refused, during the reign of Mary, to re-acknowledge the authority of the pope.

After preaching a sermon against Melanchthon Latimer was won over to the Reformation by Thomas Bilney in 1531. Latimer was one of the most famous preachers in England. His motto was abolish the sermon and nothing will be left. As bishop of Worcester he prescribed that all priests and religious should have a complete Bible in English; at the very least they should have the New Testament in English. He forbade preachers to cancel sermons in favor of any ecclesiastic ceremony whatsoever. The statue of Mary in the cathedral of Worcester he called "our great Sibyl." After having the statue stripped of its precious stones and other decorations he finally had it burned. In 1539 he resigned from his episcopal office in protest of the Six Articles of the king which gave protection to certain Catholic teachings and practices. In the final years of Henry VIII he was imprisoned in the Tower of London. During the reign of Edward VI he did not wish to resume his episcopal office since he wanted to dedicate himself completely to the office of preaching.

Ridley had studied at the Sorbonne and at the University of Louvain. He was gradually won over to the Reformation by a Reformation document about the Lord's supper and by discussions with Cranmer and the Calvinist-oriented Peter Martyr. In 1539 he preached against the Six Articles, was suspected of heresy, but was able to retain his ecclesiastic offices; shortly after

214

Henry's death he became bishop of Rochester and later of London.

Hooper, originally a Cistercian monk, was won over to the Reformation by the writings of Zwingli and Bullinger. Suspected of heresy he fled to the continent, stayed in Zurich from 1547 to 1549 and returned to England a convinced Zwinglian. He rejected the Lutheran concept of the last supper. For him the expression "to eat the body of Christ" meant nothing other than "to believe in Christ." After his return to England he became the court preacher of the lord protector and later was consecrated bishop of Gloucester. In the dioceses of Gloucester and Worcester he had the altars replaced by tables, decided that communion should be received while standing and refused to wear the liturgical vestments. He preached once or twice every day. In a certain sense therefore he must be considered a precursor of the free churches rather than of Anglicanism as finally formulated under Elizabeth I.

From what has been said thus far about the time of Henry's reign it is clear that even after 1533 the development of Anglicanism along Reformation lines was accompanied by much hesitation. The pope's name was removed from liturgical books in 1535. In 1536 approval was given to distribute Coverdale's English translation of the Bible. In the name of the king the convocations of Canterbury composed and promulgated the Ten Articles. These were based on the Augsburg Confession and were divided into five doctrinal and five practical articles. The early Christian creeds, the sacraments of baptism, penance and the eucharist were accepted, as also were the teachings of justification by faith alone and sacred Scripture as the ultimate norm of revealed truth. Many ceremonies and abuses were abolished. In 1537 the *Bishop's Book* was published by order of the king: *The Institution of a Christian Man,* a concise doctrine of faith that elucidated the Ten Articles. A revision of the English translation of the Bible was completed in 1538. This first authorized publication of the Bible was called the Great Bible. It was the only one from which readings could be presented during religious exercises and also the only one which was to be placed on an easily noticeable lectern in the church. Although the mass continued to be offered in Latin the use of the English language was promoted as much as possible. The veneration of statues and the use of candles were abolished. Those monasteries still in existence were finally closed in 1539.

The king's reaction to all this became particularly noticeable in the increasing number of processes against heretics and in the Six Articles of 1539, also in the *King's Book* of 1543. The Six Articles concerned transubstantiation, the reception of communion under one species, the celibacy of the priesthood, religious vows, private masses and oral confession. The purpose was to set certain bounds on the further implementation of the Reformation. The *King's Book* of 1543 replaced the *Bishop's Book* of 1537 and explained the teaching of the church with a more Catholic slant.

In 1544 the Latin litanies were replaced by the English litanies composed by Cranmer. These were soon to be incorporated into the *Book of Common Prayer.*

Thus we have reached the eve of the first definite attempt at a complete implementation of the Reformation in the Church of England.

Henry VIII died on Jan. 28, 1547. In his last will and testament he had appointed his son Edward, born in 1537 from his marriage with Jane Seymour, as his successor under the guardianship of an executive council of sixteen members. To this council also belonged the uncle of the new king and on this occasion he received the title of Duke of Somerset. The uncle immediately constituted himself president of the council and within a few weeks took sole supremacy for himself as lord protector of England, contrary to the obvious intention of Henry's last will and testament. A convinced Protestant he was particularly attached to the Calvinist teachings, except in questions concerning the relation between church and state. He considered himself and his council to have full competency in ecclesiastic matters and regarded Cranmer and the other bishops as instruments to enforce his will. The bishops Gardiner of Winchester and Bonner of London denied however that the prerogative of royal supremacy could be handed on to the council. Their protests only resulted in their incarceration. But neither was Somerset able to maintain his position. He was outflanked, accused of treason and finally done away with by Warwick, duke of Northumberland, who succeeded him after his execution early in 1552. Warwick had no personal religious convictions but continued on the course of the Reformation for political reasons.

In 1547 immediate and drastic measures were taken to enforce the Reformation in the Church of England. For this purpose official preachers were appointed to preach against the practice of Lenten fasting, against the sacraments, against the veneration of the saints and their images. At the request of the council Cranmer composed *The First Book of Homilies* for the use of the parish clergy. Its purpose was to prevent what was called "free" preaching. The council suspended all bishops from exercising their power until a general visitation of the churches could ensure the execution of all the abolition decrees. The result of this visitation was that a number of suspected bishops were replaced by reform-minded bishops. There was a violent outbreak of vandalism when all art treasures which promoted or were reminiscent of Roman superstitions were removed from the churches.

In 1548 all blessings and other solemnities of Candlemas, Ash Wednesday, Palm Sunday, Holy Thursday, Good Friday and Holy Saturday were abolished. On Easter Sunday communion was to be distributed under species of both bread and wine in all churches. An English modification of the communion service composed by the Lutheran archbishop of Cologne, Hermann von Wied, was introduced.

The year 1549 also saw the introduction of a complete vernacular liturgy according to the first draft of the *Book of Com-*

217

mon Prayer, the official Anglican church book. By an Act of Uniformity all other ecclesiastic ceremonies were prohibited under pain of heavy fines and possible imprisonment and the use of the *Book of Common Prayer* was made obligatory. The introduction of this liturgical book implied the abolition of the sacrifice of the mass. That this was intended appears from the fact that the altars were destroyed and replaced by tables.

In 1550 the Latin pontifical, containing the rite of ordinations, was abolished. It was replaced by an English order of service for the ordination of bishops, priests and deacons according to the data of Scripture. Most of the Roman customs and usages were done away with. The new formula for ordination retains the historical and juridical apostolic succession but precludes on some important points a dogmatic and theological interpretation in the Roman Catholic sense.

Meanwhile, for lack of English theologians in sufficient number, Cranmer had begun to make abundant use of the advice of reformers like Calvin and Bullinger, as well as the effective assistance of theologians and preachers who had settled in England at Cranmer's invitation. Some of these were Bucer, Peter Martyr (Vermigli), à Lasco and Mikron (Martin Klein), natives of Alsace, Italy, Poland and The Netherlands (Ghent) respectively. In 1549 Bucer was appointed professor of theology at Cambridge, Peter Martyr at Oxford. Also in 1549 à Lasco organized a community of refugees in London for which Mikron served as preacher in 1550. Calvin's future collaborator John Knox, also reformer of Scotland, was court preacher in London from 1551 to 1553. None of these theologians was a pure Calvinist though each inclined toward Calvinism. Both Mikron and Peter Martyr had received their Reformation training in Zurich and à Lasco had also begun as a Zwinglian.

All these advisers made their own contributions to the further development of ecclesiastic and liturgical reforms. In particular they insisted on and greatly influenced a revision of the *Book of Common Prayer*. The revised *Book of Common Prayer* replaced the old one in 1552 by a new Act of Uniformity.

Considering the pronounced Swiss-Reformed character of this liturgy it is all the more remarkable that the Forty-two Articles (later reduced to thirty-nine), published in 1553 as a summary of Anglican teaching, is not based on Reformed teaching but on the Lutheran Augsburg Confession and on the writings of Luther and Melanchthon. All this indicates that in setting its provisional course the Church of England availed itself of the most diverse sources of the Reformation.

It is of course incorrect to say that the reform under Edward VI was enforced from without and that it had no antecedents in the preceding period. But neither is it correct to say that this Reformation was only of a passing nature and that it did not truly and permanently determine the character of Anglicanism.

From a Catholic point of view the drastic measures of Cranmer, the lord protector with his council and the parliament under Edward VI left the original Catholic Church in England in ruins. After the brief Catholic reaction in the reign of Mary Tudor (1553–1558), which we will pass over in silence, the Anglican Church of England would finally see its definitive formation. To this day its foundations are in essence typically Reformational.

The Book of Common Prayer

The *Book of Common Prayer* is, together with the Thirty-nine Articles, the most important source for a proper understanding of Anglicanism. The edition still flourishing in the Church of England dates from the year 1662. It is the fruit of the restoration after the Presbyterian-Congregationalist interval (1645–1660) which in the life of the Church of England was a typical counterpart to the Catholic interlude under Mary Tudor (1553–1558). The *Book of Common Prayer* was revised and ecumenically enriched in 1928 but because it was vetoed by the British parliament it has not gained a legal status.

The *Book of Common Prayer* or Prayer Book has gone through four editions, in 1549, 1552, 1559 and 1662. The first edition was only a provisional draft and was considerably changed under the influence of the Reformation. The revision of 1559, completed early in the reign of Elizabeth I, was practically canceled in 1662. In purpose and content the book of 1662 fairly well agrees with that of 1552. In essence and principle it is a Reformation book, differing only in minor points from the more extreme liturgical books of the Reformation.

In the composition of the *Book of Common Prayer* the intention was to apply the Reformation principles to the pre-Reformation Latin liturgy. Its contents are certainly Reformational. This is especially clear when they are compared with the contents of the missal, the breviary, the ritual and the pontifical. The drastic simplifications, the omission of numerous texts and prayers, the abolition of practically all ceremonial actions and the recasting of the mass into a communion liturgy all reflect Reformation principles. If there are any Catholic elements in the Anglican liturgy they have been take from the original liturgy in the conviction that they could be preserved since they were not contrary to the principles of the Reformation. Apart from some very rare exceptions, for example the blessing of baptismal water before the administration of baptism, there is no reason to consider the elements that were taken over as *per se* non-Reformational.

Cause for debate is the question of how the Lord's supper is to be understood according to the text of the *Book of Common Prayer*. This question can be properly asked and answered only if the text of the liturgy is explained in the light of the sermons and writings of those who composed it. If this is done one must necessarily conclude that historically speaking the Anglican liturgy is perfectly in agreement with Reformation principles. The composers of the holy communion service carefully avoided any signs in their liturgy of the controversy on the Lord's supper among the reformers themselves. They did not opt for any particular theory but honored the reality of the Lord's supper as a sacrament instituted by Christ.

The question whether the Anglican liturgy presupposes the real presence of Christ in the Lord's supper can be answered in the affirmative only with the express reservation that nothing binding was taught about the manner of this presence. There are in the Anglican churches the most diverse opinions about the way in which this is to be explained. In any case it is true that the composers of the *Book of Common Prayer* understood this presence according to Reformation principles, in the same manner the presence and operation of Christ is understood by the Lutheran churches as well as by most of the Reformed churches.

The well known black rubric proves clearly that the Anglican custom of receiving communion while kneeling down should not be interpreted in a Catholic sense. The black rubric is the only rubric in the *Book of Common Prayer* which according to law must be printed in black instead of red, and even then a different size type is to be used. Anglo-Catholics are of the opinion that not much importance should be attached to this rubric since it was hurriedly added to the 1552 edition after it had received the approbation of parliament. This posthumous addition was the result of the fear that had seized young King Edward while he heard John Knox declare in a sermon that kneeling down was a proof of idolatry. However if the rubric was contrary to Anglican teaching it would certainly have been left out in the revision of 1662. Catholics may have much sympathy for the catholicizing convictions of Anglo-Catholic Anglicans but they cannot have much respect for the arbitrary and irresponsible manner in which they try to reason away definite historical facts and official data in defense of their faith. For, in order to avoid incorrect interpretations of the precept to receive communion while kneeling down, the black rubric states emphatically "that thereby no adoration is intended or ought to be done, either unto the

221

Sacramental Bread or Wine there bodily received, or unto any Corporal Presence of Christ's natural Flesh and Blood. For the Sacramental Bread and Wine remain still in their very natural substances, and therefore may not be adored (for that were Idolatry, to be abhorred of all faithful Christians)."

The Thirty-nine Articles also expressly excludes acceptance of the Catholic teaching on transubstantiation and the sacrifice of the mass, as well as the Catholic devotions and practices based on these teachings. Similarly the Anglican ordination ceremony excludes the interpretation that this rite gives to the ordained priest the power to offer the sacrifice of the mass. When in 1896 Pope Leo XIII declared Anglican orders invalid this action was not opportunism but was based on objective reality. Where irrefutable truths and facts are concerned the Catholic Church has never been guided by opportunism in its judgments. The Roman-oriented group among the Anglo-Catholics—who prefer to speak of holy mass instead of holy communion or holy eucharist—interpret the *Book of Common Prayer* in this respect in flagrant contradiction of the obvious intention of the text and the rubrics of the liturgy, as well as of the intention of the composers.

Obviously this is meant neither as an attack on Anglo-Catholicism as such nor on Anglicanism. It is strictly a matter of clarifying the situation as it really is. From the point of view of the Reformation the *Book of Common Prayer* must be considered both in form and content as an achievement that has never been equaled. The Anglican churches were the only ones to succeed in transforming the pre-Reformation Catholic liturgy into a specifically Reformation liturgy in a professional and responsible manner.

The complete title of the *Book of Common Prayer* reads: *The Book of Common Prayer and Administration of the Sacraments and Other Rites and Ceremonies of the Church of England.* This means that it is a matter of the liturgy of the entire Church of Christ (the "catholic" or "universal" Church) as celebrated in the Church of England in the vernacular and according to its own customs. This is an undeniable expression of a catholic awareness in the sense of a continuity with all Christianity. It is the same awareness that leads the Reformed churches to consider themselves not new churches founded at the time of the Reformation but the original church founded by Christ, only reformed.

In their application of the principles of the Reformation to the liturgy of the Church the composers of the *Book of Common Prayer* worked according to the following procedure. Taking the pre-Reformation Latin liturgical books they translated them into the vernacular and collated them in one book. In doing this they purged and simplified the original books to a considerable extent. All texts, prayers and actions which in their opinion were contrary to the criteria of the Reformation were omitted. This applied also to songs, hymns and lessons not contained in sacred Scripture, except for the early Christian *Te Deum* and what were called the lesser and greater doxologies or *Gloria Patri* and *Gloria in Excelsis*. Any saint not mentioned in the New Testament was removed from the calendar. Prayers addressed to God imploring the intercession of the saints and prayers for the dead were omitted. The liturgy of the eucharist was reshaped in such a way that it was clearly transformed into a communion service minus the sacrifice of the mass. This service is accordingly called holy communion, or the Lord's supper. Moreover for practical reasons the liturgy was considerably simplified and abbreviated in order to suit the needs of the people. The hours of the breviary were limited to a morning and an evening prayer. The psalms, instead of being divided over a week's period, were divided over a month; they are sung in the biblical sequence. Two lessons occur in both the morning and the evening prayer: one from the Old Testament and one from the New. These were selected in such a way as to have the entire Old Testament read once a year and the entire New Testament twice a year. In no other Reformed church does the reading of the Bible occupy such a prominent place. In the fore-mass, now called the ante-communion service, the original orations, epistles and gospels for Sundays and feast days were incorporated with little change. But all the changeable parts of the original mass liturgy (introit, gradual, alleluia verse, tract, offertory and communion prayer) were omitted.

The communion service is usually held in connection with the morning and the evening prayer. This used to take place only a few times during the year but now occurs more frequently as a result of Anglo-Catholic influence. The greater part of the congregation used to leave the church after the morning or evening prayer so that only the communicants attended the celebration of the eucharistic service. This is still true in most places. Even more than the morning or evening prayer the communion service is celebrated with the greatest possible simplicity. Anything that might possibly add lustre to the service, such as vestments, assistant priests, incense, etc. was abolished. All services are read slowly, clearly and audibly. They are followed word for word, consciously and with great attention, as in all Protestant churches. If a person has a thorough knowledge of both the Roman Catholic and the Anglican religious services and does not judge by superficial impressions he will certainly not doubt the Reformation character of the *Book of Common Prayer*. This applies also to its other sections: the fixed prayers, the English litanies, the baptismal services, the minor catechism, confirmation, the marriage service, the service for the sick, burial and the penitential service on Ash Wednesday. Particularly is the latter service a typical example of the replacement of a Roman ceremony with a service of distinct Reformation character. After the Book of Psalms we find Forms of Prayer to be used at sea, the service for the Making, Ordaining and Consecrating of Bishops, Priests and Deacons, a service for the annual celebration on which His Majesty began his happy reign, and the Articles of Religion.

Finally it must be observed that each of the autonomous

Anglican churches has its own *Book of Common Prayer,* constructed in the same way as that of the Church of England but also showing distinct personal marks. The most catholic and ecumenical is the revised *Scottish Prayer Book* of 1929.

The stabilization of Anglicanism

The execution of Cranmer in 1556 and the cruel scenes of the final years of Mary's reign in various parts of England when about three hundred Anglicans were executed had aroused latent anti-Roman feelings within a large part of the English population. A general rising was prevented only by the death of Queen Mary on Nov. 17, 1558, the same day that Cardinal Reginald Pole, archbishop of Canterbury, died. Elizabeth, Henry VIII's disinherited daughter from his marriage to Anne Boleyn, was proclaimed successor to the throne by Nicolas Heath, lord chancellor and archbishop of York.

Her accession to the throne on Jan. 15, 1559 was the great turning point in England's history. Half a century of continual unrest and mismanagement caused by royal advisers and "protectors" who were out for nothing but honor, self-promotion and wealth had brought the country to the brink of disaster. However beginning with Elizabeth's reign the country came back to life and began to develop steadily. Not only did English literature reach its zenith in the works of Shakespeare but the increasing trade and prosperity were also laying the foundation for the nineteenth century hegemony of England in world commerce, and for the rise and expansion of the British empire.

From a religious point of view the reign of Elizabeth (1559–1603) meant the stabilization of Anglicanism. This is generally referred to as the Elizabethan settlement. The Church of England, having become the established church, was referred to as the establishment.

In the relations between church and state the title of supreme head, which Henry VIII had appropriated to himself, was after months of discussions and against the wishes of the queen changed to supreme governor. The Supremacy Act of April 29, 1559 attributed to the ruler of the realm the power of supreme governor in matters ecclesiastic as well as temporal. On the same day parliament passed a law, by a majority of only three votes, abolishing the mass. A new Act of Uniformity, on June 24, 1559, made the *Book of Common Prayer* of 1552 obligatory, with only a few changes having been made.

Of the sixteen bishops who were still living only one took the oath as prescribed by the Act of Supremacy. The other fifteen bishops were removed from office and deprived of their liberty in one manner or another; one escaped; five died before the end of the year. Elizabeth appointed Matthew Parker, the former court chaplain of her mother, the new archbishop of Canterbury. He was "ordained" bishop on Dec. 17, 1559 in the chapel of Lambeth Palace according to the ordinal of the *Book of Common Prayer*. The ordination was performed by four bishops, two of whom had been ordained bishops under Henry VIII according to the Catholic rite. During the ordination one of the bishops wore a cope, two were vested in surplices and one in a black gown. A few days after his ordination Parker consecrated a number of new bishops for the vacant episcopal sees. Parker died in 1575, was succeeded by the then archbishop of York, Edmund Grindal, who was succeeded in turn by John Whitgift after his death in 1583.

Revision of Cranmer's Articles of Religion met with great difficulties both in parliament and with the queen, first in the convocation of 1563 and later in 1566. The number of articles was reduced from forty-two to thirty-nine. Finally, after a last revision in which Jewel played the main role, the text was settled on and accepted in 1571.

In 1570 Queen Elizabeth was excommunicated and deprived of her unlawful throne. Anyone who had taken the oath of allegiance to her was absolved from his oath: "We now by these letters release them and deprive the said Elizabeth of her pretended right to the throne, and every other right whatever aforesaid: We command all and singular the nobles, the people subject to her and others aforesaid, never to venture to obey her monitions, mandates, and laws" (English translation of the Bull of Excommunication *Regnans in Excelsis* in Hughes' *The Reformation in England*, 3, 418–20).

The break between England and Rome had now become final and irreparable. The queen as well as the populace began to see Rome as an enemy and threat. Ultimately Elizabeth decided to persecute her opponents. In the second half of her reign she executed one hundred and twenty-three priests and sixty laymen who either secretly or in some other manner had practiced the Catholic faith by celebrating mass or exercising other priestly functions or by cooperating as laymen.

Anglicanism owes its independent character to a battle on two fronts: one against what it held to be Roman aberrations in teaching and practice; the other against what it held to be puritanical deformations of the Reformation principles and a puritanical misunderstanding of the original intentions of the reformers.

The influence of the Reformation had increased in power because many of the Anglican preachers, clergy and theologians had fled to the continent (Frankfurt, Strasburg, Zurich and Geneva) during the reign of Queen Mary. Even at that time the English community of refugees in Frankfurt was divided into those who were in favor of the Prayer Book, and those who were against it, i.e. followers of Cox and followers of Knox. After his return to England Cox became the Anglican bishop of Ely. Knox later became the Calvinist reformer of Scotland. When the exiles returned in 1559 their Reformation convictions had been strengthened. Those who were appointed to leading offices in the life of the church regularly tried to obtain advice from the reformers of the continent, particularly Bullinger. The influence of Zurich on the stabilization of Anglicanism was greater than that of Geneva for it was precisely the nonconformists and puritans who appealed to Calvin and Beza, while the Anglicans appealed to the churches of Zurich and Berne.

In no other country did the stabilization of the reform movement have to take account of so many contradictory factors as in England. Nor did any other country experience so many varying influences. That in this web of opinions and tendencies the Church of England did not lose its way was due to the moderation of its leaders. They strove, according to the preface of the *Book of Common Prayer,* "to keep the mean between two extremes, of too much stiffness in refusing and of too much easiness in admitting any variations."

In this connection one usually speaks of the *via media* of Anglicanism. This is alright provided the *via media* is not looked upon as a middle path between the Catholic Church and the Reformation. For in principle Anglicanism is entirely on the side of the Reformation. The *via media* refers to the method of reform. It is a matter of avoiding extremes, such as Puritanism. The *via media* means that only those teachings and practices of Romanism were rejected which the Reformation considered contrary to the testimony of sacred Scripture. At the same time many elements were preserved which puritanism had unjustly rejected because of an exaggerated one-sidedness and extremism.

The Anglican Reformation did not have a primarily doctrinal character but a liturgical one. Most of its attention was given to the transformation of the Catholic liturgy into a liturgy with a biblical and Reformational basis as contained in the *Book of Common Prayer,* which is truly the most impressive creation of the Anglican Reformation. It operated with great caution on the subject of doctrine. In its composition of the catechism it limited itself to what was absolutely necessary. The Anglican Reformation did not want to bind itself to an extensive, detailed confession since it did not want to add to or take away from the undivided Church of the first centuries.

In this respect the Elizabethan settlement, the final formulation under Elizabeth, built on Cranmer's Reformation under

Edward VI. The *Book of Common Prayer* of 1559 was practically identical to that of 1552. The only changes consisted in the omission of the black rubric (reintroduced in the Prayer Book of 1662), the addition of a table of Old and New Testament lessons for Sundays and feast days, the insertion of a new rubric concerning ecclesiastic vestments (which, except by later Anglo-Catholics, was never applied) and some incidental changes in the litany. The most important change was the expansion of the formulas for the distribution of communion and for the giving of a blessing. From the Anglican point of view these formulas are typically ecumenical. Still used in the Anglican churches they derive from a combination of the original Catholic formula and the new Reformation formula as listed in the Prayer Books of 1549 and 1552.

The distribution of communion (under both species) takes place with the words: "The Body (Blood) of our Lord Jesus Christ, which was given for thee, preserve thy body and soul unto everlasting life. Take and eat (drink) this in remembrance that Christ died for thee (that Christ's blood was shed for thee), and feed on him in thy heart with thanksgiving." When the cup is presented the latter phrase is replaced by "and be thankful."

Out of reverence for the mystery and an awareness of the insufficiency of human formulations Anglicanism has never taken part in the controversies on the Lord's supper which occurred in other churches. It did however reject in principle the teaching on transubstantiation (article 28 of the articles of religion; black rubric), but it did not want to detract from what it held to be the original Catholic belief concerning the holy eucharist.

A combination like the above is also found in the words which accompany the blessing at the end of the communion service: "The peace of God, which passeth all understanding, keep your hearts and minds in the knowledge and love of God, and of his Son Jesus Christ our Lord: And the blessing of God

Almighty, the Father, the Son, and the Holy Ghost, be amongst you and remain with you always. Amen." The first part has been taken from the Lutheran liturgy; the second half from the Catholic liturgy. The morning and evening prayer on the other hand is concluded with the Pauline blessing, commonly used in Reformed churches: "The grace of our Lord Jesus Christ, and the love of God, and the fellowship of the Holy Ghost, be with us all evermore. Amen."

This synthesis of liturgical elements from the most diverse churches is symptomatic of Anglicanism in general. In this synthesis Anglicanism is not conscious of jeopardizing truth. Rather it is convinced in principle that in this way it does full justice to the whole content of revelation while at the same time keeping in line with sacred Scripture.

Sacred Scripture is acknowledged to be the only absolute norm of faith and morals. However in its explanation and application of the Bible Anglicanism attaches great—though relative—value to the Catholic tradition of Christian antiquity and to the consensus of the Church fathers. It is convinced that its attitude in this connection is in perfect agreement with the original intentions of the reformers. To the Anglican a Roman concept of tradition, as distinct from the Anglican concept, does not exist.

It has already been shown that the final establishment of the Church of England as the Anglican state church in a juridical sense dates from the reign of Queen Elizabeth. With the increasing tension between the Anglicans who accepted the establishment and the puritans who objected to conforming to the legally defined situation, it became more and more necessary to give the Anglican Reformation a theological basis. This was done in the second half of the reign of Elizabeth, mainly by Whitgift, Hooker and Jewel, the founders of classical Anglican theology. While they shared with the puritans the common basis of the sixteenth century Reformation they created, in reaction to puritanism, their own Anglican theology. Without a thorough study of the writings of these theologians it is impossible to form a correct notion of the quite personal character of Anglicanism.

The complete works of Richard Hooker were republished in 1836 by John Keble, one of the three principal leaders of the Oxford movement. Hooker's main work, *Of the Laws of Ecclesiastical Polity,* also appears in the popular Everyman's Library. The complete works of Whitgift and Jewel were, like the correspondence of Matthew Parker (first Elizabethan archbishop of Canterbury), republished by the Parker Society and appeared in Oxford around 1850.

For understandable reasons Anglo-Catholicism put the sixteenth century Tudor theologians in the shadow of the seventeenth century Stuart theologians, usually referred to as the Caroline divines, after the reigns of Charles I (1625–1649) and Charles II (1660–1685).

An extensive and excellent anthology of the writings of the latter theologians is that by More and Cross published in 1935 by the Society for Promoting Christian Knowledge (SPCK) under the title *Anglicanism.* It appears from the lengthy introduction that the composers of this edition expressly intended to interpret Anglicanism from the point of view of Anglo-Catholicism.

From a comparison of the writings of the Tudor and Stuart theologians with one another as well as with those of the sixteenth century reformers, with the spirit and content of the *Book of Common Prayer* and with the Thirty-nine Articles, one must agree with the following conclusion of Hugh F. Woodhouse in his extremely incisive study of *The Doctrine of the Church in Anglican Theology 1547–1603,* published in 1954 by the SPCK at the request of the Church Historical Society:

It is right to respect and revere the Caroline divines, but in actual fact they were either adding to, changing, or destroying the first story of a house already built. They were not pioneers of post-Reformation Angelican thought; they were exponents thereof; a second generation. This is not universally recognized. It has been said that documents before 1662 are "not authoritative"—a statement doubtful in itself. However, in this thesis we have not been quoting documents; Anglican fathers of the sixteenth century have been our study and they were writers loyal to the ethos of their Church, possessing knowledge and ability. . . . Those therefore who seek the genealogy and affinity of the Church of England must make a study of the Tudor Anglican divines (186–187).

The above citation should suffice to show how in our own day—though usually hidden to the eyes of a distant observer—a battle goes on within the Anglican churches about a renewed and purified understanding of the true nature and of the real, original and most profound essence of Anglicanism. We must however agree with the Anglo-Catholics that the Tudor theologians should not be considered as the only representatives of pure Anglicanism. Anglicanism has never really come to a complete rest; it is still in process. This is precisely one of its most characteristic marks. Perhaps never before in history has anything been established with so little permanence as the Anglican establishment under Elizabeth I.

Characteristic features and principles of Anglicanism

In the preceding sections of this chapter passing mention has been made of some of the distinguishing features by which Anglicanism differs from other forms of Christianity. A summary of these distinguishing features gives us the following picture of Anglicanism.

First, although of all the autonomous Anglican churches the Church of England is the only state church, Anglicanism also has a distinctly national character in the other churches. Anglicanism bears the clear stamp of a definite people in language, mentality and culture. With some exceptions in missionary countries English is the language of the liturgy. It is also the official language of the Anglican communion of churches. In mentality, atmosphere and culture Anglicanism everywhere and at all times betrays its English origin. It gives an impression of quiet, orderliness, control and importance. It is a Christianity of the practical and sound mind. It leaves each person free in the practice of his faith as long as he does not impose his personal views or those of his group on the entire church. The principal reason for the battle against puritanism lay in the exclusivism and absolutism of the puritans.

Secondly, Anglicanism has a pronounced liturgical character. It is the liturgy of the *Book of Common Prayer,* and not a commonly accepted confession, which forms the principal bond uniting all Anglicans within one communion of churches. The nonconformists were not so much Englishmen who could not agree with certain Anglican confessional writings but Englishmen who objected to the liturgy and the church ordinance.

It is because of the liturgical character of Anglicanism that Anglicans in the practice of their religion show few anthropocentric inclinations. They do not go to church for their own sake, to be esthetically touched or to be edified. Their common purpose is to practice the daily prayer, to listen to Scripture and to worship God. An English churchgoer has motives and criteria for religious services quite different from those of Protestant churchgoers in other countries.

Thirdly, Anglicanism has a remarkably biblical character. In few Christian churches are the Old and the New Testament read to the congregation with so much care and reverence as in the Anglican church. An Anglican does not order his life according to a moral system but according to the example of the biblical witnesses of faith of the Old and New Testaments. Particularly in evangelic Anglican circles the criterion in every situation is the answer to the question: what would Jesus do? The practical, moral and religious life of every day is a "walking in his steps." Religious life has an ascetico-mystical character. But an Anglican does not like to speak of his religious experience nor does he like to theorize or speculate about religious matters. The biblical piety of Anglicanism, with its sense of antiquity, sobriety

233

and order and its respect for erudition and culture, still shows a close connection with the biblical humanism in which the Reformation is rooted.

Fourthly, Anglicanism has a distinctly ecumenical character. This trait is based on an inner structure and tendency which, as it were, automatically stimulates ecumenical activity. We have indicated how Anglicanism from its very beginning and during its development experienced influences of the most diverse origins. In this process Anglicanism displayed a great capacity for assimilation and integration. Despite the fact that the state originally strove for uniformity and despite the fact that during the sixteenth, seventeenth and eighteenth centuries it took strict measures against nearly every movement that promoted nonconformity with the customs and institutions of the church, the adherents of the various movements always remained partly within the church. This is why Anglicanism, although outwardly uniform, developed within the widest possible comprehensiveness. There is scarcely a single form of Christianity which is not in one way or another found in the Anglican churches. Consequently Anglicanism offers, through its inner disposition and variety, points of contact for practically all Christian denominations in all possible expressions. It is quite incorrect and unjust however to say that the inherent ecumenical disposition is to be explained by a lack of principle. If Anglicanism gives this impression it is because there is question of "a lack of principle for the sake of principle."

Fifthly, Anglicanism has more an historical and practical rather than a theological and speculative character. It pays more attention to facts and events than to theological constructions and interpretations. It considers the latter as very human and therefore of very relative value when compared to the factual, objective data of revelation and the universal Christian tradition. The data of revelation have an historical character, the character of salvific events. These events—among others the institution of the sacraments of the Lord's supper and baptism, the foundation of the visible church on the first Pentecost and the expansion of the apostolic office instituted by Christ into the threefold office of bishop, priest and deacon—must be acknowledged and respected.

On the other hand Anglicanism tends to shy away from a too profound theological reflection. It leaves the facts as they are but at the same time leaves the greatest possible room for differences of opinion as regards the theological interpretation and the practical application of these facts. Only among the extreme groups, among the Anglo-Calvinists of the sixteenth century and among the Anglo-Catholics of the twentieth, has theology occupied a greater place than is usual in Anglicanism.

The scanty appreciation of theology is expressed in the formation of the Anglican clergy. Originally it was sufficient for the admission to the diaconate if the candidate had obtained a BA or MA degree. The prerequisites for these degrees do not include theology but only the historical, literary and philosophical branches of learning. For some time now the requirements have been changed. In preparation for the ecclesiastic office a candidate must now have at least a year's residence in a theological seminary, several years if he has not previously followed academic studies. Academic studies for the degrees of bachelor of divinity or doctor of divinity, after a master's degree has been obtained, may be pursued at the university but this is not necessary for the admission to the office. There are even bishops who have never officially studied theology. This is a disadvantage in that part of the Anglican clergy has but little and sometimes insufficient knowledge of the theological principles of Anglicanism. Most preachers build on the conventional viewpoints of the religious milieu in which they grew up, on common sense and on personal experience. This applies *a fortiori* to the Anglican lay people. Therefore someone who wants to become acquainted with Anglicanism should not let himself be guided by the information of lay people or the parish clergy, but should get in touch with specialists who dedicate themselves *ex professo* to a scientific study of Anglicanism.

The classical Anglican principles as they have been elaborated and defended by the leading theologians of the sixteenth century —Whitgift, Hooker and Jewel—differ from the Lutheran and Reformed principles in a formal rather than a material respect. As regards the Reformation vision of the gospel, conscience, the authority of Scripture, the nature and competencies of the church and the relation between church and state the Anglican theologians agree in principle with the Lutheran and Reformed theologians. The one important material difference is the Anglican conviction that the episcopal structure of the church extends as far back as Scripture and that it has its foundation in the clear testimony of sacred Scripture. According to the preface to the Anglican ordinal:

It is evident unto all men diligently reading holy Scripture and ancient Authors, that from the Apostles' time there have been these Orders of Ministers in Christ's Church: Bishops, Priests, and Deacons. Which offices were evermore had in such reverend estimation, that no man might presume to execute any of them, except he were first called, tried, examined, and known to have such qualities as are requisite for the same; and also by public Prayer, with Imposition of Hands, were approved and admitted thereunto by lawful Authority. And therefore, to the intent that these Orders may be continued, and reverently used and esteemed, in the Church of England: no man shall be accounted or taken to be a lawful Bishop, Priest, or Deacon, in the Church of England, or suffered to execute any of the said functions, except he be called, tried, examined, and admitted thereunto, according to the Form hereafter following, or has had formerly Episcopal Consecration or Ordination.

For the episcopal order Anglicanism appeals to its institution by Christ and the apostles which, on the basis of sacred Scripture and the Church fathers, cannot but be accepted as a fact. Facts cannot be argued away and Anglicanism wants to honor this truth. But what it certainly does not wish to do is to declare as binding any theological interpretation or further commentary by the church which is not clearly based on Scripture.

Here we touch on one of the most important principles of Anglicanism: the historical, that is, the nonjuridical, nontheological and nonspeculative approach to questions on which Christianity is divided. It is clear from the writings of the sixteenth century Anglican theologians that the facts which concern the church are not put on a level with the facts of salvation. With the latter stands or falls the entire work of salvation. Without Christ's work the church would not exist. The structure of the church belongs to the *bene esse* (the wellbeing) of the church, not to its very being, its *esse*. Anglicanism accepts and respects the facts concerning the wellbeing of the church and considers them as the best criteria for the institution of the church, but in typically Reformation manner it does not consider salvation and the distribution of grace dependent on them. Hence Anglican churches have never officially doubted the sacramental distribution of grace of the nonepiscopal churches of the Reformation. At a recent Lambeth conference the Anglican communion of churches even stated that the offices, sacraments and ministrations of these churches have evidently been blessed by God.

The official Anglican teaching on the historical episcopacy can therefore be summarized as follows:

The historical episcopacy is an evident and factual datum. Consequently Anglicanism does not see why the episcopacy should be abandoned. It belongs to the wellbeing of the Church. To the Reformation churches which have abandoned it it is a defect and a loss. However this defect does not mean that the offices and sacramental ministrations are not blessed by God. But since the historical episcopacy is, according to sacred Scripture and the customs of the ancient Church, a given fact an organic reunion between episcopal and nonepiscopal churches is impossible unless this fact is accepted by the entire reunited church. Any reunion whereby one or more of the churches should abandon this positive and actual fact would be a regression. The presbyterial church order is also a good although imperfect arrangement. If this imperfect order should be integrated into an episcopal church it would not only not be lost but would return to the originally intended perfect fullness of the office given to the church by Christ and the apostles.

The Anglican theologians of the second half of the sixteenth century were most closely related to the Reformed theologians, then to the Lutheran theologians, and only after this, by way of the Church fathers, to the oriental theologians. They respected Thomas Aquinas and the Counter-reformation theologian Bellarmine insofar as they were in keeping with Reformation principles. The papacy and the late medieval papal church was, in the most vigorous language, unanimously rejected by the Anglican theologians. In this respect they certainly did not yield to the Reformation theologians of the continent. The Church of England maintained official relations mostly with the churches of the Reformed type. At the synod of Dordrecht the Church of England was represented by the bishop of Llandaff. Relations with the Reformed churches were obviously based on the presupposition that these were sister churches. Neither in classical Anglican theology nor in the official attitude toward Lutheran and Reformed churches is there any indication that Anglicanism, because of its notion of the church, failed to consider the Reformation churches as true parts of the catholic Church founded by Christ on earth.

Besides the difference in church organization there was another important point on which Anglicanism differed from Calvinism from the very beginning. This concerned the government of the church, the exercise of ecclesiastic discipline and the relation between church and state. However this difference does not touch on the integrity of the Reformation principles of Anglicanism since this same difference also existed in Switzerland among the Reformed churches themselves.

In the seventeenth century Anglican theology begins to shift from the Calvinist to the Arminian teaching on predestination, man's free will, the irresistibility of grace and the perseverance of the saints. In imitation of Calvin Anglicanism has always shied away from a too rationalistic and detailed teaching on predestination and from a pietistic-puritanical attempt to conclude, from religious experience or visible signs, whether or not this or that person is predestined.

Apart from the above-mentioned differences there are no other serious material differences between Anglican and Reformed teaching and theology. Consequently when the differences that formed the basis of the struggle between Anglicanism and puritanism are considered it appears from the sermons and writings of the sixteenth century theologians that these differences were of a formal nature. The principal reason why the Anglicans rejected certain puritan teachings and reforms was not so much because they had a different opinion; rather their objections were mostly directed against the attitude, method and mentality of the puritans. According to the Anglicans the puritans attributed too much authority to a human exegesis and theology, quite arbitrarily left certain scriptural data out of consideration and gave to other data a dubious explanation which, without further ado, was identified with the pure word of God. The Anglicans also found that the detailed manner whereby the puritans dealt with minor points was creating unnecessary controversies that led to an undermining of the unity of faith.

Against the puritan theologians the Anglican theologians contended that while Scripture actually gave some general directives to questions of an ecclesiastic and liturgical nature, it certainly did not contain detailed and binding percepts on such questions. Questions concerning these subjects would arise only gradually with the growth and expansion of the church and would have to be solved according to the best available human and historical insights. Thus the best criterion would be that church ordinances and liturgy should contain nothing that is clearly contrary to the intention of Scripture. The Anglicans were convinced that not only the doctrinal pronouncements of the councils of the fourth and fifth centuries and the writings of the Church fathers should be respected and left unchanged unless Scripture clearly required it, but that the same also held for the structure of the church and the liturgy as it had crystallized in the course of the first four centuries. The Anglican church ordinance and liturgy are the application and elaboration of this cautious and positive principle.

It must be said that in the field of church order and liturgy the Anglican theologians had a much more profound practical knowledge than did the puritans. The latter were not interested in historical research on church regulations and liturgy, for then they would only read those institutions, regulations and customs that could already be found literally in the New Testament.

The puritan objections against the *Book of Common Prayer* were based more on feeling and prejudice than on a knowledge of the facts. An outstanding example is the conflict which threatened to arise between the Church of England and Zurich. The church of Zurich, after taking into account a number of incorrect citations and interpretations submitted by the puritans, had handed down an unfavorable judgment on the contents of the Prayer Book. In a letter to Gualter, Cox the bishop of Ely complained about this premature judgment based on slander: "Would that someone of your piety had not so openly laid down a judgment without a correct understanding of the origin and development of the English Reformation." In his answer Gualter apologized, saying he was unaware that his puritan sources of information were capable of so distorting the facts. He confirmed the apology of Zurich by dedicating the first of his subsequent writings to the English bishops. This incident typifies the relations between the puritans and the Anglicans at that time. Cox's wish however is still quite applicable when it comes to presenting and judging Anglicanism.

Anglicans regarded puritanism as an insufficiently motivated and highly redoubtable disruption of the church. Anglican theologians frequently opine that the puritans went from one extreme (the Roman) to the other.

The main Anglican objection against the puritans was, even more than against their teachings as such, directed against their attempts to impose on others their vision of the institutions, authority and discipline of the church as the only vision in harmony with sacred Scripture, and that the church was based not on human but on divine authority. The Anglicans saw in this traces of a regression to the Roman concept of authority, since they taught that neither a church ordinance nor the forms of liturgy were based on divine (scriptural) authority. According to Whitgift and the founders of the establishment the church ordinance and the liturgy belonged to those matters which, at the order of the prince, the magistrate or possibly the representatives of the people, should be arranged in accordance with general Christian practice, the wellbeing of the people and the interest of the state.

Anglicanism today still leaves a generous margin of freedom in this respect and, as has been clearly demonstrated in recent years, it is quite open to change, expansion and adaption. In this regard however Catholics often display just as poor an insight into Anglicanism as do Lutheran and Reformed Christians.

From uniformity to comprehensiveness

The Anglican Reformation had set as its aim a new religious unity of the entire English people within one church and with one common form of religious service based on one common form of belief.

After each revision the *Book of Common Prayer* was by an Act of Uniformity made obligatory as the only admissible form of religious service. Sanctions were also laid down for any transgressions of this rule or for purposely avoiding Anglican church services.

Until the end of the eighteenth century Catholics as well as nonconformists and other dissenters were prosecuted for transgressing the Act of Uniformity. But although the state officially upheld the statute of uniformity these attempts to preserve unity and uniformity were in reality not very successful, neither in general nor as regarded the religious unity of the people. Nor, for that matter, as regarded unity within the Church of England.

Under the enforced exterior uniformity of the establishment, the product of the Elizabethan settlement, tensions among the various groups within the church increased rather than decreased after the death of Queen Elizabeth in 1603.

It may be said that the queen, supported by Whitgift and most of the bishops, gained by the establishment a victory over the puritan resistance movement. But under James I (1603–1625) and Charles I (1625–1649) this movement gradually began to gain the approval of the people, of part of the clergy and even of some bishops. Anglicanism enjoyed the protection of the king, puritanism the representation of the people. Against the limited capacities of the Stuart kings stood the growing prestige and influence of the House of Commons. Carpenter states that "if Henry VIII taught the House of Commons to work under the ruler, and Elizabeth to work with the ruler, under the Stuarts it employed the higher respect it now enjoyed and its perfected routine to work against the ruler." The more the king, in collaboration with the archbishop of Canterbury, endeavored to harmonize the church interior, the use of liturgical vestments and the church service with the prescriptions of the *Book of Common Prayer* the more the resistance against it grew within the bosom of the church people, and therefore within the House of Commons.

Meanwhile Anglican theology was inclining more and more to the principle of a *via media* between Romanism and Protestantism. The Caroline divines regarded the catholicity of the Church of England as its most important attribute and its Protestantism as something incidental and passing, particularly

242

if it deviated from the teaching, institutions and customs of the undivided Church of the first few centuries. They read and interpreted sacred Scripture not in the light of the Reformation but in that of the Church fathers. Moreover in the controversies between the Calvinists and Arminians they sided with the latter. Just as the puritans were unable to distinguish between catholic and Catholic Christianity so also did the Caroline divines risk losing sight of the distinction between Reformation and second generation Protestantism.

From a theological point of view the period of the Caroline divines can be termed the most fruitful period in the history of Anglicanism, both because of the number of native theological writings and because of the flourishing of religious exercises. In connection with the former mention must be made particularly of the *Preces Privatae* (Private Prayers) by Andrewes and the *Rule and Exercises of Holy Living* by Jeremy Taylor. These two devotional books went through numerous editions and are to this day still used for spiritual reading.

A remarkable figure among the Caroline divines was William Chillingworth (1602–1644). He had become a Catholic in 1629 and had attended the Jesuit college at Douai to study for the priesthood. He returned to England in 1631 and promptly returned to the Anglican Church. He wrote a book on *The Religion of Protestants, a Safe Way to Salvation* 1637.

The best known representative of the Caroline divines is William Laud, archbishop of Canterbury from 1633 to 1645. A very learned man he is also the greatest prelate the Church of England has produced since the Reformation. He firmly rejected Roman Catholicism as a "gross superstition" but also called the Calvinist doctrine of predestination "an idea which I abhor from the depths of my soul. For it makes God, the God of all mercy, into the most cruel and unreasonable tyrant of the world."

The Caroline divines derived more from the heritage of the Reformation, were more anti-Roman and differed less in matters of principle from the Tudor theologians than was suggested in

243

later times. The increasing tension between Anglicans and puritans, which around the middle of the seventeenth century was to result in a serious eruption, was partly based on prejudice, shortsightedness and misunderstanding. When the eruption finally came Anglicanism almost suffered a complete and permanent defeat.

From 1640 to 1660 England was for all practical purposes governed by the Long Parliament, in which the puritans predominated. In 1640 occurred the sudden explosion of the "Protestant underworld." Numerous churches were destroyed; Anglican religious services were frequently disturbed; in spite of uniformity numerous puritan conventicles arose in London and elsewhere. As a result a general collapse of ecclesiastic life ensued. In 1641 twelve bishops were imprisoned by order of parliament; in 1643 parliament appointed a commission to remove all sculpture and stained glass windows in churches; in 1645 the *Book of Common Prayer* was abolished as a papist book and replaced by a puritan *Directorium;* in the same year Laud the archbishop of Canterbury was unjustly accused of popery and executed; in 1646 the Church of England was reorganized on a presbyterial basis; in 1647 the Calvinist-presbyterial Westminster Confession with its covenant theology was composed; in 1649 King Charles I was decapitated.

An important change was made under Cromwell's rule (1654–1660) when the Presbyterian discipline gave way to Congregationalist freedom and tolerance (cf. 298 f), although Cromwell kept alive the opposition against popery and prelacy (Romanism and Anglicanism). Had the puritan hegemony been able to maintain itself the Anglican church would have been reduced to an insignificant number of faithful hopelessly fighting for a lost cause.

However the year 1660 brought with it a complete reversal. With the happy advent of the new King Charles II (1660–1685) the Anglican bishops also returned, this time to stay.

Since that time the puritans have for the most part withdrawn into their own church organizations (cf. 276 ff).

Even more precisely than that of 1559 the *Book of Common Prayer* of 1662 tried to keep the mean between Roman practices and extreme Calvinist teachings. The black rubric opposing the adoration of the sacramental bread and wine was reincorporated. Moreover a new rubric at the end of the baptismal liturgy rejected the Calvinist teaching that baptism is no guarantee for the regeneration and eternal salvation of dying infants. This rubric states "that baptized children who die before they have committed any actual sins are surely saved." And before the administration of baptism a new prayer was added to bless the baptismal water "to the mystical washing away of sin."

Since the revision of the Prayer Book in 1662 there can be no doubt that the Anglican baptismal rite implies the complete Catholic baptismal teaching. The eucharistic service on the contrary has retained the Reformation character of a communion service without the sacrifice of the mass, the elevation and the adoration.

It is the general opinion of Anglo-Catholic writers that the Prayer Book of 1662 must be regarded as "the great victory of the cause for which Laud and Charles I gave their lives. It has given final security to the Anglican position against puritanism" (More-Cross, *Anglicanism*, vol. 52). In a way this is true but it is only half the truth. Apart from the changes mentioned the Prayer Book of 1662 hardly differs from that of 1559. It still contains numerous components which in origin and intent are typically Reformation-minded. Nor should it be overlooked that the evangelic Anglicans, despite the revivals of the eighteenth century, apparently do not have serious objections against the Prayer Book. And it is certainly true that they would have such objections if the Prayer Book was contrary to the original and essential principles of the Reformation.

The effects of the theological insights and convictions of the

Caroline divines have always remained limited to a rather small elite however since religious development after the restoration of 1660 took on a quite different aspect. In his very instructive book *From Puritanism to the Age of Reason* 1950 Cragg describes this development as dominated by three phenomena: the eclipse of Calvinism, the influence of the Cambridge platonists and the rapid rise and development of latitudinarianism. "In its youthful vigor, Calvinism would have been a significant power. But it had exhausted its reserves in futile controversies. . . . It had degenerated into an abstract scriptural dogmatism."

The second half of the seventeenth century was characterized not by a struggle between the puritans and the Anglican concepts of the church, the office, sacraments and liturgy but rather by a bitter attack by Anglican theologians against Calvinist theology. Not only had the scene of battle changed in a very short time but a new spirit had awakened in Anglicanism which is still manifest today. It is the spirit of a wise and humble modesty, open to all arguments, clearly aware of the limits of theology and filled with a profound aversion to an aprioristic dogmatism which demands acceptance without motives or investigation.

The Cambridge platonists regarded the individual conscience, led by reason and enlightened by revelation, as the only authority in religious matters. They rejected not only any ecclesiastic magisterium binding in conscience but also the authority of the Bible. They distinguished the essential from the accidental elements in religion. The essential content of sacred Scripture, they argued, could be easily understood by the mind. They emphasized the ethical and practical character of religion and rejected any separation of and opposition between theology and philosophy, faith and reason. They tried to prove the truth of Christianity on rational grounds, opposed in principle any form of coercion of conscience and produced a veritable mountain of writings on tolerance and freedom of religion.

Toward the end of the seventeenth century the latitudinarians

246

had undeniably gained the upper hand in Anglican theology. In substance they agreed with the Cambridge platonists, especially in their contention that Calvinism was a theology that dishonored God. But they were not philosophers. They were purely practical men of sound reason. They were professed enemies of any form of religious emotionalism: "If the will and the emotions have a voice in the matter, truth does not stand a chance." They also rejected "a superstitious veneration of the past," that is, respect for tradition. Their apologetic method was a negative one: they defended the Christian faith by proving the unreasonableness of unbelief. They also thought that faith is secure only if it is built on a secure foundation of a rationally responsible natural theology. In sum, their confidence in human reason was greater than their confidence in the direct word of God.

In any case the end of the seventeenth century brought with it a complete change in the religious climate of the Church of England. From this period also dates the development of the terms high and low church Anglicanism. The first term was originally used only in a pejorative sense in reference to theologians said to be vying for the king's favor by defending the divine right of the monarchy. For this reason they were called high flyers. A serious use of the terms high church and low church appears first in an essay entitled *Catholicism Without Popery* 1699, with the subtitle "Essay to make the Church of England into a means and example of unity for the entire Christian world." According to this essay the Church of England unites high and low church people into one communion so that members of the high church are building a bridge toward the churches of the Catholic type, those of the low church toward the churches of the Protestant type. The terms had however a political rather than a theological content. Also the term low church was at that time practically synonymous with latitudinarianism. The low churchmen were also mockingly called no churchmen because of the minor importance they attached to questions and institutions of an ecclesiastic nature. The name was later transferred to the adherents and supporters of the evangelic revivals of the eighteenth century.

The eighteenth century is usually referred to as the age of reason, the period of the enlightenment. This certainly did not leave the Church of England untouched. The religious climate began to show growing signs of rationalism, moralism and deism.

Nonetheless, in connection with the situation of the Church, some objections can be offered against the exclusive label age of reason.

In his original Storrs Lectures at Yale University, under the title *The Heavenly City of the Eighteenth Century Philosophers,* Carl L. Becker points out that both within and without the Church we have for centuries lived in a spiritual climate that is typically intellectual: "There were, no doubt, great differences between Voltaire and St. Thomas; nevertheless, both also had much in common. What they had in common was the deep conviction that the truth of their beliefs could be proved on rational grounds." Orthodox theology was "ruthlessly rational." What happened in the eighteenth century was not that reason finally began to have some authority but rather that reason, for centuries the principal champion of the Christian faith, now began to turn against that same faith it had previously defended.

Whatever the truth to this contention it is within this context that we must understand the strong anti-intellectual reaction which has pervaded practically all of Protestantism ever since the nineteenth century, and which even now is still on the increase.

A second objection to classifying the eighteenth century as the age of reason par excellence is the fact that—at least in England—the eighteenth century witnessed two powerful, typically irrationalists revivals: the evangelic and the Methodist revivalist movements. Both movements arose within the Church of England but the latter also created the opposition between church

248

and chapel and for the most part separated itself from the Anglican Church (cf. 318 ff).

The evangelic movement of the eighteenth and the Oxford movement of the nineteenth century changed Anglicanism in many respects. Both were a reaction to and a protest of the rationalist lack of faith and undermining of belief in the eighteenth century. The two movements are closely allied, even to the extent that several leaders of the Oxford movement were converted to a personal and conscious practice of the faith because they had been raised in an evangelic-Anglican milieu.

The evangelic movement considerably strengthened the Reformation character of Anglicanism. In contrast to Methodism it refused to break with the church and its liturgy. It regarded the ecclesiastic forms as indispensable aids—although at times as necessary evils. Preaching, as the real means of man's salvation, should not be doctrinal or moralistic but must be a lively, powerful appeal to man's emotions. The central theme was the salvation of the sinner through the all sufficient sacrifice of reconciliation and the precious blood of Christ. In every man's life faith was a matter of a personal, deeply lived conversion to the service of God. Liturgy was deformalized and enlivened by the incorporation of hymns, sometimes sentimental, sometimes persuasive, often sung to melodies intended to excite the person to fever pitch. The evangelics did not shy away from religious enthusiasm and emotionalism. It was a matter of a sensible religious experience allied to pietism and Methodism (cf. 267 ff, 279 ff). The practice of faith became anthropocentric. Evangelics, when leaving their religious services, were either enthusiastic or disappointed, depending on whether or not they had been edified, touched and moved. Even though evangelism was a reaction to the Anglicanism of the low church the evangelics are at times erroneously classified with low church Anglicans because of their aversion to formalism and the sacramental and ceremonial aspects of religious life. The evangelics still occupy an important place in world Anglicanism.

No other movement has so changed and embellished the appearance of the Anglican churches as the Oxford movement (1833–1845). Opponents and enemies who pretended not to understand the intention of this movement called its leaders ritualists or tractarians (after their publication of *Tracts for the Times*). The Oxford movement was by no means aimed at exteriorization. In fact it is because of this movement that Anglicanism has not degenerated into an exteriorized, formalized state churchism. It is because of the Oxford movement that Anglicanism has reawakened to an understanding of the deepest nature of the church as an inscrutable mystery rooted in the mystery of the incarnation.

Although in some ways it shared the views of the Caroline divines of the seventeenth century the Oxford movement was also a reaction to high church state Anglicanism. An exact classification of the Oxford movement is difficult since no two leaders of the movement had exactly the same purpose in mind. From John Keble's famous Assize sermon on national apostasy, which gave the movement its first impulse, it appears that the most profound elements were at stake; it was a matter of the radical conversion and return of the entire people to the faith of their fathers.

From the very beginning the Oxford movement differed from high church Anglicanism, a difference whereby it unintentionally agreed with Calvinism. Like Calvinism the Oxford movement regarded the church as a community in a class by itself, distinct from the state. The church had its own authority, its own life and its own self-determination which did not admit to intervention by the state or the world. The Oxford movement held that the church is either the original apostolic Church with its own independent plenitude of power received from Christ or that it is not a church at all. The question proposed by the Oxford movement was: what should be changed? and what should be done in order to have the Church of England function as the Church of Christ, to have it believed, acknowledged and accepted as such?

It is general knowledge that John Henry Newman, later a cardinal, together with a number of fellow workers was, after a great deal of interior struggle, forced to arrive at the sad conclusion that the Church of England could no longer be transformed into a church since it simply neither was nor could be a church in the ancient Christian and truly catholic sense of the word.

The immense significance of the Oxford movement is that for the first time since the Reformation the dilemma "either the Catholic Church or the Reformation" presented itself again and within a Reformation church. This dilemma was re-presented as a living fact, quite real, deadly serious and existential and not, as in other instances, in an interesting, romantic, esthetic and theoretical manner sans engagement which could never be taken seriously. No one who was able to fathom the importance of this event could doubt its outcome. All one has to do is read Newman's *Apologia pro Vita Sua* and particularly his King William Street Lectures of 1850, published under the title: *Certain Difficulties Felt by Anglicans in Catholic Teaching Considered in Twelve Lectures Addressed in 1850 to the Religious Movement of 1833.* The return of Newman and his friends to full communion with the Catholic Church in 1845 marked the official end of the Oxford movement and (from the viewpoint of the Catholic Church) in principle the end of Anglicanism. What was here taking place was but a weak foreshadowing of what will happen if and when the dilemma "Catholic Church or Reformation" becomes an actual and urgent question in the World Council of Churches.

The end of the Oxford movement was by no means the end of its influence on Anglicanism. On the contrary no other movement has ever influenced Anglicanism so effectively and permanently even in our own time. Not a single flank in the low church, the liberal broad church or the high church has been able to escape its influence. Everywhere eyes have been opened to the requirements which must be demanded of a responsible form of religious and ecclesiastic life. Everywhere the institutional character of the church as a creation of the state is beginning to be considered of no importance when compared to the organic and mystical character of the church as the communion of the faithful, as the church of Christ and as a mystery of faith. Everywhere the sporadic celebration of the holy eucharist of a century ago has given way to weekly celebration. Everywhere the horizon has broadened.

Where the Oxford movement has not incorporated itself into the Catholic Church it has continued its solitary way through the world of Anglicanism and has gradually developed into what is now often referred to as Anglo-Catholicism. In contrast to the old high church Anglicanism, which was fairly well restricted to the higher clergy and the better classes, Anglo-Catholicism has grown into a truly popular movement. It is found in the better circles, it is found in the middle class, it is found in the slums. It also occupies an important place in the missions.

A serious mistake is to classify Anglo-Catholicism as high church Anglicanism or as a direct development thereof. The old high church Anglicanism must be looked for among the moderate Anglicans of the conventional and traditional Tory type. And high church Anglicanism has political overtones, something entirely foreign to Anglo-Catholicism.

It is no longer common practice to use the words high, broad, and low to indicate the various groupings in Anglicanism. The use of such words leads to misunderstanding: that the Anglican church is the high church while the other English churches are the low church, whereas high, broad and low actually indicate only the various nuances within the Anglican churches. A popular—and ignorant—use of the terms high and low is based on the interior of the church and its service: the more austere the lower, the more solemn (flowers, candles, vestments) the higher.

This opinion completely overlooks the fact that a solemn service in St. Paul's cathedral has nothing to do with Anglo-Catholicism and that an Anglo-Catholic service can be quite austere. Anglo-Catholicism actually has little or nothing to do with high or low.

Anglo-Catholicism has given Anglicanism as wide a comprehensiveness as possible. The former distinctions between high, broad and low were still within the limits of what could be accepted by the standards of the Reformation. By its vision of Christian revelation, of Christian faith and of the nature of the church with its hierarchy, its sacraments, its communion of saints, its liturgy, its spirituality, its religious orders, its devotions and its forms of pastoral care and apostolate Anglo-Catholicism has crossed the sharp line of demarcation which separates the Catholic Church from the Reformation. But the Catholic Church contends that such a crossing of lines within a Reformation church is strictly impossible, and was therefore compelled in 1896 to declare invalid the Anglican ordinations as understood by Anglo-Catholics. This understanding of Anglican ordinations is moreover contrary to authentic Anglican teaching.

Within the Anglican churches Anglo-Catholicism is a new and foreign element. It rejects the Reformation on principle. It regards as branches of the Catholic Church of Christ only the Roman, Eastern and Old Catholic churches, together with the Anglican churches. The well known branch theory is not Anglican but Anglo-Catholic. Anglo-Catholicism considers the eucharistic service as a service of sacrifice and communion, has reintroduced the eucharistic vestments of the priest and has began to speak again of holy mass. It has also restored to its former place oral confession, not to mention all the other sacraments, and has reintroduced the reservation and adoration of and the blessing with the blessed sacrament. It also promotes the veneration of Mary and the saints and, last but not least, has called back to life a system of religious orders.

Older and newer forms of Anglicanism coexist peacefully and a number of transitional forms have arisen. Among the evangelics as well as the Anglo-Catholics can be found all the various gradations from orthodoxy to liberalism. As a result Anglicanism today displays a complexity and a variety of doctrines and practices without rival in the history of Christianity. Even among Anglo-Catholics alone one can clearly distinguish four different types: liberal Anglo-Catholics (who have inherited Catholic modernism), and Anglo-Catholics of Eastern Orthodox orientation, Old Catholic orientation and Roman orientation. Among the evangelics one finds groups that are Calvinist, Arminian, Lutheran and free church in orientation. The ideal of the large group of moderate Anglicans is that all these various groupings will favorably influence one another, that they will all make their own contributions to the Anglicanism of the future and that Anglicanism will grow into a new and closely integrated unit. This ideal will be all the more closely approximated, according to Headlam, former bishop of Gloucester, to the degree that Anglicanism will become "more catholic in worship, more evangelical in appeal, more modern in mind" (Church Congress 1928). Thus understood Anglicanism is on its way to becoming a microcosm of all Christianity. This all embracing character finds its clearest expression in the hymns which, since the revival movements of the eighteenth century, alternate with the liturgy of the *Book of Common Prayer*. There is in the Anglican churches a practically unlimited freedom in the use of hymn books. The best known are *Hymns Ancient and Modern, Songs of Praise* and the *English Hymnal*. In these books songs by Bernard of Clairvaux, Thomas Aquinas, Francis Xavier and Newman are found side by side with songs by Luther, the German pietists and from the puritan psalm liturgy. There is also a choice of English songs of every possible historical and spiritual origin, with a richness and variety of content which reflects the song and prayer of all of Christianity.

Finally the Anglican comprehensiveness also has a spatial aspect. Apart from the British Isles, where besides the Church of England three other autonomous Anglican churches exist (Scotland, Ireland and Wales), Anglicanism has also expanded to the United States and from there to Japan, China, the Philippines, Liberia and Central America, and to all parts of the British empire. In Canada and Australia provinces of the Church of England were formed, and in the United States, India, South Africa and New Zealand autonomous Anglican churches were founded. And in addition to the general traits that are everywhere applicable Anglicanism in all these lands also has its own peculiar traits (see *The Anglican Communion* 1948). The various churches and provinces of world Anglicanism all together form the Anglican communion. Since 1867 all the bishops meet approximately once every ten years under the presidency of the archbishop of Canterbury at the Lambeth conference.

The number of Lambeth conferences held thus far amounts to nine, the last of which was held in 1958. After each Lambeth conference an extensive report is published which consists of an encyclical letter from the assembled bishops of the Anglican communion, the resolutions adopted and the committee reports on the topics discussed. In 1948 the bishops were divided into seven committees for the discussion of the following subjects: the Christian doctrine of man; the church and the modern world (human rights, the church and war, Palestine, the church and the modern state, Communism, education, the church militant, the Christian way of life); the unity of the church; the Anglican communion; the church's discipline in marriage; baptism and confirmation; proposed Chinese canon on ordination of a deaconess to the priesthood.

A glance at the subjects and proceedings of the Lambeth conferences leads one to conclude that these conferences have for almost a century been the prototype of the ecumenical world conferences. As with the assembly of the World Council of Churches the resolutions of the Lambeth conferences have but a moral authority, not a binding force.

The Anglican communion at present embraces more than three hundred dioceses of which forty–three belong to the provinces of Canterbury and York, twenty–seven to the churches of Scotland, Ireland and Wales, more than one–hundred to the Protestant Episcopal Church in the United States of America, and almost one–hundred and fifty to the churches in Australia, Asia and Africa. The number of baptized Anglicans is estimated at fifteen to twenty million of which some four million make their Easter communion.

Anglicanism and the ecumenical movement

If by ecumenism is understood the effort to achieve as wide a comprehension as possible, as complete a synthesis as possible and the closest possible integration within one all comprehensive but nonauthoritative, ecclesiastic bond of whatever truth, liturgy, piety and activity can be found in Christianity, then the Anglican churches of our own day must be considered ecumenical par excellence. Anglicanism has gradually developed into a microcosm of Christianity and, to all appearances, into a prototype of the future world church. This has come about by its dynamic openness to all sides, by the influences it has undergone from all possible forms of Christianity, by its present comprehensiveness and by its development into a worldwide church communion.

Practicing Anglicans are well aware of this. They regard their church as perfectly suited to the establishment of ecumenical contacts in all directions. The Anglican churches have a pronounced ecumenical character and are animated by a well developed sense of vocation. As early as the seventeenth and eighteenth centuries frequent private as well as semi-official Anglican proposals were made to launch discussion about intercommunion or possible reunion with the Catholic Church, and with Eastern Orthodox, with Lutheran and Reformed and with the free churches. In the middle of the past century the ecumenical activity achieved an official status as a result of the establishment of the Anglican communion and the institution of the Lambeth conferences.

Considering the numerous negotiations which the Anglican churches have held on all fronts for almost a century the visible results are very slight. It has become quite obvious that the Anglican comprehensiveness plays not only a stimulating but also a restraining role. As soon as reunion in a certain direction becomes serious it is often countered by the objections of Anglicans who are seeking reunion in another direction. Still a large number of bishops rise above contrasts and conflicts. But they often find it difficult to keep the ship of the *Ecclesia Anglicana* on even keel. Usually the realization of ecumenical ideals has to be postponed for the sake of internal peace.

In 1878 the second Lambeth conference appointed three different committees to consider and study: 1 the ecumenical possibilities with regard to the various Christian groups in the English-speaking world; 2 the relations between the Anglican communion and the Scandinavian and other Reformed churches, the Old Catholics and other "reforming" churches; 3 the relations with the Eastern churches.

This action clearly shows that even half a century before the beginning of the ecumenical movement, and seventy years before the foundation of the World Council of Churches, the Anglican communion was thinking of a possible reunion of all Christianity, that it was inspired by a well defined ecumenical ideal and that it took concrete steps toward the realization of this ideal. It did not leave a single part of Christianity out of consideration.

The committee in charge of studying relations with the Catholic Church reported the following negative result:

The Committee with deep regret felt that, under present conditions, it was useless to consider the question of Reunion with our brethren of the Roman Church, being painfully aware that any proposal for reunion would be entertained by the authorities of that Church only on condition of a complete submission on our part to those claims of absolute authority, and the acceptance of those other errors, both in doctrine and in discipline, against which, in faithfulness to God's Holy Word, and to the true principles of His Church, we have been for three centuries bound to protest.

Therefore from the very beginning, in its relation with the Roman Church, the Anglican communion placed itself on the side of the Reformation churches. The only semi-official attempt to arrive at a mutual understanding between Catholics and Anglicans since that time were the Malines conversations of 1921–1927. These were held under the direction of Cardinal Mercier and the extreme Anglo-Catholic Lord Halifax. Even some Anglican circles protested against these conversations. The report of the then Anglo-Catholic bishop of Truro (the well known liturgist Frere) describes how difficult it was to establish some rapport between Anglo-Catholics and Roman Catholics. Even with all the apparent similarity in doctrine, theology, ecclesiastic practice and liturgy there exists an almost insurmountable barrier between the two groups. This barrier is not so much the result of material points of difference as of the diametric opposition between the Roman and Anglican mentalities.

The Anglican churches first formulated their joint ecumenical standpoint at the third Lambeth conference in 1888. They believe that a reunion of all of Christianity could be achieved on the basis of the acceptance of the following articles:

1 The Holy Scriptures of the Old and New Testaments, as "containing all things necessary to salvation," and as being the rule and ultimate standard of faith.
2 The Apostles' Creed, as the Baptismal Symbol; and the Nicene Creed, as the sufficient statement of the Christian faith. (Note the distinction between symbol and statement.)
3 The two Sacraments ordained by Christ Himself—Baptism and the Supper of the Lord—ministered with unfailing use of Christ's words of Institution, and of the elements ordained by Him.
4 The Historic Episcopate, locally adapted in the methods of its administration to the varying needs of the nations and peoples called of God into the Unity of His Church.

The visible unity of the Church therefore has not yet been realized but must still be achieved. Furthermore it is clear that articles one to three are based on the Reformation principles concerning Scripture, confession and the sacraments.

The stumbling block is the fourth article about the historic episcopate, particularly for the churches which are convinced that only a presbyterial church ordinance is in agreement with sacred Scripture. This article has unjustly been regarded as a *conditio sine qua non* which the Anglican churches think they must of necessity impose on other churches. This attitude reflects a lack of understanding of the Anglican mentality however. The Anglican churches based the Lambeth Quadrilateral not on their own subjective insights but on an acknowledgement of objective facts. It is their opinion that for a general reunion acknowledgement of the historic episcopate is clearly demanded by the history of the church, by the virtually universal opinion of Christianity for more than eighteen centuries and by the obvious data of sacred Scripture.

In the Lambeth Appeal of 1920, intended as an appeal to all Christian peoples to reunite, the Anglican churches gave a more extensive presentation of their ecumenical position. The appeal contains nine paragraphs which represent the fruit of ecumenical negotiations and discussions over the preceding twenty-five years. To prevent any misunderstanding it is stated emphatically that the Lambeth Quadrilateral should not—as some dogmatically inclined churches suppose—be taken as a minimum confession which everyone must accept if they wish to belong to the church. All those persons who have been baptized in Christ and believe in him are true members of the church of Christ. It is therefore not a question of return or submission but of a joint effort to restore the unity which has been lost.

The completely new formulation of the Lambeth Quadrilateral shows how closely the Anglican churches have observed reactions since 1888, and how ready they are to enter into self-criticism and change in order to integrate and negotiate the positive elements of other churches. The formulation of the fourth article was completely renewed. The historic episcopacy, though intended, is not mentioned by name. The new text reads as follows:

A ministry acknowledged by every part of the Church as possessing not only the inward call of the Spirit, but also the commission of Christ and the authority of the whole body.

The Anglican churches acknowledge the ministries and sacraments of the nonepiscopal churches as manifestly blessed by God. In reunion the acceptance of the historic episcopate should never lead the churches involved to deny the riches of grace which they have already received from God during their separation. Consequently the Anglican view is that any possible reunion should never be the result of capitulation or dogmatic submission. A transitional phase would necessarily be required so that special adjustments could be effected in order for the reuniting churches to grow freely into a new and close unity without being forced by higher authorities. If mention should be made of an ecumenical condition it would be that no single church should *per se* and in all things take account only of its own heritage. Rather all churches should be willing to be corrected, complemented and enriched by one another.

Of all the churches actively participating in the ecumenical movement the Anglican churches are the only ones which—long before the meetings of the first great world conferences On Life and Work and On Faith and Order—were animated by a genuine ecumenical awareness. Long before these meetings they were the only churches which had prepared a concrete plan for reunion based on expert knowledge of conditions and on serious reflection of the ecumenical problem. An example of this search for unity within the Anglican communion is the current negotiations between the Church of England and the Methodist Church for a possible merger sometime in the future (see 318).

It is part of the tragedy of the ecumenical movement that most of the Protestant churches, instead of responding to the Anglican attitude, showed only misunderstanding and a lack of appreciation. Moreover, ever since its establishment in 1948 and particularly during the world conferences of Lund (1952), Evanston (1954) and New Delhi (1961), the World Council of Churches has set out on a course which has little in common with the principles and aims of Anglican ecumenism.

The Anglican churches are officially affiliated with the World Council and are sufficiently represented in all the different committees. Still it is difficult to avoid the impression that the ecclesiological and ecumenical principles of Anglicanism, as well as those of the Eastern churches, are not really incorporated and applied in modern ecumenical thinking. Modern ecumenical thought moves rather in a continental-Reformational and American-Protestant direction.

But the Anglican churches have not stopped their ecumenical efforts toward a real and visible reunion with other churches, nor have they failed to achieve concrete results.

In this connection mention must first be made of the complete intercommunion established in 1931 between Anglicans and Old Catholics. It is true that the latter, with characteristic caution, first voiced their doubts and hesitations. But they were easily satisfied, so much so that an Anglican bishop is reported to have declared: "We did not find it difficult to satisfy them." This expression gives a surprisingly clear picture of the situation that exists between Anglicans and Old Catholics.

It is doubtful whether the Old Catholics showed much understanding of the typically Anglican approach to the ecumenical problem. There is sufficient reason to fear that they saw Anglicanism too exclusively through the eyes of Anglo-Catholics. They do not seem to realize that they have entered into a union with a church in which the major part of the clergy and the lay people regard the catholicity of the church in a Reformational or generally Protestant sense.

It can therefore be said that the sacramental intercommunion between Anglicans and Old Catholics rests on a fictitious or at

261

the very least a weak basis since both sides, while possibly proceeding from identical historical and practical presuppositions, certainly differ in their dogmatic and theological presuppositions. The facts presented in this chapter show that the Anglo-Catholic viewpoint within the Anglican churches is a forced one and that dogmatically and historically it rests on unreal grounds. Consequently an intercommunion which supposes that the Anglo-Catholic viewpoint is the actual and authentic viewpoint of Anglicanism must fundamentally rest on error.

The same cannot be said of the ecclesiastic reunion in South India between Anglicans, Presbyterians, Congregationalists and Methodists. This reunion, which may be considered a prototype of what the Anglican churches are hoping for, is thus far the greatest triumph of Anglican ecumenism. The Church of South India, a result of the union in 1947 at Madras, is one of the purest manifestations of the ecumenical principles of Anglicanism. It also corresponds with that vision of reunion of the free churches of England and America which the archbishop of Canterbury had presented in his famous sermon of Nov. 3, 1946 at the University of Cambridge on the subject "A Step Forward in Inter-church Relations." Thus it was no surprise when the archbishop, during the inauguration of the Church of South India—at which time three Anglican churches ceased to exist and were incorporated into this new church—expressed his hope that the day might eventually come when not a single Anglican diocese would remain, since they would all be reunited into a richer and broader communion of churches.

It was perfectly in line with Anglican ecumenism that the church assembly of the Anglican Church of England agreed, by a large majority of votes, to enter into full intercommunion with the Church of India. Some restrictions were applied which will be valid for the period of transition. But inside observers know that these restrictions serve to set at rest the consciences of the weaker brethren who find themselves oppressed. These restrictions pertain particularly to the Anglo-Catholic members of the Church of England who, when the plan for reunion of South India was first suggested, launched a powerful protest. In appeasing the Anglo-Catholics the Anglican churches have thus far gone to extremes. It is understandable that the resolution to enter into intercommunion with the Church of South India caused a crisis in certain Anglo-Catholic circles. However, from the Anglican point of view, this resolution was in perfect agreement with the principles which have characterized Anglicanism since the sixteenth century.

Conversations have also been going on between the Anglicans and Presbyterians of England and Scotland. These conversations led to the publication in 1957 of the report: *Relations between Anglican and Presbyterian Churches.* The report is of extraordinary importance from an ecumenical point of view. The compilers on both sides had come to the conclusion that "the questions arising between Episcopalians and Presbyterians lay at the heart of the differences evidenced by other divisions in the Body of Christ, and that a notable act of reconciliation between them could not fail to introduce a new and promising element into the whole field of ecumenical relationships." A reconciliation between the two systems of church order in Great Britain would to their mind "bear fruit over a much wider area" (3).

The ecumenical situation described in this report is sympathetic to the ecumenical situation throughout the whole world: "If it should be supposed that two Church systems which have grown apart through centuries of time can be reconciled, either by unilateral surrender or by pious thinking, unaccompanied by definite, and perhaps difficult, processes of change, then the hope of a reintegration of Christendom becomes completely unrealistic" (6).

In 1958 the Lambeth Conference paid considerable attention to the report, as also to the report published in May 1958 by the General Assembly of the Church of Scotland. It also discussed a Schema of Church Union in Ceylon and a Plan of Church Union in North India and Pakistan. With regard to the Roman

263

Catholic Church the report on Church unity prepared for the Lambeth Conference states that "although the Roman Catholic Church retains the conviction that the only goal of re-union must be submission to the Papacy, there are some welcome signs of an increasing recognition by the Roman authorities of the importance of the ecumenical movement" (II, 48).

Anglican reaction to the Second Vatican Council has been open and critical. Dr. John Moorman, bishop of Ripon and leader of the Anglican delegates at the council, said in an interview published in the Anglican weekly *Church Times* that he believed the Anglican communion as a whole "would be prepared to accept the fact of the papacy, though they would find great difficulty in recognizing the basis on which the primacy rests." The bishop-observer also noted that if there is to be a final unity among Christians "there will have to be a central head of the Church, and that head will clearly have to be the Bishop of Rome." Another observer-delegate, Dr. John W. Sadiq, Anglican bishop of Nagpur, India, was quoted elsewhere in a similar sense. Both opinions must of course be regarded as private.

The Anglican churches are faced with a difficult ecumenical dilemma. On the one hand they do not wish to estrange their Anglo-Catholic members needlessly for then reunion would be achieved at the expense of a schism, a result they obviously want to avoid. On the other hand the experiences of the past twenty-five years have taught the Anglicans that they cannot move in two opposite directions at the same time. Over their dedicated ecumenical efforts looms the shadow of the Christian dilemma: Catholic Church or Reformation? This is the dilemma all ecumenical efforts must ultimately confront.

4

From Reformation to World Protestantism

The road which the Reformation has traveled, from its rise and stabilization in the sixteenth century to the reintegration and consolidation of many different churches in the bond of world Protestantism of the twentieth century, has had many ups and downs. Periods of indifference and neglect of the faith were often followed by unexpected revivals and reactions which effect a new deepening and practice of belief. In the midst of an apparently growing splintering and dispersion the first attempts were made to arrive at some rapprochement and collaboration by means of alliances and world leagues, supra-ecclesiastic youth movements and international mission conferences, all of which finally led to the rise of the ecumenical movement and the foundation of the World Council of Churches.

It is in this perspective that the reader must view what we have to say about Protestantism in this fourth chapter. If in the preceding chapters we have restricted ourselves to a consideration of the three principal types of reformed Christianity, we will now direct our attention to the movements, free churches and sects which have arisen in the course of more than three centuries and which, especially in the eyes of the Catholic spectator, have given Protestantism such a terribly complicated character.

The Catholic reader should also bear in mind that his ideas

265

on the division of Protestantism are one-sided and often exaggerated. It is not true that each Protestant church has its own belief and that a Protestant would therefore have to choose from as many beliefs as there are churches. In fact the division of belief in Protestantism is really only a question of tensions and conflicts between at most three or four opposite ecclesiastic and doctrinal standpoints. The division of faith is generally a division which exists not so much between the churches themselves as between the different parties, directions or modalities within one and the same church. What Protestantism by means of its own interior strength has been able to achieve in our century in the fields of reunion, collaboration, the missions and evangelization is truly astounding. All indications are that Protestantism is busy overcoming the declines and divisions of previous centuries.

Corresponding to the three types of Protestantism dealt with in the preceding chapters are three groups of churches in which the Reformation movement of the sixteenth century has assumed a fixed and permanent form. The large number of these churches does not in itself point to a division of belief; rather it is the result of the fact that the Reformation was everywhere introduced by order of the prince or the magistrate. Consequently the number of independent churches coincided fairly well with the number of countries or free cities where the Reformation was introduced. All these churches were state churches or national churches, each with its own liturgy in the vernacular. From a religious point of view there were hardly any significant differences among the churches of one and the same group.

The ecclesiastic and doctrinal differences between the three groups themselves however were considerably greater. Yet even these differences were always of minor importance since the three groups did have their common origin in the sixteenth century Reformation and were rooted in the same basic principles of this Reformation.

By means of discussions and exchanges of letters the reformers did what they could to preserve the awareness of unity and communion among the Protestants of all churches. The polemics of the seventeenth century (and also of the late sixteenth century) did much to carry to extremes the ecclesiastic and theological differences between Lutherans, Reformed and Anglicans and to solidify the estrangement between the different groups of churches.

The fact that since the sixteenth century Protestantism gradually took on an increasingly complicated character and that it finally began to present a picture of ever-increasing confusion and progressive decomposition must be attributed to the continual rise of new movements and currents and to the rise of numerous free churches and sects.

The new movements and currents within the original state or national churches often resulted more from a difference in emphasis rather than from a disagreement over an article of belief. The problem was to decide which element in religion should receive the main emphasis: true doctrine, genuine and deep piety, or self-sacrificing, dedicated and practical service of one's neighbor. Yet at the same time there was an increasing attention to the vision of the gospel, to the interpretation of the Bible and finally to the nature and value of religion and Christianity. The most important of the movements and currents which have succeeded one another since the end of the sixteenth century are puritanism, pietism, rationalism, Methodism, modernism, the evangelic or Reformation revival, the theological movement of Barth and the ecumenical movement with its sporadic catholicizing revivalism as an accompanying phenomenon.

In practically all the state or national churches within the three mainstreams of Protestantism these movements have successively made themselves felt and have left permanent traces. From these movements and currents arose new parties and organizations, new directions and modalities. These new developments did not always succeed one another but often continued to exist, sometimes side by side, at times even irreconcilably, within the churches concerned. The consequences of this situation cannot be overlooked if one wants to form a clear picture of the present unity and division in Protestantism.

One such consequence is that Protestants of one direction or modality, even though they belong to quite different churches, consider themselves allied in spirit; at the same time they are more or less estranged from members of their own church who favor a different direction. This situation has frequently led to religious contacts despite the walls of separation between the churches. It has also resulted in the rise of international alliances, movements and unions the members of which belong to the same type, but to different churches. Although there are insurmountable walls of separation in modern Protestantism which keep the various groups at a distance from one another, these walls of separation frequently are no longer barriers between the original churches, but between the factions within the individual churches.

Moreover when a person is attempting to determine what is taking place among Protestants today he must also bear in mind that the traditional barriers between the three main groups of Lutheran, Reformed and Anglican Protestantism are no longer considered invulnerable. Furthermore he must remember that the theological and ecclesiastic points of dispute between these three groups have lost much of their significance in the light of the more weighty problems the parties within one and the same church are faced with. A consensus between Lutherans and Reformed is no longer surprising, but a consensus between Reformed and liberals within the same church often belongs to the realm of the impossible. A consensus between liberal evangelics and extreme Anglo-Catholics within the Anglican Church is out of the question; on the other hand intercommunion between the Anglican Church of England and the united Church of South India is quite feasible.

The first, most important and most basic cause of the Protestant division of belief is the rise of the movements and currents we have just mentioned. This factor must also be borne in mind when we speak of the free churches. Although these free churches have by their number and diversity contributed considerably to the vast complexity of Protestantism, they have not essentially enlarged the division of belief. The free churches do not have their origin in the rise of new beliefs but rather in the will to hold fast to the original beliefs of the great national churches, or in the desire to give new life to these beliefs and to improve the practice of them. In most, though not all instances the cause which led the free churches to separate themselves from the national or state churches have long since lost their significance. It is therefore not at all strange that reunions take place between national churches and free churches, or between free churches themselves.

Free churches, like the great national or state churches, are churches rooted in Reformation principles; but they have separated or freed themselves from these national churches for reasons which, while accidental, were at the same time of great subjective importance. Differences in the notion of authority often played an important role in these separations. Practically all the free churches contended that the state has no authority in matters ecclesiastic and religious. In this respect the free churches were the pioneers of the separation of church and state, a principle later adopted by most of the national churches.

The free churches also disagreed with the national or state churches on the manner in which ecclesiastic authority should be exercised, and on the form this authority should take. The Presbyterian churches, which originated in England, refused to conform to the legal establishment of the Anglican Church of England because they considered the episcopal institution and any form of episcopal authority contrary to sacred Scripture. Other free churches separated themselves because they found that personal freedom of conscience was jeopardized by a binding ecclesiastic authority (creed, fixed liturgy, ecclesiastic law). Usually these churches emphasized the perfect autonomy of the local community or congregation (Congregationalists, independents). The Remonstrants in The Netherlands can be compared to the English Congregationalists as far as their notion of authority and sense of independence is concerned. But the Remonstrants did not leave the Dutch Reformed Church of their own free will. They were excommunicated by the synod of Dordrecht in 1619 because of their teachings on predestination, grace, free will, man's cooperation unto salvation and the possibility of losing the state of grace (Arminianism).

Other churches separated themselves because of a practice of piety or a form of evangelization either forbidden or rendered difficult by ecclesiastic authorities. They sprang from the revivalist movements which by prayer and song attempted to give new life to religious feelings in a time of cold rationalism or barren formality. Thus arose the Methodist churches in England, America and later in almost all Protestant countries. In a certain sense the Baptists can be numbered among the free churches, although the original Anabaptists and Mennonites should be considered sects.

A large number of free Lutheran churches arose in Germany either in reaction to an enforced union with the Reformed or to the barrenness or liberalism of state Lutheranism.

The Society of Remonstrants in The Netherlands has its origin in Reformed Protestantism. From the structure of its religious service it is clear that this society is not willing to sacrifice its relationship with Reformed Protestantism. In some respects the Remonstrants resemble Anglicans, in others Congregationalists. Their name stems from the "Remonstrance" which they addressed to the states general in 1610 in protest against the spirit of intolerance of Calvinist orthodoxy and against the doctrines Calvinist orthodoxy tried to impose on the Protestant communities in The Netherlands. The synod of Dordrecht (1618–1619) condemned the teachings of the Remonstrants (also called Arminians after their principal theologian Arminius). After this condemnation they formed the Society of Remonstrants. Like the Congregationalists they refused to acknowledge any authority of synods over local communities, as well as any binding magisterium. The entire Society eventually embraced modernism.

The Baptist Society in The Netherlands originated with the baptist movements of the Anabaptists and Mennonites in the sixteenth century. As the result of a number of disputes and disagreements many of them decided to join the Reformed churches. Large numbers of Mennonites later emigrated to America where they split into numerous separate groups.

Many of the free churches succeeded in escaping the pressure of the state by emigrating to America. In the United States the free church type is predominant. Of all the Protestants in the world 65 per cent still belong to one of the great national churches, and 30 per cent to one of the free churches. The remaining 5 per cent belong to the host of generally small sects. It is a serious mistake to attempt to put Protestantism in a bad light by pointing to the large number of these sects. This attitude betrays a lack of insight into the Protestant situation and does not take into account the fact that the oldest of these sects, such as the Anabaptists and the Mennonites, were often just as cruelly persecuted in the Protestant countries as were the first adherents of the Reformation in Catholic countries. It is actually something of a miracle of unity that the present descendants of those persecuted sects are now fraternally and harmoniously cooperating in the ecumenical movement, as though there was nothing to forgive and forget. Thus in many ways they can serve as an example to many Christians of Protestant and Catholic background.

The sects have sometimes been called the "step-children of Christianity" or the "unpaid accounts of the church." They pay little or no attention to the teachings and practices of the official church and have separated themselves from the church either on grounds of "special divine revelations" or in express protest against the church. By preference they emphasize precisely those truths and practices which seem to be supported by the testimony of holy Scripture and particularly by the preaching of Christ, but which are nevertheless either not given or only scarcely given their due in the preaching and practice of the church. To this extent the sects might be called complementary movements. On the other hand however the sects usually reject important and sometimes essential elements in the teaching and practice of the church.

There have been sects ever since the beginning of Christianity. We will limit ourselves to those sects which still exist today and which have arisen not from within the Catholic Church but from within the churches of the Reformation.

Theologically speaking a sect is a religious community which has its own peculiar type of piety, spirituality and mentality in contrast to that of the church. The national churches of the Reformation agree with the Catholic Church in that they acknowledge offices, creeds and sacraments and are consciously rooted in the teachings and practices of the Church of the first few centuries. They have separated themselves from the Catholic Church on grounds similar to those resorted to by the later free churches when they separated themselves from the national churches of the Reformation. Both the national churches and the free churches expressly consider themselves "church" and have actually preserved the church type in their appearance and activities.

From a religious phenomenological viewpoint therefore it is a mistake (usually a result of antipathy) when Protestants regard the Catholic Church as the "largest sect" or when in turn Catholics disqualify all Protestant churches as "sects." For the sect type is distinguished from the church type not so much by separation and isolation, or by its strength in numbers, but by its own proper and specifically different form of religiousness.

The principal norm by which to judge whether a religious society belongs to the free churches or to the sects is whether in its teaching, organization, liturgy and concept of society it is akin to the churches of the Reformation, or whether its teachings and religious practices are foreign to the Reformation tradition.

Not all sects have removed themselves from the tradition of the Reformation to the same extent. And it is sometimes difficult to determine which sects have so removed themselves that they can no longer be considered a part of Protestantism. But it can safely be said that the Mormons, the Jehovah's Witnesses, the supporters of the Baha'i religion, the Swedenborgians, the Christian Scientists and the Anthroposophic Christian Society members are no longer truly Protestant.

Moreover there are also religious and spiritual currents and societies which owe their origin to a world of faith and thought entirely apart from or even opposed to Christianity: freemasonry, the humanist league, the free catholic church, theosophy, the "star of the east," the Rosicrucians, Sophism, Bahaism, Mazdaznan. It is obvious that these groups have nothing to do with Protestantism and the Reformation and that they cannot therefore be advanced as evidence for the "hopeless division of Protestantism."

The sect type is opposed to the church type. It is an unmistakable characteristic of practically all sects that they have a hostile attitude toward the church. This is often accompanied by an antipathy toward the world, the state and society. In some instances they manifest an inclination toward a more or less communistic form of society. Almost all sects give a somewhat exalted, eccentric or odd impression. For this reason Kurt Hutten gave to his book on the sects the title of *Seher—Grübler—Enthusiasten* (Seers—Musers—Enthusiasts). This book, which is the most captivating and most complete book on the sects, appeared in Stuttgart in 1950, and has gone through several editions. As a counterpart to this book there appeared in 1953,

273

by the same publisher, the work of Ulrich Kunz on the free churches: *Viele Glieder—Ein Leib* (Many Members—One Body). These two titles clearly express the fundamental distinction between sects and free churches. In The Netherlands there appeared in 1953 Boerwinkel's booklet on the problem of the sects: *Kerk en Sekte* (Church and Sect). Because of the author's congeniality with the sect mentality he has written with much understanding and devotion. He numbers the Baptists, who are on the borderline, among the sects and not among the free churches.

Both Hutten and Boerwinkel attempt to create some order from the chaos of sects by classifying them under a number of groups. Hutten distinguishes apocalyptic (adventist) medical, occult, perfectionist, ministerial and incarnationalist sects. Boerwinkel views the sects primarily as corrections of the church and divides them into three groups—according to the correction of a lack of faith, a lack of hope or a lack of charity.

A totally different concept of the sect type is found in an interesting book by John S. Whale, *The Protestant Tradition* 1955. As a Presbyterian Whale leaves Anglicanism entirely out of consideration. He reduces the Protestant tradition to three main sources: Luther, Calvin and the sectarians. By sectarians he understands the dissenters or separatists who could not abide the state church. His chapter on the sect type actually refers to the free churches and not to sects in the true sense. His analysis of the sect type according to personal, voluntarist and spiritual principles therefore does not refer to sects in the sense in which we use the term, following Hutten and Boerwinkel.

The oldest Protestant sects arose during the time of the Reformation from the Baptist movements in Switzerland, Germany, The Netherlands and England: namely the Anabaptists and the Mennonites. Bypassing ecclesiastic tradition they based themselves entirely on sacred Scripture and in particular on the gospels. They denied that an ecclesiastic institution with offices, sacraments and a fixed liturgy, with a magisterium and a binding creed, was in agreement with the intentions of Christ. Their criticism applied not only to the Catholic Chuch but also to the new churches of the Reformation which they regarded as "only half a job." Their attitude toward the world, the state and the "unchristian" society was one of reserve. They rejected infant baptism and the real presence of Christ in the supper of the Lord and opposed participation in armed conflicts and the swearing of oaths. The activity of the Anabaptists was often revolutionary.

The Baptists, who emigrated from England to America and to the other countries of Europe, reject infant baptism but they do not stem from the original baptist movements. They have gradually come close to the church type so that they can now be classified among the free churches. Hutten and Kunz also list the Quakers among the free churches even though the Quakers do not acknowledge ministries, sacraments, liturgy and creeds and have a form of meeting entirely foreign to any ecclesiastic tradition.

Thus if not only the English Presbyterians and Congregationalists but also the Baptists and Quakers of the seventeenth century and the Methodists of the eighteenth are numbered among the free churches, England must be regarded as the cradle par excellence of the free church system. Second is Germany with its many forms of evangelic-Lutheran *Freikirchen*. With the exceptions of the Catholic-Apostolics and the Seventh Day Adventists, who both date from the early half of the nineteenth century, actual sects did not arise in England. In Sweden, early in the eighteenth century, Swedenborg became the father of an occult sectarian movement. A related movement, Lorber-Gesellschaft, arose in Austria in the early nineteenth century.

All other existing sects have their origin in America or Germany. In the United States there arose the Mormons, or Church of Jesus Christ of the Latter-day Saints (early nineteenth century); the Christian Scientists (middle nineteenth century); the perfectionist Church of the Nazarenes, an outgrowth of Methodism (middle nineteenth century); the Jehovah's Witnesses (end of the nineteenth century); and the Pentecostals (early twentieth century). The German sects all date from the twentieth century: the Kelle society, the Philadelphia society, the Brethren of Jesus Christ, the Baha'i religion, the Christian Society, the restored Apostolics and the Evangelical Church of John.

Whereas the free churches generally make a real contribution toward a unity of Protestantism the sects do not play a significant role in the process of development from Reformation to world Protestantism. Therefore the sects need not be considered at further length.

The most important movements

In the following two sections we will describe the most important movements and free churches which have arisen from the time of the Reformation. A chronological order will be followed in these descriptions.

The distinction between the various movements (and the directions and modalities which arose from them) is found primarily in the area of the practice of faith, not in the content of faith. In principle each movement can be acceptable to any one of the Protestant churches—Lutheran, Reformed or Anglican. There is however a connection between movement and doctrine inasmuch as the latter gives a distinctive stamp to the particular movement in each church. In other words the movement may imply a new accentuation of accepted doctrines and at times may lead to profound changes, e.g. modernism. The movements differ among themselves in that some are of an intellectual nature, others of an ethical, mystical or practical nature. Another difference is that some have an individual, others an ecclesiastic character.

The most important movements which have successively influenced Protestantism are: puritanism, pietism, rationalism, Methodism, modernism, Reformation revivalism and finally the ecumenical, (church) organizational, liturgical and catholicizing movements which sprang from a new ecclesial awareness. All of these movements, in greater or lesser degree, still influence the Protestant national churches of our day.

Puritanism was a protest movement which arose in the Church of England under the reign of Queen Elizabeth (cf. 194 ff). At the root of this movement was the same concern which had originally led Calvin on the road toward the Reformation, namely "the taste for the pure religion" (cf. 126 f). The words of Christ: "God is spirit, and those who adore him must adore him in spirit and in truth" address the puritans very strongly. The means of communication between God and man is the word. "An image, a book, a form, a beautiful building, an extensive and ornate service can become an idol which distracts the soul by assuming the place of God." Thus does Henderson formulate the puritan fear of beautiful churches and elaborate services.

The puritans considered the most important task of the Reformation to be the imitation of the prophets of the Old Testament in their efforts to convert the people who had fallen into idolatry and superstition to the service of the one, true and living God, and to root out anything that in any way whatever resembled idolatry and superstition. According to the puritans the Church of England had failed in its duty.

The protest of the puritans was directed particularly against the *Book of Common Prayer,* though not so much against the content of the prayers, texts and admonitions as against the rubrics which concerned the church interior, liturgical vestments and various ceremonials.

According to the puritan norm everything that was not expressly and in so many words prescribed in the Bible had to be radically removed from church buildings and religious services. All that was allowed to remain in the church was a pulpit and a Bible. During the ministration of baptism there would be added a temporary baptismal font, during the ministration of the Lord's supper a temporary table in the nave of the church—and not in the sanctuary. All the fixed altars and baptismal fonts, statuaries, paintings and stained glass windows were removed, also all the ornamentals with which the religious service used to be enhanced: candles, flowers, carpets and other decorations, thuribles and other cult objects. Liturgical vestments, from the simple surplice to the vestments for mass, were replaced by the black "Geneva gown." As far as ceremonies were concerned the puritans were particularly offended by making the sign of the cross on the forehead of the person to be baptized, by the reception of communion while kneeling down, by the blessing of the wedding ring and by several funeral customs.

Despite their objections to the Anglican church ordinances and liturgy the puritans remained in the Church of England— under continual protest from the latter—in hopes that they would finally succeed in having the puritan reform introduced. The two principal champions of the puritans during the six- teenth century were Thomas Cartwright and Walter Travers. Thomas Cartwright, by his *Admonition to Parliament* of 1572, provoked an answer by Whitgift, *Answer to the Admonition* 1573. In the meantime Cartwright had to take refuge on the continent where he became a preacher of the English puritan communities of Antwerp and Middleburg. From the continent he addressed two other answers to Whitgift. A similar paper war was waged a few years later by Travers and Hooker, both masters of the temple in London. Hooker's masterpiece, *Laws of Ecclesiastical Polity,* was the product of that war. Travers' Latin work on the church ordinances according to the word of God and on Anglican deviations was translated into English by Cart- wright in 1574. All these writings together form the principal source for the study of the controversies between puritans and Anglicans. As was seen in the preceding chapter the puritans gained a brief victory in the middle of the seventeenth cen- tury. But since the Anglican restoration in 1660 puritanism has had only a very minor influence within the Church of England.

The puritan ideal of the religious service has been best realized in the Reformed churches of The Netherlands, in the Presbyterian churches of Scotland, England and America and in the Protestant churches of Switzerland and France. The central place in the religious service is given to the preaching of the pure word of God. The sermon is preceded by a reading from Scripture chosen *ad libitum* from which the text of the sermon is usually taken. The service is opened and closed by an extemporaneous prayer. The songs during the service were originally only psalms in verse; later evangelic songs were also introduced. These songs are also chosen *ad libitum* by the preacher but generally they are related to the subject of the sermon. The present liturgical movement, in turn, is a reaction to and a protest against a puritan extremism.

Pietism, like puritanism, can be regarded as a protest movement. It was not however a protest against a definite church order and liturgy but against an exclusively objective and at the same time an all too rationalistic dogmatism. Pietism defended the subjective practice of faith and religious experience. It held that a purely rational faith was worthless and championed a personal living faith which, apart from being based on the external word of God, also rested on an interior emotional experience of God's work in the soul.

Pietism took several forms, depending on the milieu in which it originated. The puritan-Calvinist pietism of England and The Netherlands differs in some important respects (particularly with regard to the experiential relation to predestination and election) from the Lutheran pietism in Germany and other countries. The later Anglican pietism of the eighteenth century has taken on a particularly Methodist form, but even apart from Methodism it is clear that there is a pietistic strand running through the history of Anglican spirituality.

Generally it was not the intention of pietists to leave the church to which they belonged. However their aversion to dead formalism, together with their existential life of conscience, led them, often against their will, into conflict with ecclesiastic authorities. In many instances, when cold religious services and dry, doctrinal sermons became unbearable, they had recourse to similarly minded friends or else they formed small pious gatherings. In most countries these gatherings or conventicles were opposed by the higher authorities. In the eyes of their opponents the pietists were abnormal fanatics.

The pietist movement meant a revival of asceticism and mysticism in Protestantism. During the seventeenth century it established a surprising new link with Catholicism. Not only the *Imitation of Christ* by Thomas à Kempis but also many other Catholic mystical writings were restored to honor by Protestant pietists, and even by puritan pietists. There arose a need for ascetical and spiritual exercises. In some instances even monastic communities were established.

Pietism in England dates from the second half of the sixteenth century (William Perkins and others). This puritan pietism reached its prime in the figure of the Presbyterian Richard Baxter (1615–1691), whose writings also influenced the rise of pietism in Germany.

In his excellent work on *The English Free Churches* Horton Davies calls Baxter "the first exponent of ecumenism in England." Baxter was extremely averse to ecclesiastic disputes. At the restoration of 1660 he tried to act as intermediary between the Anglicans and puritans. His opinion was that "all those who accept the Apostolic Creed as a compendium of faith, the Our Father as a compendium of piety, and the Ten Commandments as a compendium of duty, are true Christians and members of the Catholic or Universal Church of Christ" (cf. 172). He preferred to call himself not puritan, Anglican or Presbyterian but catholic. He regarded questions of an ecclesiastic, dogmatic or liturgical nature as subordinate to questions about the care of souls and the spiritual life. The most important of his more than one hundred and fifty writings is the now classical pietist-mystical *The Saint's Everlasting Rest.*

The father of German pietism is Philipp Spener (1635–

1705). He held that no one should be admitted to the office of preaching unless he could testify to his personal regeneration through the spirit; unless on the basis of personal experience he knew himself to "be born of God" and consequently—according to a phrase from Scripture—"incapable of sinning again." Spener also won Francke, professor of theology at Halle, over to pietism. Through Francke's fierce battle with the theological faculty of Leipzig pietism became a public and ecclesiastic matter. His battle was against the penetration of philosophy into faith, against dogmatism and homiletics and against everything that stood in the way of the spontaneous operation of the spirit.

German pietism gave the impulse to a revival of mysticism. The principal representative of Protestant mysticism was Gerhard Terstegen (1697–1769). His *Geistliches Blumengärtlein inniger Seelen* (A Spiritual Anthology for Interior Souls) contains songs which are at present sung in churches of all countries. One mystical song is especially popular:

> God reveals his presence—
> Let us now adore him,
> And with awe appear before him.
> God is in his temple—
> All within keep silence,
> Prostrate lie with deepest reverence.
> Him alone
> God we own,
> Him our God and Savior;
> Praise his Name for ever.
>
> O thou Fount of blessing,
> Purify my spirit,
> Trusting only in thy merit.
> Like the holy angels
> Who behold thy glory,
> May I ceaselessly adore thee.
> Let thy will
> Ever still
> Rule thy Church terrestrial,
> As the hosts celestial.

The pietists knew themselves to be pilgrims and strangers on this earth. They looked for another fatherland. They also realized man was destitute. They were concerned not only about the salvation of their own souls but also about those of others. And they had in mind not only the spiritual needs of the soul but also the material needs of the body. They rediscovered love. For this reason pietism supplied the first impulse to the rise of Protestant missions among the pagans and also to the founding of homes for widows and orphans and for the materially destitute.

On the one hand pietism has often led to separatism because the atmosphere in the churches was too cold and too stifling for their religious feelings. But on the other hand it has also contributed to a penetration of church walls and has led to a first interconfessional contact over these walls. However there was a dark side to this first ecumenical attitude inasmuch as it was born from a disparagement of ecclesiastic and dogmatic forms, from a belittling of the ecclesiological problem and from an indifferentism in regard to elements in the reality of revelation, elements which from a Catholic point of view are precisely those of the greatest importance. Thus pietism has often led to a false irenics, that is, to an irenic attitude which is acceptable only on condition of a neglect of essential data of faith. This attitude also explains why pietism was well nigh powerless in the face of the rationalism of the enlightenment, and why it unwillingly prepared the road for the religious superficiality and undermining of faith in the eighteenth and nineteenth centuries. Nevertheless, at a time when the faith was weakened and the spiritual life in a state of utter distress, pietism remained active in the hearts of many. Although one must be critical of pietism for its one-sided neglect of ecclesiastic and doctrinal values, one should never forget that the evangelic revivalist movements of the nineteenth century received their most powerful impulses from pietism, and from Methodism.

In Germany, The Netherlands and England the first half of

the twentieth century saw a strong reawakening of a mystical approach to Christian life and faith. This Protestant attention to mysticism has given birth to numerous writings, among which those of Evelyn Underhill and Dean Inge occupy first place. In this connection we must mention the song of Bathurst, in which the *via mystica* is heralded in an exceptionally simple manner:

> O Savior, may we never rest
>   Till Thou art form'd within,
> Till Thou hast calm'd our troubled breast,
>   And crush'd the power of sin.
>
> O may we gaze upon Thy Cross,
>   Until the wondrous sight
> Makes earthly treasures seem but dross
>   And earthly sorrows light:
>
> Until, released from carnal ties,
>   Our Spirit upward springs,
> And sees true peace above the skies,
>   True joy in heavenly things.
>
> There as we gaze, may we become
>   United, Lord, to Thee,
> And, in a fairer, happier home
>   Thy perfect beauty see.

This whole attitude now seems a thing of the past. A powerful antipietistic and antimystic reaction was started in the twenties by Brunner. His work on *Die Mystik und das Wort* (*Mysticism and the Word*) was a passionate protest against all emotional piety. About the same time there arose the tornado which bears the name of Barth, not to mention the revival of the existentialism of Kierkegaard. All this seems to have put an end to any form of pietist-mystical piety, at least for the moment.

From a religious point of view the post-war world has undergone important changes. There is a deeply rooted distrust of anything resembling a religious or mystical experience. Religious life has become more matter-of-fact, more naturally realistic, more practical, more businesslike. The vague religious experience has had to make way for the clear and secure word of God. We are suddenly living in different times. The pietist-mystical irenic-ethical Protestantism of religious geniality, the Protestantism pictured by Bouyer when he looked back, exists no longer.

This Protestantism of the past held to the happy medium between an all too practical Methodism on the one hand and an all too rational modernism on the other. We must now give some attention to these two movements.

Methodism, like puritanism, originated in the Church of England. It soon went its own way and led to the foundation in England, America and other countries of a great number of churches that differ from one another in organization, liturgy and theology. In some of these churches Methodism reflects a kinship with the puritan-Calvinist pietism; in others it has a pronounced Arminian character as regards doctrine, preaching, mission and the care of souls.

The two founders of Methodism are the brothers John (1703–1791) and Charles Wesley (1707–1788). The former became the organizer, missionary and theologian while Charles was the poet of the movement. Even in their youth each had undergone pietistic influences. In their student years at Oxford they founded a Holy Club the members of which exercised themselves in a rigorous way of life, pleasing to God, according to the directions of Law's *Serious Call to a Devout and Holy Life.* As Anglicans of the high church tradition they emphasized the regular reception of holy communion. Both of them became clergymen in the Church of England. Their interest in missionary activity brought them into contact with the Herrnhutters (Moravian Brethren; cf. 108). After that time the pietist-Lutheran vision of the gospel determined the content of their preaching (Hildebrandt, *From Luther to Wesley* 1951).

Methodism was born in 1738. During a religious evening

284

service John Wesley underwent a conversion while he was listening to a reading of Luther's preface to his commentary on the Epistle to the Romans. This conversion was typically ethico-practical. It released in John Wesley a zeal for conversion which reminds one of Francis Xavier. In forty years' time he traveled about 300,000 miles on horseback, always preaching to thousands of listeners and encouraging everyone to convert to Methodism.

Methodism is related to pietism in its emphasis on personal religious experience and practice of the faith. The difference is that pietism stresses personally experienced regeneration and Methodism personal conversion. Pietism has more of a mystical contemplative character, Methodism more of an ethical active character. The fundamental contrast in pietism is between spiritual death and spiritual life, in Methodism between sin and holiness.

Methodist preaching describes the misery of a life of sin. It offers salvation and redemption through the blood of the lamb. It testifies to the glory of liberation and purification through the precious blood of Christ. It urges people to make a personal decision for or against Christ, now, at this very moment. It struggles as it were for the salvation of the lost soul. It tries to bring the sinner to repentance, to move him by urgent emotional appeals and promises, until finally the moment arrives when the sinner surrenders, when he breaks with his sinful past and begins a new life of joy and gratitude, a life totally dedicated to God and neighbor. One of the characteristics of Methodism is that its effects are contagious, that the sinner who has been saved pities the lot of those who have not yet been converted, that he too begins to preach and testify everywhere and at all times to the redeeming and atoning blood of the savior.

Methodism regards conversion as a definite aversion—not only to a sinful life but also to a frivolous, worldly life. It has an ascetical and exclusive character. Before his conversion the sinner was involved in worldly reading matter, he took delight

285

in worldly pleasures, songs, plays and dances. After his conversion the redeemed Christian reads the Bible and devotional
books, he sings religious songs at home and at the meetings, he
abstains from alcohol and usually from smoking, he no longer
participates in grandiose feasts and no longer visits such places
of worldly pleasure as taverns, dance halls, fairs or theatres. The
true Methodist loathes the world, which rushes headlong to its
destruction, and he tries as much as possible to tear people away
from its frivolous pleasures.

Methodism agrees with Lutheranism in its vision of the gospel,
that is, in justification by faith alone. It differs from Lutheranism inasmuch as it emphasizes the duty of the sinner, justified by
faith, to exert himself as much as possible in the struggle to
achieve holiness. It differs from Calvinism in that holiness is
pursued not only by a "walking in the way of God's commands"
but also by an express attempt to be perfect. Conversion means
that the sinner has now done away with sin. Though there are
Calvinist Methodists, most Methodists incline to an Arminian
vision of sin, the freedom of man and man's cooperation toward
beatitude, made possible by the redemption of the will.

Like the above mentioned movements Methodism lacks its
own proper doctrine. It is usually nondogmatic and has paid
little attention to theology. A recent attempt to summarize
Methodist theological principles was made by Burtner and
Chiles in *A Compend of Wesley's Theology*. A profound and
acute work on perfectionism is Flew's *The Idea of Perfection in
Christian Theology* 1934. Flew finds that in this respect perfectionism is related to the Anglican Oxford movement (cf.
250 ff).

More than has pietism, Methodism has given a powerful
impulse to the rise and development of mission work. It also
lies at the root of the origin of the Salvation Army, a type of
convert work later adopted by many churches. Finally the spirit
of Methodism also influenced the rise of the first Young Men's
and Young Women's Christian Associations, Student associa-

286

tions, the Buchman movement and the Moral Rearmament movement. The MRA has its roots in the Buchman movement.

The principal sources for a study of the spiritual climate of Methodism are the *Journal of John Wesley,* his sermons and his letters. Other sources are the revivalist songs of Charles Wesley and of other Methodist hymn writers, and finally the very extensive Methodist literature which can be found in the bibliography at the end of Leslie Church's *The Early Methodist People.* The most important Methodist songs can be found in *The Methodist Hymn Book* and other Methodist collections of songs.

Songs, always chanted to stimulating and sometimes even exciting melodies, occupy an important place in the meetings of the Methodists and in their life at home. All possible facets and nuances of the life of faith, prayer and religious sentiment are expressed in the many hundreds of Methodist songs. The more restrained songs have also been incorporated into the official hymnals of almost all Protestant churches. A very well known and beloved song of Charles Wesley is:

> Jesu, Lover of my soul,
> Let me to Thy Bosom fly,
> While the gathering waters roll,
> While the tempest still is high:
> Hide me, O my Savior, hide,
> Till the storm of life is past;
> Safe into the haven guide,
> O receive my soul at last.
>
> Plenteous grace with Thee is found,
> Grace to cleanse from every sin;
> Let the healing streams abound;
> Make and keep me pure within;
> Thou of Life the Fountain art;
> Freely let me take of Thee;
> Spring Thou up within my heart,
> Rise to all eternity.

Modernism brings us face to face with the deepest tragedy which Protestantism has experienced since the Reformation.

Though its way was prepared by eighteenth century rationalism and liberalism its real origin is found not so much in philosophical theory as in the application of the methods of modern science to the sources of revelation. The modernist view of Christianity was heralded by the appearance in 1835 of a book by Strauss: *Das Leben Jesu kritisch bearbeitet* (A Critical Study of the Life of Jesus). Since that time modernism rapidly invaded all Protestant national churches and most of the free churches. In most cases it led more to a mystical than to a rationalist consideration of Christ, but in all cases it led to a total revolution in the vision of the nature of Christianity.

It cannot be denied that according to the testimony of holy Scripture and according to the creeds of the Catholic Church as well as of the Reformation, the Christian faith is based on a unique, special and extrinsic divine revelation. But modernism consciously and on principle broke with this presupposition. What up to that time had been held by Christianity as a unique, specific, universally and absolutely valid revelation was reduced by modernism to a product of the human mind. Thus, *eo ipso,* the very concept of basing the faith on a heteronomous authority, a heteronomous organ of authority above and beyond human reason, human conscience and religious experience, was nullified.

If modernism continued to speak of revelation, faith and authority these terms were used in an essentially new sense and meaning. Modernism never denied the existence of God, even if a theistic consideration of God often threatened to fade in a pantheistic one. The spirit of God is revealed in the wonders of nature and in the awareness of God which is found in all peoples and religions. The fact that of all the prophets and founders of religions Christ is the one who has most clearly testified to God and revealed him, made him known, better than did any other prophet, does not, as far as modernism is concerned, deprive other religions and spiritual currents of their revelatory character. The act of faith is not based on the fact that a certain source of revelation is *a priori* held to be infallible and authoritative; rather it rests on the conviction that whatever presents itself as revelation must be able to vindicate itself as true before the tribunal of reason, conscience or religious sentiment. The proclamation of the word is not based on the acceptance of an objective content of faith which at Christ's command must be faithfully preserved and handed on throughout the ages, but on a conviction, measured by personal and autonomous norms, concerning the nature, sense and value of religion and Christianity.

This radical reversal of the concept of the nature of revelation, the act of faith and authority necessarily entailed inevitable consequences for the actual content of modernist preaching. The books of sacred Scripture were equated with the holy books of other religions. They were counted as world literature and consequently were also interpreted according to the same linguistic and historical methods and according to the same intrinsic criteria applied to any other written sources. Moreover the study of comparative religion considerably gained in importance. It supplied an understanding of the forms which religions can take and made the mind more attentive to what is essential and what is accidental in religion. Finally the natural sciences and the still younger psychological and social sciences gave new insights into the interconnection between phenomena and into what could be accepted as possible or probable, and what should be rejected. Man's horizons have seldom undergone such enormous changes in so short a time as in the past hundred years. And all these new developments were applied by modernism to the content of the sources of revelation, which had thus far been regarded as unassailable.

Modernism rejected the doctrine of the Blessed Trinity and the incarnation; it denied the divinity of Christ (except in a figurative sense), his virgin birth, his miracles and the salvific significance of his death; it rejected the teaching of the vicarious and redeeming passion and death of Christ and the sacrificial character of his death on the cross; it denied the corporal resurrection of Christ, "the empty tomb" and the reality of the Pentecost miracle; it rejected the teaching on the fall and original sin; it no longer regarded sin as a radical break with God but as mere human weakness; it attributed to the human will the ability to perform supernaturally good works without special divine help (i.e. grace); in short, it denied all salvific events and relegated the biblical and ecclesiastic notions of Christ to the realm of myth and legend.

Although in the past twenty-five years modernism has attempted to arrive at a more positive and traditional consideration of Christ, in principle the problem has changed but little. A significant proof of this is Bultmann's recent appeal for the demythologization of the New Testament. His *Entmythologisierung* (Demythologization) is concerned with the question how the Christian kerygma can be divested of its so-called mythological framework, which is unacceptable to modern man, without losing any of its original content and meaning. Bultmann's appeal, together with the reactions to it, can be found in the four volumes of *Kerygma und Mythos* (1951–1955).

The tragedy of Protestantism is that while the Reformation found itself compelled to take up arms against the Catholic Church on behalf of the absolute authority of the word of God, for more than a century in practically all the great Protestant national churches hundreds of "ministers of the divine word" were, Sunday after Sunday, denying and combating the truth of the content of the Christian faith, so that in the hearts of thousands the faith in Christ as the son of God and as the redeemer of the world was being undermined and obliterated. Instead of leaving the church to which they belonged because they had lost their faith in the God-man, the preachers of modernism used their position in the church to combat the faith; and all the while the Protestant churches were incapable of rectifying the situation.

The reactions which followed upon modernism have been mentioned earlier in this book. On the one hand they led to serious schisms, but on the other also to a Reformation revival and to a struggle for a new church ordinance and confession within the afflicted churches (cf. 148 ff, 254).

Liberal Protestantism cannot simply be identified with rationalism, liberalism or modernism. It represents a mentality which is as old as Protestantism itself. It is difficult to say what it actually teaches but in any case it has always been averse to any effort to determine the Christian teaching once and for all and to declare it binding. It has preserved an openness to the understanding of the Bible as well as to human thought and culture. It is an attitude rather than a definite teaching. It must be regarded as the heir of the Renaissance and humanism. It was born of the spirit of an elite which was able to maintain a high degree of spiritual freedom in regard to ecclesiastic pronouncements and theological dogmatism. It is found in all the national churches and many of the free churches owe their origin to the liberal mentality.

This mentality does not in itself necessarily lead to a denial of the facts of salvation or of the fundamental dogmas of the Christian faith. But it cannot be denied that the liberal mentality has been especially open to the influence of rationalism and modern philosophy and science; hence the fact that liberal Protestantism, during the heyday of rationalism and modernism, practically coincided with those movements. To this extent liberal Protestantism can be regarded as the expression of a serious crisis of faith which Protestantism has had to face.

In a sense liberal Protestantism was treated by orthodox Protestantism in the same way Catholic apologetes treated the Reformation. With little ado liberal Protestantism was rejected and combated by orthodoxy without any effort made to understand the problem. This problem imposed itself on believing Christians as a result of the spiritual and cultural development which western European man experienced in a brief span of time.

Liberal Protestantism was faced with the most serious and most dangerous challenge ever presented to Christian faith. It was confronted with a great number of new discoveries and insights which were causing real difficulties of faith for many serious Christian thinkers versed in philosophy and science. In self-defense against this problem orthodoxy anxiously clung to the doctrine which it had received without ever trying to make a real contribution to the study and solution of the new problems. Liberal Protestantism accepted the challenge and was almost shipwrecked. In the past century it has had to traverse the depths of an almost deadly crisis of faith. In principle it seems to have overcome this crisis, at least in those liberals who, around the twenties of this century, experienced the swing toward a rightist modernism. In the second printing of his book on the directions in the Dutch Reformed Church Haitjema even maintains that the development of liberal Protestantism over the past twenty years can be typified as "a gradual return to the classical confession of Christ" (219). In view of the renewed struggle concerning the demythologization of the New Testament however the question can be asked whether this vision is not all too optimistic.

The rationalism, liberalism and modernism of the preceding two centuries have at least had one good effect in that they have aroused the positive Christian conscience, they have pointed the way to a new examination of the actual content of revelation and they have mobilized the hidden reserves of faith.

The Reformation revival of our own day owes its existence to the reaction which modernism called forth by its literary-historical criticism of the sources of revelation. And the revival of the Catholic Church in many of the Protestant countries, the question of conscience asked of Protestantism by the Swiss theology of the twenties and finally the meetings with other churches in the ecumenical movement have all forced Protestantism to reflect on its *raison d'être,* on the most profound and most vital

292

principles of the Reformation and on the nature of the Church and the life of the Christian.

Finally an observation must be made about the catholic or catholicizing movements within Protestant churches at present. In the past fifty years much has been said and written about evangelic catholicity. In The Netherlands there appeared a thesis under this title by Boissevain and in Germany a collection of essays and conferences by Heiler. In England a collection of articles by a number of contributors from various countries was published under the title *Northern Catholicism* 1933. At present the expression Reformed-catholic is growing in popularity.

In Germany Heiler, professor at Marburg since 1920, is the animating spirit of the evangelic catholic movement and is editor of the periodical *Die Hochkirche* (The High Church). Even as early as 1933 an extra edition of *Die Hochkirche* mentioned similar movements in Switzerland, France, Italy, Scandinavia and The Netherlands (*Die evangelisch-katholische Bewegung im ausserdeutschen Protestantismus*).

In this movement there is no question of a rapprochement with the Catholic Church. Rather its intention is to rediscover typically catholic values which have unnecessarily gone astray in the Reformation, and to reintegrate them into Reformed Christianity. On the one hand this movement does not want to derogate in any way from the Reformational understanding of the gospel: it does not intend to sacrifice the freedom of the Reformation; but on the other hand it works zealously toward the restoration of the liturgy—particularly the celebration of the eucharist in its original Catholic form, the commemoration of the Blessed Virgin and the saints, Catholic spirituality, religious orders, the episcopal office and the apostolic succession.

Centers of evangelic or Reformed-catholic endeavor in Germany are the *Michaelsbruderschaft* and the *Oekumenische Marienschwestern* (Brotherhood of St. Michael and the Ecumenical Sisters of Mary); in France the evangelic-catholic monastery

293

of Cluny Taize; in Switzerland a circle around Cullmann and Leuba with its periodical *Verbum Caro;* in The Netherlands the Reformed Catholic Community. All these groups are aiming at the realization, in the Reformation churches to which they belong, of a catholicism without papacy, without a living magisterium, without "new dogmas," without the use of Latin as a cultic language and without what they hold to be Roman defects.

The prototype of such Reformed-catholic movements is the Anglican Oxford movement. When judging the *raison d'être* and the sense of such a movement the question must be asked whether it is still in accordance with the principles of the Reformation, or whether in principle it is no longer Reformational but authentically Catholic. In the first instance there is a danger of a pseudo-Catholicism. In the second the Catholic basis is seriously meant, but at the same time it is certain that in a Reformation church Catholicism, like Anglo-Catholicism, can at best be tolerated and can never be regarded as legitimate. Thus it is condemned to remain a foreign element in a milieu in which it does not belong, in which it will not be able to take root, in which it will never be able to be itself. Then there applies what Newman said of the Oxford movement, namely that it will never be able to find its full development and its real home anywhere but in the Catholic Church.

Anglosaxon free church Protestantism

Anglosaxon free church Protestantism is mainly of English origin. Although it owes its existence to various reactions against Anglicanism in England the movement reached its fullest development in the United States. Many of the first settlements in America had a distinctly religious character. They were founded by nonconformists and dissenters who emigrated to America in order to organize a church and society according to their religious convictions without being restrained or disturbed. There were also emigrants from Germany and The

294

Netherlands who had left their country for similar reasons. The result was that the Protestant national church type appeared late in America and that it is a minority in comparison to the free church type. Generally speaking the character of American Protestantism is determined and dominated by the latter.

As far as external unity is concerned it is remarkable that in America—apart from the Catholic Church with its forty-three million members—only the Protestant Episcopal Church forms an ecclesiastic unity. All other church types are distributed over a great number of denominations. This is the result of the fact that, in contrast to Anglicanism, their origins lay not in any single country but in various countries of different languages. Moreover the immigrants of the various national origins settled in different areas which were often separated by miles of desolate, uncultivated land. The number of branches of Lutheranism in the United States for example is remarkably great. While this diffusion of Lutheranism is partly due to differences of language and national character it is also a result of the orthodox, pietistic and liberal groups organizing their own denominations—in marked contrast to what these groups did in the Lutheran lands of Europe (cf. 106 f).

To the free church type belong five principal groups which are mainly of English origin: Presbyterians, Congregationalists, Baptists, Quakers (Society of Friends) and Methodists. There are also groups from other European countries, for example, the Mennonites from The Netherlands, and such groups as the Disciples of Christ or the Fundamentalists which arose in America through separation from former groups.

Even a summary review of the origin, history, characteristics and activities of the more than one hundred independent denominations in America would fill a volume. The best book on the subject is Neve's *Churches and Sects of Christendom* 1952. A person who wishes to learn more about American Protestantism is also advised to read the interdenominational quarterly *Religion in Life* (A Christian Quarterly of Opinion and Discussion). The ecumenical movement has given rise to the amalgamation of churches of the same group, so that now the number of denominations has been reduced by more than half. Moreover, partly with a view to missionary activity and the protestantization of South America, a close, even financial cooperation has been initiated in the National Council of Churches of North America. Some sixty denominations belong to this federation.

Shortly before the meeting of the third world conference On Faith and Order at Lund in 1952 there appeared in *The Christian Century* an article by van Dusen, one of the leading figures in the ecumenical movement and a representative of the Presbyterian Church in the United States, denying that the participants in the ecumenical movement represent either a Catholic or a Reformation type. According to van Dusen this contrast overlooked another contrast of at least similar importance, namely the contrast between European and American Protestantism. He correctly urged that the latter be considered a proper form of Christianity and that it occupy a more important place in ecumenical discussions. Van Dusen also said that European Protestantism, with its typically theologico-dogmatic and ecclesiastic approach to the ecumenical problem, had disproportionate influence.

Therefore Anglosaxon free church Protestantism must be regarded as a separate type. Apart from some extreme groups, such as the Fundamentalists, there are for all practical purposes only historical differences among the various free churches. A spectator might sometimes get the impression that American Protestantism is hopelessly divided. But with regard to its vision of the gospel, of the nature and function of the church, of the Christian's place in the world and of the missionary task the differences which originally existed have been considerably reduced. From a liturgical point of view we can also speak of a leveling of differences since religious services everywhere are beginning to manifest a similar structure, and since the churches, in their new liturgical books and hymnals, have adopted many prayers and songs from one another. Many theological and ecclesiastic problems which still occupy the old European churches no longer interest American free church Protestantism. The biggest problem is a practical one, namely how the world can be won for Christ in as short a time as possible.

The principal means to achieve this aim is a large-scale distribution of the Bible in simple, affective words adapted to modern life and suited to the needs and problems of modern man. In this respect American Protestantism—not to mention the Protestantism of the young Asiatic and African missionary churches—has achieved a sense of unity still lacking in the old Protestantism of Europe, weighed down as it is with theological and ecclesiastic traditions. American Protestantism has its own peculiar mentality and spirituality which all the churches share and which relegates the original differences to the background. The reputed division of American Protestantism is more shadow than substance and many American Protestants consider it meaningless.

A summary characterization of the main groups of Anglosaxon free church Protestantism therefore is of an historical rather than an actual importance.

As far as church order and the original teaching are concerned the Presbyterian churches of England and America are similar to the Calvinist-Reformed churches of Geneva, France, The Netherlands and Scotland. In England the Presbyterian-minded puritans tried as long as possible to remain within the Church of England and to reform it in a presbyterial spirit. Only when this failed did they try to establish after 1660 an English Presbyterian church. It was not until the arrival of William of Orange in 1688 however that this was finally achieved. In America the first general synod of the Presbyterian Church in the United States took place in 1716. During the eighteenth century Presbyterianism in England almost floundered as a result of rationalism and liberalism. Through the initiative of Scottish immigrants the remnants were united into the Presbyterian Church of England in 1863. The Presbyterian churches of America and England experienced a struggle over their confession similar to that which the Dutch Reformed Church underwent, and they have likewise suffered from frequent schisms. The "official" confession is the Westminster Confession of 1647.

The Congregationalist churches of England and America, like the Presbyterian churches, originated from the struggle between Puritanism and Anglicanism. These churches too, as far as doctrine is concerned, are of Calvinist-Reformed descent. But they differed from the Presbyterian churches from the very start—not only by their sense of independence or in their relationship to the state, but also in their individual make-up.

The principal difference between the Presbyterians and Congregationalists lay in the notion of the church. The Presbyterians placed the unity of the church above the independence of local communities; the Congregationalists emphasized the strict independence of local communities. The latter considered the local church the fullness of the church. According to the Presbyterians ecclesiastic decisions concerning doctrine, church order and liturgy had to be made by the general synod as the highest ecclesiastic authority; according to the Congregationalists only the local church could make such decisions. If therefore the Congregationalist churches later united into one national and ultimately into one international union, this union has the characteristics of an alliance rather than of a church. In the survey by Peel and Horton on *International Congregationalism* the Remonstrant Brethren and the Union of Free Evangelical Congregations in The Netherlands are numbered among the Congregationalist communities.

Like the Remonstrant Brethren Congregationalism has always objected on principle to ecclesiastic discipline and to binding confessions. It has always demanded the highest personal, moral and religious integrity of its members. It has always aimed at a community of an elite rather than a community of saints. It has a

298

Baptist tendency inasmuch as it attributes real value to baptism only when it is joined to a personal conviction of faith. In this respect it has in mind a rationally justified conviction rather than a personally experienced regeneration or a sudden conversion.

The principles of independence naturally implied that the Congregationalists could more easily separate from the Church of England than could the Presbyterian-minded. For this reason they were also called separatists. But since this separatism was subject to severe punishment the first communities had to meet in secret. Thus the Congregationalists frequently took refuge in The Netherlands (Browne and Ainsworth in 1580; John Robinson in 1618).

Browne is the author of the Congregationalist Institution: *A Book Which Sheweth the Life and Manners of All True Christians,* printed in Middleburg. Flourishing Congregationalist communities of English refugees sprang up in Amsterdam and Leyden but for various reasons were unable to make themselves at home in The Netherlands. In 1620 they joined the pilgrim fathers and emigrated in the Mayflower to New England. In his farewell address at Leyden John Robinson rebuked the Dutch Calvinists for their tenacity: "They take root where that great Divine [Calvin] left them, even though he had not had an insight into all things. This is a disaster which must be greatly pitied."

As in the case of the Presbyterians the Congregationalists in England were able to organize only in 1688. They too adopted the Westminster Confession as the official norm. Despite (or perhaps precisely because of) their aversion to binding confessions and doctrinal discipline they suffered far less than the Presbyterians from heresies, ecclesiastic disputes and schisms. In contrast to the Presbyterians they had a weekly celebration of the Lord's supper and attributed great importance to the careful consecration of the bread and wine.

In 1931 the Congregationalist churches merged with the

Christian Churches (Disciples of Christ) to form the Congregational Christian Churches. A quarter of a century later, in 1957, the General Council of the Congregational Christian Churches merged with the Evangelical and Reformed Church to form the United Church of Christ. In Philadelphia in July 1961 final actions were taken to establish the United Church of Christ in the United States. Inclusive membership of the United Church of Christ is now more than two million faithful.

The Baptist churches are likewise of English origin and are an outgrowth of Congregationalism. The first separation took place on Dutch soil when John Smyth and his followers withdrew in 1609 from the Congregationalist community of English refugees in Amsterdam.

The Baptists can be regarded as consistent Congregationalists. Not only did they consider infant baptism meaningless unless followed by a personal acceptance of the faith, they also rejected it completely as contrary to sacred Scripture and without value for beatitude. In this respect they agreed with the Anabaptists and Mennonites; they also may have felt the influence of the latter while they were in Amsterdam. However the Baptist churches did not originate directly from Anabaptism.

The Baptists also pushed another Congregationalist principle to its limits, namely the purely spiritual character of religious services. Not only did they reject fixed forms of prayer but they also discarded community singing since it does not always correspond to the emotions of the moment of some of the members of the community. This extremism was abolished however toward the end of the seventeenth century. The Baptists also refused to allow mixed marriages, their celebration of the Lord's supper was preceded by an agape, and some communities celebrated the washing of the feet. But all these special characteristics for the most part disappeared in time. From a theological viewpoint the Baptists chose the side of Arminianism and were the first defenders of religious tolerance. They were also opposed to human respect. Thomas Helwys, leader of the Baptists in

England, gave his life for this cause in 1616 during his imprisonment.

One of the best known Baptists is John Bunyan. His spirituality betrays traits of puritanism, pietism, Congregationalism and even Methodism. He experienced a sudden conversion while reading Luther's commentary on the Epistle to the Galatians. As a precursor of Methodism he preached everywhere while traversing the country and spent many years in jail. It was in prison that he wrote his famous work *The Pilgrim's Progress* (1675). It described the "being a Christian" as an heroic, militant journey through the midst of the greatest dangers, and with the most unexpected meetings, toward the eternal city of God, the heavenly Jerusalem:

> Who would true valor see,
> Let him come hither;
> One here will constant be,
> Come wind, come weather;
> There's no discouragement
> Shall make him once relent
> His first avow'd intent
> To be a pilgrim.
>
> Whoso beset him round
> With dismal stories
> Do but themselves confound;
> His strength the more is.
> No lion can him fright,
> He'll with a giant fight,
> But he will have a right
> To be a pilgrim.
>
> Hobgoblin nor foul fiend
> Can daunt his spirit;
> He knows he at the end
> Shall life inherit.
> Then fancies fly away,
> He'll not fear what men say;
> He'll labor night and day
> To be a pilgrim.

301

Meanwhile the Baptists had divided into two groups because some had returned to the Calvinist doctrine of predestination. The General Baptists, to whom Bunyan belonged, taught that Christ died for all men; the Particular Baptists, like the Calvinists, taught that Christ died only for the elect.

In America the Baptist denominations are divided into three main groups and some twenty-five smaller groups. Membership of the Southern Baptist Convention was last reported (1962) at ten million, the National Baptist Convention, U.S.A., at five million, and the National Baptist Convention of America at two and a half million. The smaller but nonetheless influential American Baptist Convention has a membership of approximately 1,500,000. Total American Baptists are numbered in the 1964 *Yearbook of American Churches* at 21,643,000. It should be noted however that these figures do not include children of parents who are Baptist. In Baptist communities, as in most Congregationalist communities, only baptized adults are considered members. Baptists have founded mission churches in practically all European countries on both sides of the iron curtain.

The Quakers are on the borderline of the sect type. They are not really a church society, do not acknowledge ecclesiastic ministries and have no creed, sacraments or liturgy. They are united into a Society of Friends. They use no titles and address one another with a "thou" or "thine."

The name Quaker originally had a pejorative meaning in reference to the emotionalism of the earliest Quaker meetings. The movement began as a reaction to the ecclesiastic system of Christianity. The Quakers were especially scandalized by the religious disputes and by the fact that Christians were persecuting one another over differences in beliefs. The Quakers want to overcome evil by good alone. They apply the sermon on the mount literally. They invite the poor and the oppressed to share their meals. They are also conscientious objectors to military service. At one time they frequently disturbed religious services by suddenly interrupting the preacher to protest against his mendacious distortion of holy Scripture.

In their meetings the Quakers observe lengthy periods of silence and open themselves to the "interior light." There is no fixed order of service. Whoever feels impelled to do so pronounces a free, spontaneous prayer, reads aloud some scriptural texts, delivers a speech or sings a hymn. The gathering takes place in the greatest possible silence, peace and unity.

The movement owes its existence to the activity of George Fox (1624–1691). He was a searcher, had been born into the Anglican Church of England, was for a time a member of the Baptist movement and in 1649 for the first time protested unexpectedly in the middle of a church service. The Quakers were, like other adherents of free churches, persecuted and many of them emigrated to America, where William Penn established the movement in 1680.

The Quakers had long felt the need for a more theological delineation of their beliefs however. The most important theologian of the Quakers is Robert Barclay. His *Apology for the True Christian Divinity* is still the standard work of reference for the study of the theology of the Quakers. Actually it was a theology which stirred a certain unrest among the peace loving Quakers. Early in the nineteenth century doctrinal disagreements divided the Quakers into four different groups: the orthodox, the Hicksites, the Wilburites and the primitives. But the Quakers have always excelled in human charity. William Temple, the former archbishop of Canterbury, once said: "We differ from the Quakers in every respect, but they certainly are the best Christians."

The Methodist churches owe their existence to the activity of the Wesley brothers (cf. 284 ff). These churches are very numerous and differ among themselves in theology and church organization. Although the Wesley brothers would have preferred to remain within the Church of England their mobility and sense of independence, their emphasis on the general priesthood of the faithful, their activity and the peculiar character of their meetings unwillingly led to the rise of communities separate from the church. The effect of their conversions made it impossible to keep the converts within the limits of the conventional church system.

In 1784 John Wesley confirmed, by an imposition of hands, Thomas Coke as superintendent for the Methodist communities that had sprouted in Amsterdam. In England the Methodists were no longer attending the official church services. They gathered in barns, camps, private homes, chapels or in the open air. Imperceptibly groups were formed which organized themselves more or less on ecclesiastic lines but at the same time retained individual characteristics. Only in the course of this century have they come to a closer union as a result of the ecumenical movement. In this manner the Methodist Church arose in England in 1932 with more than a million members. In America Methodism is divided into a great number of churches—Calvinist and Arminian, episcopal and nonepiscopal—with a membership of some thirteen million. Like the Baptists the Methodists are engaged in a widespread missionary activity not only in non-Christian countries but also in the Catholic countries of South America and Europe.

The Disciples of Christ merit our special attention since they separated from the existing churches because of the scandal of divided Christendom—although by their action they added to the great number of denominations which regard the unity of all Christians as their primary goal. The movement arose early in the nineteenth century. Anticipating the future unity of all Christians the Disciples of Christ called their church association simply the Christian Churches. Here is that curious phenomenon whereby a Protestant community does not seize on the catholic principle of the visible unity of the church as a motive to return to the Catholic Church, but as a motive to give existence to a new unity church. The Christian Church of the Disciples of Christ could therefore be regarded as a foreshadowing of the new world church which some participants in the ecumenical movement consider as their ultimate goal. Ever since its birth the ecumenical movement has found powerful moral and financial support from the Disciples.

The Disciples of Christ regarded their movement as one toward complete restoration of divided, degenerated and seriously dilapidated Christianity. They called their movement The Restoration Movement and designed a plan of restoration entitled "Declaration and Address." Articles of religion were condemned as articles of division which only stand in the way of Christian unity. It is not a creed or a church ordinance but discipleship which must form the basis of Christian unity. The place to encounter Christ is not the church but the Bible. The sacraments of baptism and the Lord's supper were understood symbolically. Although infant baptism was not rejected many Disciples had their children baptized only at a later age.

The two founders of the community of Disciples were Thomas Campbell and his son Alexander. The latter lived to witness the rise of modern biblical criticism which presented serious difficulties to the Disciples because of their exclusive biblicism. Alexander Campbell could not prevent a division of the unity loving Disciples. A progressive and a conservative group were formed. In the struggle over fundamentalism which broke out in the United States in the early part of this century the conservative group of the Disciples sided with the fundamentalists.

The fundamentalists belong to different denominations. They hold strictly to the literal sense of the absolutely unassailable text of the Bible (creation of the world in six ordinary days of twenty-four hours, chronology of the Bible, etc.). During the First World War they distributed numerous writings in which they tried to prove that the results of excavations and other scientific investigations plead in favor of the literal understand-

305

ing of the Bible, thus proving the fundamentalists to be correct after all.

Kierkegaard and Barth

It can be said that, despite contrasts, protests, conflicts and schisms, the development of Protestantism had not been truly disturbed before Kierkegaard and Barth appeared on the scene. The activity of these two men brought a decisive halt to Protestantism (and indirectly to all Christianity) in its march through history. No other men in the world of Protestantism since the beginning of the Reformation have, in the same sense and measure as Kierkegaard and Barth, acted as prophets of doom, troubling the conscience of Christianity.

There are, no doubt, differences between Kierkegaard and Barth. Søren Kierkegaard (1813–1855) was a poet-philosopher whose reflections are contained in letters, diaries, aphorisms and occasional writings; Karl Barth (born in 1886) is a theologian of great stature who—apart from numerous other writings— has given a lifetime of labor to his *Church Dogmatics,* now numbering ten volumes and by no means complete.

The resemblance between Kierkegaard and Barth lies not primarily in the fact that Barth, in the form, content and intention of his works, consciously builds upon the work of Kierkegaard, though there is a connection in this respect. The resemblance in question lies rather in their function in Protestant Christianity, namely that of prophets of doom, troublers of the conscience of Christianity.

Both acted compulsively because the Christian situation alarmed them, because they considered the Christian existence to be in danger. Against all convention both made it their aim to achieve ultimate truth and reality; both made things difficult for themselves and for others; both undermined a false sense of security and unmasked false appearances; both have scandalized many; both have been disregarded, incorrectly interpreted, misunderstood and ridiculed; both have been set aside. Kierkegaard died a recluse, Barth has already been deserted by many of his followers.

Kierkegaard and Barth have something in common as a result of which the world, particularly the Christian and ecclesiastic world, refuses to accept them. This something does not lie in the fact that they have formed for themselves certain convictions which differ from most. This is true of all figures who have played significant roles in the history of Christianity. This something lies rather in the fact that their activities are a condemnation of the Christian existence as such, as it actually manifests itself in the modern world. Basically both of them are concerned with the question whether today it is still possible to find Christians, true believers. Theirs is a question of whether Christianity as a religion still has something to do with Christ, whether Christians themselves have not done everything in their power to render Christianity insipid, powerless and tasteless, whether Christianity has perhaps ceased to exist. This causes scandal because nobody likes to see himself deprived of his illusions, to have unmasked before him as vain appearances the very things he considers solid reality. The fact that Barth's alarm has taken on a specifically theological form is in this connection of minor importance.

Kierkegaard was born in Copenhagen, studied theology, but never became a preacher. The milieu in which he matured was overshadowed by the Danish Lutheran state church, but his words are addressed to all Christian people. Kierkegaard posed the question whether the relation between Jesus Christ and the official representatives of religion (scribes, pharisees and priests) is perhaps a relation that applies to all times. His question was whether in our own world Jesus would fare any better than in the Jerusalem of the past, whether the conflict between Jesus and the religious leaders of the people of his time is perhaps not the prototype of the everlasting conflict between Christ and official religion.

The development of Protestantism had been smooth enough until Kierkegaard appeared on the scene with the thorny question whether this official Protestantism with its ecclesiastic, theological and religious disputes about doctrine, church order, liturgy, piety and politics, whether this official Christianity was perhaps on the side of official Jewry in the days of Jesus, that is to say, in opposition to Christ. Will Christ recognize as his own work this Christian activity and this bourgeois Christianity which has resulted from it? Or will Christ perhaps say that Christians with all their orthodoxy, pietism, rationalism and revivalism have really achieved nothing but the abolition of Christianity? Are perhaps Christians not the greatest enemies of Christ?

Kierkegaard did not propose any new doctrine, any new church, any new liturgy, any new form of piety, any new theological system, any new political party. Neither was it his aim to abolish what was already in existence or to replace it with something better. Neither did he intend to join a different church. He might have been a member of any church and, like Christ in his time, he would have acknowledged and respected the actual ecclesiastic authorities. But he would have been faced with the same conflict in any situation.

Kierkegaard typified the true Christian as a disciple-contemporary of Jesus, that is, as someone who finds himself in the same situation as Christ, as someone who, together with Jesus, finds himself here on earth "on his way to Jerusalem" to die with him. The great danger which threatens the Christian is not false theology, doctrine, piety or politics but the danger of being scandalized at Jesus, of denying and deserting him in the situation of the moment, the decisive moment.

Like all the other figures in the rise and development of Protestantism Kierkegaard too was strongly affected by certain words from sacred Scripture. For Kierkegaard they were the words about the stumbling block, about scandal, about being persecuted and rejected, about the danger of being misled or misleading oneself, and in particular the words of Jesus about the condition of the religious leaders, sinners and publicans, of the early rulers of this world. For Kierkegaard, to be a Christian means to be in a certain existential relation to God, a relation which becomes real only when man becomes a disciple-contemporary of Christ.

Kierkegaard took a particularly strong stand against two means by which man tries to escape from the existential decision to be a disciple-contemporary, namely the esthetic-religious sphere in which man enjoys religion and the intellectual-speculative sphere in which man denies the distance which separates him from God and is satisfied to be a spectator.

English translations of the works of Kierkegaard have been published by the Princeton University Press and the Oxford University Press by Swenson, Lowrie and Dru.

In one of his last works, *Training in Christianity* 1850, Kierkegaard, after an edifying meditation on the consoling words of Jesus: "Come hither to me, all ye that labor and are heavy laden, I will give you rest," suddenly imposes a decisive halt on all devoutness and edification. Almost pitilessly he transposes the still unsuspecting reader from the dreamland of pious meditation into the stark reality of the existential decision for or against Christ.

A similar halt was imposed on Christianity and on the theological world by Barth in his small pamphlet *Biblische Fragen, Einsichten und Ausblicke* 1920 and in his 1918 commentary on the Epistle to the Romans, drastically revised in 1921.

The Barthian tornado has spared no person or thing. Nineteenth century Protestant theology, natural theology, pietism, sectarianism, the Roman Church, Catholic theology, even the ecumenical movement, not to speak of Christian culture, Christian politics, humanism and the totalitarian ideologies, were all ripped open in Barth's disastrous judgment of God's word. It must be said however that Barth was prepared to be the first to bow his head to this condemnation and that he has extended this condemnation to all man-made religiousness and with no respect for persons, with no personal resentments and with no ecclesiastico-political designs.

It is obviously impossible to give a brief summary of Karl Barth's theology. But if we ask ourselves what was the deepest motive of his actions and the deepest core of his testimony we will find them to be quite close to the motives that inspired Kierkegaard. Barth's testimony was directed against the plurality of pseudo-religious and pseudo-Christian efforts by which man, with regard to faith and salvation, tries to achieve certainty on the basis of private insight, emotion, experience or good-will while allotting but a secondary role to God, God's revelation and God's salvific act. Barth was concerned with the acknowledgment of God's salvific act as the absolutely unique foundation on which salvation rests and with the acknowledgment of God's word as the absolutely unique foundation on which faith rests. He unconditionally rejected any other foundation, such as the talking about God, the relation to God or religious activity in the name of God, in short, religious existence from any other source (*von anders woher*).

Any attempt to give a rational foundation to revelation, any effort to ascend to God by means of pious exercises and practices that disregard God or put him in second place, any form of self-sanctification or religious activism which pretends that salvation depends on oneself are all forms of pseudo-religion. According to Barth these are forms of a religiousness which have as their foundation something other than the humble acknowledgment of and unconditional surrender to the only fact which really counts, the fact that "God is with us in Christ." All these forms have no significance or value in the relationship between God and man.

We must not underestimate the force of this condemnation, which really signifies the final destruction of any form of vainglory and any sort of religious possession which man in his

310

audacity has obtained from some other place (*von anders wo-her*). It is certainly not Barth's intention to destroy faith, hope and charity as long as their only true source lies not in us but in God.

The ecumenical movement and the World Council of Churches

Attempts to strengthen or restore unity and collaboration among Protestants are practically as old as the differences of belief and the schisms which led to the present division of Protestant Christianity.

The past hundred years have seen the rise of many international institutions and world organizations that have united Protestants of the most disparate churches: the Evangelical Alliance, the World Organization for the Defense of Protestantism, the World Organizations of the YMCA and the YWCA, the Student Christian Movement, the World Organization for the Promotion of Friendship between Nations through the Intervention of the Churches, the International Missionary Council.

Moreover churches with a common confession and organization have allied within universal alliances. Thus arose the Anglican Communion of Churches, the Presbyterian World Alliance, the Ecumenical Methodist Conference, the United Church of Christ, the Baptist World Alliance, the Lutheran World Federation.

Some of these federations and councils have exercised an important and even direct influence on the organization of the ecumenical movement and the World Council of Churches. It was only in some very exceptional cases that the desire for a closer union sprang from the liberal mentality of "unity rather than division." Rather the ecumenical endeavor was born precisely from the deepening of faith which caused the Reformation revival, and from the necessity of building up a wall against

311

liberalism and other causes of religious indifferentism and deterioration of faith.

Catholics have all too often judged the ecumenical movement from their own viewpoint and without taking the necessary trouble to obtain a sufficient understanding of its real motives and intentions and aims. And we must add immediately that it certainly took no great amount of time before at least some of the participants in ecumenical conferences showed some understanding of the real foundations of the Catholic viewpoint.

The present ecumenical movement dates from the years immediately following the First World War. It manifested itself originally in two forms: a practical form and a theologico-dogmatic form. The first practical world conference On Life and Work met in Stockholm in 1925 under the direction of the Lutheran archbishop of Upsala, Nathan Söderblom; the first theological world conference On Faith and Order met in Lausanne in 1927 under the direction of the Anglican bishop of West New York, Charles Brent. The purpose of the Stockholm conference was to arrive at a general Christian statement concerning the critical world situation in all its socio-ethical aspects; the Lausanne conference had a similar purpose concerning differences in belief and the ecclesiastic division of Christianity. After thorough preparations by various committees both conferences held second meetings in 1937 in Oxford and Edinburgh respectively. At both conferences it was decided to amalgamate the two movements into one single ecumenical movement and to incorporate this movement in a World Council of Churches in which the churches concerned would be officially represented. This council was finally established during a first assembly in Amsterdam in 1948. The number of churches which officially joined the World Council amounts to about two hundred: Lutheran, Reformed, Anglican and free churches, as well as Old Catholic churches and several Eastern churches.

From the very beginning the ecumenical movement proposed as broad an aim as possible. It never intended to be a pan-

Protestant movement but rather aimed at embracing all Christianity. If in the course of events since 1948 the WCC has contributed mainly to a consolidation of world Protestantism this has happened not so much by intention as by default.

The new element in the ecumenical thought, attitude and method consists in the radical change it hopes to achieve in the disposition of Christians toward one another. For centuries the leaders and adherents of the various churches and movements have found it obvious and necessary to fight one another as fiercely as possible, even with force. In contrast the ecumenical position is based on the consideration that all Christian faith and life should be built on the immense reality of God's love, mercy and forgiveness which have been revealed in Christ's sacrifice of love on the cross. It is also based on the consideration that Christ came into this world for no other purpose than to reconcile men to God and to one another through his cross and passion; on the consideration, finally, that we as Christians are standing in the way of the efficacy of Christ's work of reconciliation through our lovelessness, our lack of forgiveness and unwillingness to reconcile ourselves, and through our indifference toward one another.

Ecumenical awareness means that we have finally become aware how much, by our division and disputes, we have made ourselves into a sad and unattractive spectacle in the eyes of the distant world of paganism and of the dechristianized world around us.

Of course this awareness in itself does not remove the serious religious differences and ecclesiastic controversies which have arisen in the course of centuries. But what is totally new about the ecumenical point of view is that Christians should not only avoid contending with one another and despising one another because of these differences and oppositions, but that they must search for one another in a spirit of love which will not rest until a way has been found toward a rapprochement, toward new cooperation and toward possible ecclesiastic reunion. The ecumenical viewpoint presupposes that all Christians, in one way or another, are coresponsible for the restoration of unity. Even the conviction of belonging to the true church cannot absolve a Christian from this responsibility. For subjectively, from the human viewpoint, we are all historically and presently, individually and corporately guilty of the existing situation. We all share equally in this guilt insofar as and as often as we have failed in public and in private life to correspond to what may be expected of a believer. In this respect we have all sinned and we must all continually convert ourselves, whether we are Protestants or Catholics.

These new ecumenical thoughts, attitudes, dispositions and concerns are not as simple as they might appear. Whoever attends ecumenical conferences cannot help but realize how difficult it is for many persons not only to listen to arguments of representatives of a different church, but also to give truly patient attention to what a representative of another church—a former adversary—has to say. It is amazing how difficult it is to see the one-sidedness, the lack of understanding, the errors of faith and practice not only of others but also of one's own church when necessary. The ecumenical movement has a great ideal. For this reason alone it is not surprising that in certain respects the results have so far not come up to the original expectations.

In one respect however the results have exceeded even the greatest expectations of the first ecumenical pioneers. The fact that within twenty-five years after the first ecumenical world conferences (and despite the terrible upset caused by the Second World War) the World Council of Churches could be founded in 1948 must be looked upon as a very real and concrete result. There is also the fact that it has an official participation of nearly two hundred churches from all parts of the world. This result must to a great extent be attributed to the perseverance and organizational talent of Dr. W. A. Visser 't Hooft, the first secretary-general of the World Council.

314

The World Council of Churches, with headquarters in Geneva, is not a super church, much less a reunited church into which the member churches have been incorporated at the expense of losing their own identities. It is an official center for dialogue and cooperation. Every six years there is an assembly of those delegates who have been officially appointed by the member churches. The reports, resolutions and announcements of the assembly however do not have a binding but only a moral authority. There is a yearly meeting of a central committee appointed by the assembly. This committee of about one hundred members discusses the more urgent matters and makes preparations for the next assembly. At its meeting in Toronto in 1950 this committee adopted important resolutions concerning the relation between the church (of the credo), the churches (as denominations) and the World Council of Churches. It was emphasized that if a church chose to become a member of the World Council this decision would not entail that church's acceptance of the other member churches as churches in the full or true sense of the word. The World Council does not want to adopt the views of any particular church. It was precisely because of the multitude of views that the council brought the churches together. And the motive and aim of the council demand that no one church be *a priori* excluded from the dialogue.

It is difficult to give a proper summary in this brief compass of the many and varied themes which have been treated by the various world conferences and by the numerous study committees appointed by these conferences from the first meetings in Stockholm and Lausanne in 1925 and 1927 to the meetings in New Delhi and Montreal in 1961 and 1963. It is even more difficult to summarize what has been said about these conferences by the participants. The number of published reports on the conferences and the meetings of committees, as well as collections of studies in preparation for the world conferences, is ever increasing.

One statement which should definitely be mentioned here is

the report of the third assembly of the World Council of Churches in New Delhi. Here for the first time the ultimate end of the ecumenical movement was clearly stated:

We believe that the unity which is both God's will and his gift to his Church is being made visible as all in each place who are baptized into Jesus Christ and confess him as Lord and Savior are brought by the Holy Spirit into one fully committed fellowship, holding the one apostolic faith, preaching the one Gospel, breaking the one bread, joining in common prayer, and having a corporate life reaching out in witness and service to all, and who at the same time are united with the whole Christian fellowship in all places and ages in such wise that ministry and members are accepted by all, and that all can act and speak together as occasion requires for the task to which God calls his people.

The World Council of Churches and ecumenism

Halfway between the first and second sessions of the Second Vatican Council the fourth Conference on Faith and Order was held in Montreal in July 1963. The importance of this gathering of some four hundred theologians, historians, sociologists, church historians and lay people was its relevance to a continuing but widely differing effort by the churches to make Christian unity as manifest as possible. The Roman Catholic council naturally overshadowed the main objective of this ecumenical gathering, since the situation has utterly changed since the time of the Lund Conference.

Among the new notable issues are: 1) Faith and Order had been transformed into a department within the Division of Studies—a very considerable drop from its former position in the World Council of Churches, and it was widely thought that it had lost its original élan. It was one of the conditions made by the Russian Patriarchate before entering the World Council at New Delhi in 1961 that the work of Faith and Order should be restored on a broader basis and given more freedom as a platform for dogmatic problems essential to real unity. Since the New Delhi conference there has been a determined effort to attempt to rehabilitate Faith and Order, though it was too late to settle any major problems except the "revised" basis of the World Council of Churches.

2) For this reason the officers of the staff-committee had attempted a definition, or description, of the unity aimed at and advocated by the churches belonging to the World Council. Of course the different churches cannot regard this basis as a real confession of faith, but they have the option to recognize it as a definite outline in the search for a confession of faith. Instead of being a meeting place of dialogue and cooperation between the churches, which the WCC will continue to be, the churches must consider their participation in the life of the council as a *koinonia,* a fellowship or communion based on the testimony of the apostles as contained in sacred Scripture. This was the hope, so to speak, of those who had shaped the formula, but Montreal did not succeed in giving greater precision to this vision of unity, largely because the bulk of the sixty Orthodox delegates refused to confirm it.

3) The entry of the Orthodox churches of Russia, Bulgaria, Rumania and Poland as members of the World Council had effected a profound change. Critics can no longer regard the council as essentially Protestant in its aspirations. The hope is that Orthodox pneumatology might help the World Council to overcome the difficult problems of unity, but at Montreal there was no help forthcoming.

4) A fact of highest importance is the Roman Catholic Church's decision to participate in the ecumenical dialogue. No one's name enjoyed greater esteem at the Montreal conference than that of Pope John XXIII.

5) Within the last decade there have been numerous negotiations between member churches of the WCC. The spirit of unionism is spreading throughout the Protestant world.

In light of the many problems therefore, the main result of the Faith and Order meeting was that a very new approach and procedure must be found to overcome the formidable accumulation of problems. Another result was the impression that if the Roman Catholic Church joined the WCC this would only increase the difficulties.

Thus the assembly was unable to produce a message to the churches; it could only receive, without voting, a message from the officers of the Faith and Order Conference which begins: "We are on the way to Christian unity..."

The "spirit of unionism" referred to above however can be considered a very tangible and important result of the efforts toward unity within world Protestantism. The establishment of the Church of South India in 1957 and the formation of the United Chuch of Christ in 1961 are two prime examples of "inter-Protestant unity."

One of the most important of the trends toward intercommunal unity within world Protestantism involves the Church of England and the Methodist Church. At the beginning of the eventful ecumenical year 1964 the Church of England stood before two decisions which could transform her very nature. One concerns the transformation of the National Church Assembly, founded in 1920, into a General Synod of the Church of England. The former, in contrast to the convocations of Canterbury and York, includes a House of Laity. The plan aims to bring the historical order of the Church of England in line with the modern synodical constitution of Anglicanism which was renewed in 1963 in Toronto. A body would therefore be formed with the help of which the nature of the established church might be loosened, so that it might be able to act more freely, that is to say, independently of the House of Commons and the Crown.

In spite of a warning by the former archbishop of Canterbury, Dr. Geoffrey Fisher, the Church Assembly at the beginning of November 1963 accepted a compromise proposal put forward by the archbishops of Canterbury and York for the synodical government of the Church of England. The idea of establishing a synod sprang not from the canon law of the Catholic Church but from Calvinism, and it refers to a representative constitution of the church through a body elected by the parishes or communities, and in which the laity are also entitled to a say in questions of faith and order. However, the General Synod which is planned seems to be nothing but a façade since it leaves the convocations of York and Canterbury with the right to veto on matters of liturgy and doctrine. For this reason the *Church Times* calls this "pretence of synodical government in the Church of England disappointing." The Church Assembly would continue to exist under a different name—the "General Synod." "The Convocations will have the power to hold up the business and defeat the intentions of the larger body in which lay representatives sit with them." The proposals constitute "something less than the minimum required if synodical government, with full lay participation, is to become reality." That would mean the end of the convocations. Archbishop Fisher had proposed to add a House of Laity to each of these Convocations as the simplest way of reform.

In the debate of the Church Assembly it was stated that the primates' proposals, approved by an overwhelming majority, do not shut the door to additions or amendments. The plan may be the first cautious step in the direction of full synodical government. Later the powers of the General Synod may be increased. In any case the Church of England does not give up what it judges to be its fundamental "catholic" structure, the hierarchical or historical episcopacy which is the main instrument of its ecumenical policy.

While on the one hand Canterbury is hoping that the Second Vatican Council will reconsider Pope Leo XIII's refusal to acknowledge Anglican orders, on the other Canterbury continues the successful plan, started with the formation of the Church of South India in 1947, to reunite within the Anglican orders all Christian communities sprung from the Church of England by secession. What has succeeded in the mission field has to be achieved now in England. The "aggiornamento" of the Church

319

of England in developing a Calvinist synodical government under the cover of episcopacy is inspired by the other decisive plan which causes much anxiety among Anglican as well as Methodist congregations.

For at the end of February 1963 a "Report" was published by the *Church Times* concerning "Anglican-Methodist conversations on complete unity via full communion," to begin in 1965. The committees representing the Church of England and the Methodist Church have had their meetings in joint residential sessions at intervals since 1956. The report was signed by all eleven Anglican members and by eight of the twelve members of the Methodist committee. The remaining four Methodist members signed a dissenting report.

The majority report contains outline proposals for the coming-together of the two churches in two stages. Stage two is complete union. This however must be preceded by a stage lasting for some years at which the two churches would enter upon full communion with one another, while retaining their distinct life and identity. It is admitted that the existence of two parallel churches, side by side, in full communion, would be anomalous and unsatisfactory except as a step toward, and a means of achieving, the ultimate goal of complete unity. The report concentrates on the action necessary to achieve stage one. It is proposed that full communion should be established by the following steps:

1) The reconciliation of the two churches in a service which includes the integration by reciprocal action of their existing ministries.

2) The acceptance by the Methodist Church of episcopacy in continuity with the historical episcopate, and the practice of episcopal ordination for its ministers in the future.

3) The provision of means by which the two churches, during the period of full communion, could cooperate and grow together by consultation, common action and common devotion at all levels.

World Protestantism and world apostolate

In this and succeeding sections world Protestantism will be understood as Protestantism insofar as it has associated itself to the World Council of Churches. If by this limitation we are excluding some of the extreme-orthodox and extreme-liberal groups we do not intend this exclusion to be a value judgment. But neither is this exclusion an arbitrary one since by far the greater portion of Protestants who belong to the national churches are on the way to a new unity, namely world Protestantism.

Modern world Protestantism is the result of a process of growth. It is not a utopia. It is already a tangible reality in the world of our time, a reality which has a real basis: real harmony.

This new Protestantism is not a detailed and logically constructed doctrinal system accepted by the whole of world Protestantism. Rather it is one of its characteristics that it considers such a system valueless and useless if not impossible. World Protestantism is not a static but a dynamic reality, not an intellectual but an existential reality. It knows it is faced with numerous unsolved problems. But it is inspired by a strong awareness of unity in Christ, spirit, attitude, purpose and method. The unity of faith by which Christians are one in Christ, thus forming one body, is not considered incompatible with a certain degree of difference of opinion concerning theology, church organization or worship.

The two principal marks of world Protestantism are: real unity of belief and practical insight and a real, hitherto unknown awareness of vocation with regard to mankind.

The first mark does not contradict what we have said elsewhere about the ecumenical situation. And some ecumenical relations have arisen which do not actually rest on a real foundation. But this does not apply to ecumenical contacts or even to ecclesiasical reunions between moderate-reformed, moderate-orthodox Lutherans and Anglicans and the major part of the free churches (Presbyterians, Congregationalists and Method-ists). Among these groups, who together represent more than 50 per cent of all Protestants, a real consensus, a real *communis opinio* has arisen which forms a real, firm basis for unity and collaboration within ecumenically oriented world Protestantism. Here there is no question of a unity which though pursued with great effort is doomed to failure. It is a matter of a firm, real unity based on real agreement and harmony and which cannot easily be undone.

The original Reformation confessions, church ordinances and liturgies have not lost their meaning in world Protestantism but there is a general need to subject them to a thorough revision in the light of the present state of biblical science and studies, and in the light of modern thought and of the needs of our times. These revised confessions, church ordinances and liturgies, together with the reports and messages of the great world con-ferences of Amsterdam, Lund and Evanston, should be regarded as the principal sources for an understanding of world Protes-tantism.

As we have remarked above the World Council of Churches has not been able to integrate catholic (Eastern Orthodox, Old Catholic and Anglo-Catholic) views into its terminology and into the material content of its testimony of faith. It is question-able whether this integration will ever be possible. Hence the fact that the World Council has really become the exponent of the general opinion of the major part of Protestantism. There-fore it is quite justifiable to define world Protestantism as Protes-tantism insofar as it has officially associated itself to the World Council of Churches. It is of course quite obvious that the unity of this world Protestantism implies the avoidance of all sorts of ecclesiastic and theological nuances.

We will now limit ourselves to the second principal mark of modern world Protestantism: the awareness of vocation with regard to mankind, the awareness of coresponsibility for the spiritual and material welfare of mankind. Here there is question of the evangelization of mankind (world apostolate) on the one hand, and on the other of a clear testimony concerning the critical world situation, and of a practical collaboration in providing for the spiritual and material distress of mankind. These two themes of world apostolate and world distress were on the agenda of every ecumenical conference. In Amsterdam they were discussed as parts of the main theme: "God's Design and Man's Disorder;" in Evanston as parts of the main theme: "Christ, the Hope of the World."

The world apostolate is directed at the non-Christian peoples, at the dechristianized people of the home countries, at Roman Catholics and at the people of Israel.

The rise of the Protestant mission among non-Christian peoples dates from the eighteenth century. The mission, that is, the preaching of the gospel to all peoples and races over the whole world and to the end of time, is one of the most important tasks which Christ gave to his apostles and to the Church. During the late middle ages the awareness of this command and vocation was latent in the Church. The Catholic Church renewed its missionary activity with full vigor during the sixteenth century, particularly through the Jesuits (e.g. Francis Xavier). The Reformation churches were more than a century behind. Their renewed awareness of responsibility toward the non-Christian peoples did not spring from the sixteenth century Reformation but from the pietist and Methodist revival movements of the eighteenth century. At first the national churches, generally averse to the revivals, also had a reserved attitude toward missionary activity. As a result the Protestant missionary mentality has always borne a typically pietist-Methodist stamp. It was only during the past twenty or thirty years that some change occurred in this respect. In any event the Protestant missionary movement originated with the free churches in Germany and England and not with the national churches—with the exception of the Anglican Society for the Propagation of the Gospel in Foreign Parts (1701), which was directed mostly to emigrants.

323

The first missionary group was the Herrnhutter Community of Brethren, established in 1727 under a strong pietist influence. In 1732 this community sent its first missionaries to the Negro slaves and Eskimos of North America. Since that time the Herrnhutter mission has spread over Labrador, Alaska, California, Central America, Dutch Guiana, the former German colonies in Africa and the Himalayas.

But the great rise of the Protestant mission dates only from the last few years of the eighteenth and the first years of the nineteenth century. The first in this rather sudden renewal of activity were the free churches of England who in their organization and method pointed the way to the revival of missionary activity in Germany. Mission activity in other Protestant countries was soon to follow. From the very beginning the organization of missionary activity was not undertaken officially by the churches, but privately by missionary societies.

In England the first steps toward the formation of a missionary society were taken by the Baptist shoemaker and lay preacher Willam Carey. He published an *Examination into the Duties of a Christian to Undertake the Conversion of the Pagans.* In 1792 his inspiring preaching moved the Baptists to form what was later called the Baptist Missionary Society. In 1795 followed the establishment of the London Missionary Society formed by the Congregationalists in cooperation with Presbyterians and Anglicans. A pronounced ecumenical tendency manifested itself even then. The statutes declared that the intention was not to give pagans a determined church form but "the glorious gospel of God." It was left to the converted pagans themselves to "choose the church form which in their conviction is best in harmony with the word of God."

From the very start it was one of the marks of Protestant missionary activity that it did not spread a definite confessional church order and liturgy, but rather that it wanted to bring the gospel to the pagans by means of a free proclamation of God's word. The Protestant missionaries emphasized the need to translate the Bible into the language of the people with whom they were working. Later missionaries included not only medical doctors but also ethnologists and linguists.

In order to promote and make possible the publication of Bible translations a number of Bible societies were founded at the same time the missionary societies were being formed: The British and Foreign Bible Society (1804), The Basle Bible Society (1804) and, some years later, the Wurtemberg, Prussian and Saxonian Bible Societies. In The Netherlands the Dutch Bible Society (1814) was formed and in North America the American Bible Society (1816). Even the British and Foreign Bible Society alone has, since its foundation in 1804, distributed almost six hundred million Bibles in more than eight hundred different languages. Missiology and biblical science are therefore closely connected in Protestant missionary activity.

The first missionary societies which arose in Germany after the Herrnhutter mission date from the early part of the nineteenth century: the Berlin Missionary Society (1824), the Rhineland Missionary Society (1824), the North German Society (1828), and others. Similar missionary societies were also founded in Switzerland, Denmark, Sweden and, last but not least, America. In America alone they number almost one hundred and fifty, in England more than seventy-five. The total number of Protestant missionary societies is estimated at about two hundred and fifty.

The development of Protestant missionary activity in the past fifty years manifests three principal tendencies: the endeavor toward a closer cooperation among the great number of various corporations, an increased interest on the part of the churches and greater attention to the scientific foundation of missionary work.

One of the results of the world conference on the missions, held in Edinburgh in 1910, was the establishment of the International Missionary Council, which was later to include a great number of the existing missionary corporations. Its publication is *The International Review of Missions*. Each year the January edition carries an accurate survey of the state of the missions in the various parts of the world. Of great importance for closer collaboration among the various Protestant missionary organizations were the world missionary conferences of Jerusalem (1928) and Tambaram (1939). In preparation for this latter conference the Dutch missiologist Kraemer (later director of the Ecumenical Institute at Boissey near Geneva 1946–1955) wrote his *The Christian Message in a Non-Christian World* 1938. In 1947 Latourette completed his *History of the Expansion of Christianity,* a seven-volume work which is the most complete history of missionary activity thus far published. At the world missionary conferences of Whitby in Canada (1947) and Willingen in Germany (1952) it appeared that the question of granting independence to the mission churches had become urgent. The ecumenical character of the Protestant missionary movement is expressed not only in an increasing cooperation among the corporations but also in a strong desire for unity manifested by the young mission churches. The Church of South India came into existence as a result of a reunion of originally Presbyterian, Congregationalist, Methodist and Anglican churches. There is a close connection between the strongly ecumenical character of the missionary movement and the rise and development of the ecumenical movement.

One of the most important ecumenical-missionary societies is the International Missionary Council, which until 1961 was not a member of the World Council of Churches—partly because its members were not "churches" but missionary societies of different origins. After the second conference in Evanston in 1954 the complete integration of the IMC into the World Council was planned as a new Commission on World Mission and Evangelism. Following a period of difficult negotiations led by Bishop Lesslie Newbigin, one of the founders of the Church of South India, this integration was achieved in 1961 at New Delhi. The aim was to give a new sense of missionary responsibility to the members of the WCC and to promote the organic unity of this fellowship or federation of independent churches.

The first full meeting of the Commission on World Mission and Evangelism of the WCC was held at Mexico City in December 1963 under the general theme "God's Mission and Our Task." Official Catholic observers were present at the debates on the critical situations of the missions in all six continents. Two hundred Protestant delegates worked to bring about "a common witness of the whole Church" based on profound biblical study, and showed themselves willing to cooperate with Catholic missions.

World Protestantism and the world situation

The reports of the ecumenical world conferences, the international missionary conferences and the Anglican Lambeth conferences all confirm the growing impression that world Protestanism, insofar as it expresses itself in these reports, forms a true religious, spiritual and socio-ethical unity. This unity is anchored in a similarity of vision of the gospel and of the deepest core of the Christian faith, and in a mutual acceptance of one and the same vocation and task on behalf of all mankind in the world today.

Moreover the reports give evidence of a new religious and spiritual climate. This climate is characterized by an atmosphere of true spiritual freedom and impartiality in connection with the problems to be discussed, by a primary interest for the more urgent matters at hand, by a certain indifference with regard to current terminology, traditional formulations and conventional practices, and by the rejection of doctrinal discipline.

The reports are expressed in a language that modern man can understand. And the emphases are essentially different. Orthodox dogmatism, theological disputes and narrow churchism are things of the past in ecumenical world Protestantism, although these tendencies are still found among those relatively small groups which do not partake in the ecumenical movement. But in these churches there is also much thought and activity which no longer consider harmony and uniformity of primary importance. There is a growing insight which sees that a stubborn and fundamental rejection of new ecclesiastic, liturgical and social practices is often the result of conventionalism, formalism and absolutism. Centuries-old practices have been cast adrift. This new attitude is not the result of indifferentism. Rather it is the result of new discoveries and an essentially new situation. Our time—and especially world Protestantism—has acquired an essentially new vision of what is of major and what is of minor importance.

This change of climate also appears to influence the churches' attitudes toward the world situation, the state and politics. Only in a few places are efforts still made to hold fast to the traditional attitudes of pre-war days. By far the majority of countries —and again especially world Protestantism—manifest a real change in this respect. This change is best characterized by a determined refusal ("for the sake of the gospel and conscience") to allow the church or the Christian faith to be used as a servant of the state, as an instrument of politics or as the advocate of the interests of a certain class or party.

The roles have been reversed. On the basis of a new understanding of the gospel modern world Protestantism considers itself called to testify to God's will and intention and, if necessary, to protest no less strongly against the world, the state, civil authority and political parties whenever circumstances exist which according to the gospel are contrary to God's will and intention. Whether the world, state, authority or party call themselves Christian or not has no bearing on this testimony of the churches.

There has never been a time when Protestantism has so strongly felt the necessity for complete independence of the state and international and national politics as it does now. The struggle against an unchristian totalitarian regime and the danger of ungodliness continually threatening any political party have, in less than a quarter of a century, made Protestantism reluctant to identify with a political party on a confessional basis. There is no doubt that in Europe the increasing influence of Kierkegaard and the socio-ethical testimony of Barth have had their say in this regard. In America the attitude toward the state and politics is determined by the traditional spirit of the free churches. Without any confessional-political obligations of an ecclesiastic or religious character these churches want to co-operate—as free witnesses to Christ and in the midst of the world, the state and politics—in the construction of a better world.

In its attitude toward the world situation world Protestantism manifests some important nuances. Continental European world Protestantism generally has little confidence in a gradual improvement of the world, but lives rather in the eschatological expectation of the coming of the kingdom of God and the return of Christ at the end of time. On the other hand American world Protestantism lives in the hope that Christians will be able to realize more and more God's kingdom here on earth by means of harmonious cooperation. Generally speaking American Protestantism is inclined to regard Communism as an enemy force in principle unchristian, and to accept the American form of society on principle in order to christianize it gradually from within. European Protestantism adopts a critical attitude toward American capitalism, considers itself strongly co-guilty in the injustices capitalism has inflicted on the laborer, is sympathetic toward the socialistic form of society and does not want to exclude *a priori* any dialogue with Communism.

Nonetheless, on the basis of recent ecumenical reports, the attitude of world Protestantism toward the world situation can be summarized as follows.

The modern world situation, dominated as it is by fear, hate, selfishness, competition, brute force and the danger of a new world war and total destruction is in flagrant conflict with God's plan for the universe and with Christ's atoning work. Ecumenical Christianity has become aware that it has shared in the guilt

329

of this situation through blindness and tepidity, through unbelief (in an existential sense) and disobedience. In the battles between races, nations and classes it has looked to its own self-interest. The ecumenical reawakening demands repentance, conversion and penance. In its attitude toward the world situation it is concerned with a new "obedience in faith."

"Obedience in faith" does not mean that a man must be obedient to the laws and precepts of moral theology as it has deduced them from Christian revelation. It is rather a question of faith in a personal, dynamic and existential sense. In each situation of life the Christian has a new encounter with Christ and he is ever again faced with the choice of being obedient or disobedient to whatever Christ is asking of him in this or that particular situation. Disobedience means disbelief; true obedience is based on a living relation of faith with Christ; it is obedience in faith, not an obedience to the precepts of a church, a party or a system of morals. This obedience in faith presupposes the Reformation concept of the nature of the act of faith, conscience and of authority.

It cannot be disputed that the segregation between races and nations has penetrated into the very bosom of Christianity: "All churches and all Christians are involved in the tensions between the races and nations of the world, whether they will admit it or not" (Evanston report). This applies also to the segregation, the contrasts and the tensions between classes and political parties. In many instances Christians face each other as enemies and opponents. Often the existing situations and circumstances lead to such segregation. A Christian is guilty before God if he allows himself to be led by antipathy, passion, hate, self-interest, heartlessness and intransigence; he is not guilty if by unfeigned charity and sincere desire he endeavors to restore peace, and to promote and safeguard it. If there is but a remnant of true Christian faith left in him a person knows that the world cannot possibly be saved by the right of the strongest or by any other

330

right, but only by the charity and loving forgiveness which has its source in Christ.

World Protestantism is not satisfied however merely to define principles and norms but also applies them to practically all problems of an economic, social, national and international nature. It directs its appeals to all mankind. Through the World Council of Churches and through the individual churches it appeals to authorities and rulers whenever it finds that certain concrete measures, situations or events are contrary to the universal Christian conscience (e.g. a growth in the danger of war, irresponsible use of atomic energy, unwarranted detention of prisoners of war, neglect of homeless and displaced persons, suppression of minorities, suppression of the freedom of religion and conscience, biased administration of justice, racial discrimination).

The churches associated with the World Council must first turn within themselves to come to grips with social problems:

The vocation of the church with regard to the racial problem is to testify within its own community to the kingship of Christ and to the unity of his people. In his incarnation and in his work of atonement, Jesus Christ restores this unity intended by God from the very beginning (Evanston report).

This vocation applies not only to the relation between races but to all human relationships. It depends on the Christian whether and to what extent the church can contribute to the healing of the world:

If the church is to be to the world as salt, which preserves civilization from corruption and keeps life wholesome, there must be something distinctive about us Christians—in the way we do our daily work, in the homes we make, and in the standards by which we live. We must take our full part as citizens. Yet, in so doing, we must not forget that we are citizens of a heavenly kingdom, and inheritors of an eternal destiny (Lambeth encyclical letter 1945).

The task with regard to the world situation must therefore be seen *sub specie aeternitatis,* in a perspective of eternity.

With these presuppositions world Protestantism is of one mind concerning the defense of democratic rights, the support of the charter of the United Nations concerning the rights of man, the rejection of any form of state totalitarianism, the condemnation of war as a means of solving international conflicts. It is united in its protest against any infringement of the rights of freedom of religion (especially in those Catholic countries where the practice and spread of the Protestant religion is impeded by the state), in the promotion of improved international relations and in the defense of the rights of all neglected and ill-treated groups.

Modern world Protestantism is inspired by a strong socio-ethical sense of responsibility toward all mankind. In this sense of responsibility and in the resulting practical ecumenical activity the social awareness of the free churches—which gave the first impulse to the combat against slavery and against social abuses in the home country—has reached its full development. This socio-ethical awareness rests not only on purely human considerations but springs also from the evangelic faith that God is the creator, father and redeemer of all men. Official pronouncements, resolutions and reports of world Protestantism seldom if ever mention predestination and election of only a part of mankind. Rather they seem to presuppose the universal salvific will of God. Consequently any socio-ethical activity should be inspired by the belief that it has real value only insofar as it is seen in the light of man's eternal destiny.

World Protestantism and the Catholic Church

In defining the existing relationship between world Protestantism and the Catholic Church (quite apart from forming any judgment) two aspects must be clearly distinguished: the objective and the subjective aspects.

The objective aspect is acknowledged only by a person who believes that the Catholic Church has been called into existence by God and that the nature of the Church is based not on human insight and human discretion but on God's plan and God's institution. In other words it is acknowledged only by a person who believes that there are in the Church elements which cannot be challenged because they are founded on an unchangeable divine institution, and on divine revelation.

If by revelation is meant not only that God speaks to man by his word but also that God gives to this world a visible reality which is what it is not because we humans wish and see it so, but precisely because God decreed it thus from all eternity, then this implies that faith is belief in the revealed word, and also (on the basis of this word) belief in an objective, unassailable revealed reality which is unchangeable and which remains what it is independently of what we human beings think of it.

For Christians Christ is this objectively given revealed reality here on earth. To believe means the unconditional acknowledgment of the Christ reality as he actually is, not as we judge him, appreciate him or interpret him. The subjective act of faith ceases to be a true act of faith—in the sense of Christian revelation—whenever, instead of being founded on an objectively given reality, it rests on human insight, on human deliberation and judgment, on human needs, on a human statement of "this is the way I see it" or "this I find completely unnecessary." Revelation means that nothing is left for *me* to say in the matter, that there is nothing left for *me* to do but to believe or not believe.

All Christians who acknowledge and accept Jesus Christ as God and redeemer posit an act of faith determined by and aimed at the objectively given reality of Christ as the incarnate word, as the God-man. This is true for a Catholic as well as for a Protestant Christian. But the cardinal difference between Catholics and Protestants is that for the former the visible Church as the body of Christ is implied in the reality of the Christ mystery. As far as the here and now is concerned the Catholic's act of faith is based on and aimed at Christ as he continues to live and work in the Church. The Church should not "be trying" to conform with Christ's intention; the Church, as the communion of the faithful, should not "be endeavoring" to maintain itself or to direct itself according to God's word or to preserve unity and harmony as well as possible. The Church *is* in conformity with Christ's intention; it *is* the body of Christ; it *cannot* but proclaim the truth; it *is* the dispenser of divine grace; in short, it is what it is only because of God's decree and intention. It *cannot* be otherwise.

It is true that a Catholic believer distinguishes in the empirical Church a divine and a human aspect, but when as a believer he speaks of the Church he means the unchangeable, objectively given divine aspect. The Protestant on the contrary means precisely the human aspect when he speaks of the visible church in its earthly appearance. He does not deny that the visible church as the communion of the faithful has been willed by Christ and is directed by the Holy Spirit, but he denies that the word, authority and activity of men in the church can ever have a divine, infallible and unassailable character. Anything that belongs to the visible being of the church is subject to corruption, degeneration and loss of vitality; any visible church can fall into error; the universal church as the totality of all the baptized will always have to struggle with heresy and schism. So says the Anglican hymn "The Church's One Foundation Is Jesus Christ Her Lord." In the third stanza appear the following lines:

> Though with a scornful wonder
> Men see her sore opprest,
> By schisms rent asunder,
> By heresies distrest . . .

According to this view the visible church is, in its being and appearance, evidently dependent on human thought and action, on subjective, human factors. According to the belief of Catholics the Catholic Church is, in its authoritative and infallible

334

proclamation of the faith and in its sacramental distribution of grace, completely independent of human factors. The unity, truth and fullness of grace in the Church do not spring from any human insight or action but from Christ since the Church is the supernatural body of Christ.

Much would be gained if those Christians who are occupied with the difficult problem of the relationship between world Protestantism and the Catholic Church were willing to see this problem as a bona fide problem of faith which must be taken seriously.

Neither Catholics nor Protestants show ill will in this respect. Nor can there be question of disobedience to God's will on either part. Catholics are convinced, no less than Protestants, that their belief in the Church is according to God's word and in harmony with the intention and institution of Christ. So long as Catholics and Protestants continue to attribute each others' teachings and practices concerning the church to such human failures as pride, self-conceit, desire for power or disobedience the dialogue will remain far below a truly ecumenical level. Protestants who hold their exegesis of sacred Scripture to be irrefutable may be under the impression that the Catholic Church is the disobedient church but they themselves are no less disobedient in the eyes of Catholics, who do not doubt the divine character of the authority which Christ, through the Holy Spirit and by means of the pope and the bishops, exercises in and through the Catholic Church. Therefore there is no point in continuing to accuse one another of pride and disobedience.

If we look at the relationship between world Protestantism and the Catholic Church not from the objective point of view (from revelation) but rather from the subjective point of view, that is, from the point of view of human relations, we will find that considerable progress has been made, at least in some countries. This is true apologetically as well as ecumenically.

In the apologetic sense there is a growing conviction that the apostolate, evangelization and the proclamation of the faith

335

should be concerned exclusively with the wellbeing of the other and never with victorious conquests, cheap proselytizing and increase of numbers and influence.

Whereas Catholics and Protestants were for a long time exclusively engaged in combating, hindering and harming each other or at best in disregarding one another there is now present on both sides an apostolic zeal toward each other which, in the best instances, is truly inspired by Christian love. Many Catholics and Protestants are inspired by a sincere desire to win the other back to the complete truth. There is in this mutual endeavor something humorous and at the same time tragic. Both Catholics and Protestants are deeply convinced that the other lacks something essential. The apologetic standpoint of the two groups can be characterized as follows.

The Catholic Christian lives, according to his convictions of faith, in the consciousness that as far as faith, spiritual life, divine worship and grace are concerned the fullness of being a Christian cannot possibly be known and experienced outside full visible communion with the Catholic Church. Only within the Church and nowhere else is it possible to come to a full and true knowledge of revealed truth. Only within the Church is it possible to share fully in the supernatural, sacramental riches of grace and in the communion of saints.

The Protestant Christian, because of his view of faith, is convinced that the fullness of being a Christian rests exclusively on the knowledge of and belief in the pure, unadulterated gospel. He is convinced that man, lost because of original sin, needs only God's own word, God's own message, God's own promises in order to be saved. Regular familiarity with the Bible is the foundation of the life of prayer and faith. Spreading and interpreting the Bible are the bases of the whole apostolate of evangelization. The Protestant is convinced that the Catholic lacks the essential because in his opinion the gospel has become obscure in the Roman church, that it is no longer known, taught and preached.

336

This apologetic situation is also reflected in the ecumenical dialogue. The Protestant participant finds it perfectly obvious to go to sacred Scripture in order to find out what can be salvaged of the theological and dogmatic arguments of the participants, and what can be maintained as true. The Catholic participant finds it no less obvious to go to the Catholic Church (to that which is *de fide:* the *depositum fidei* and the authoritative interpretation by the Church) in order to see what will be left of the exegetical methods, findings and opinions of the participants and what can be maintained as true. At any rate it is highly unecumenical in a religious dialogue between Catholics and Protestants to determine beforehand that all participants should exclusively follow either the first or the second way to the truth. And such unecumenical *a priori's* are still all too often considered ecumenical.

Of considerable importance in this respect is the Feb. 28, 1950 instruction of the Sacred Congregation of the Holy Office to the bishops instructing them "not only to zealously and actively guard over this whole action, but also to prudently promote and direct it." This instruction concerns the promotion of local and semi-official meetings and discussions between Catholics and non-Catholics—the most important way the Catholic Church can take part in the ecumenical movement.

Another important factor in the relations between world Protestantism and the Church in communion with Rome was the pontificate of Pope John XXIII. This wise and beloved pontiff made it clear to all that the first thing necessary for church unity is a reconciliation between divided Christians on the basis of love and forgiveness. No matter how great the difficulties are by which the churches are divided the first and main concern is that Christians, notwithstanding their different points of view, should whole-heartedly be reconciled with one another as persons who have all been incorporated into the Mystical Body of Christ by a living faith and by the sacrament of holy baptism.

Although Roman Catholic Christians look upon the Chair of St. Peter as the Christ-given center, norm and guarantee of the visible unity of the Church, Pope John has made it quite clear that a thorough renovation of the papacy, the liturgy, the theology and the spiritual life of the Church in communion with Rome will be necessary before an actual reunion of all Christian churches will be possible.

This actual reunion, even though it implies a reunion with St. Peter and his successors, should not be conceived as a unilateral submission. It should rather be based on a free and open discussion between the various churches. As regards the place of world Protestantism in the reunited Church, not only the witness of the Reformation to the gospel but also later achievements in the life of Reformation churches should be taken seriously and be incorporated into the life of the whole Church.

Thus all Christians should pray that the final results of the Second Vatican Council will actually open a door toward closer relationships between and the ultimate reunion of the churches of the Reformation and the Church of Rome.

Index of Names

Index of Subjects

343

Date Due

APR 27 '65	CANISIUS		
NOV 14 '66			
MAY 3 '67	CANISIUS		
JAN 17 '68	CANISIUS		
AN 8 '69	CANISIUS		